4/2000

**Talking with
Michener**

I'm one of the guys who sat
around the fire and did the
talking.

James A. Michener

Talking with Michener

by Lawrence Grobel

University Press of Mississippi
Jackson

www.upress.state.ms.us

First edition
07 06 05 04 03 02 01 00 99   4 3 2 1

The paper in this book meets the guidelines for permanence and durability of
the Committee on Production Guidelines for Book Longevity of the Council on
Library Resources.

Library of Congress Cataloging-in-Publication Data
Grobel, Lawrence.
    Talking with Michener / by Lawrence Grobel.
      p.   cm.
    Includes index.
    ISBN 1-57806-139-3 (cloth : alk. paper)
    1. Michener, James A. (James Albert), 1907–   Interviews.
  2. Novelist, American—20th century Interviews. 3. Historical
fiction—Authorship.   I. Michener, James A.   (James Albert), 1907–
    II. Title.
PS3525.I19Z67   1999
813'.54—dc21
[B]   99-20065
                                                                      CIP

British Library Cataloging-in-Publication Data available

21
MICHENER
999

Contents

For Jim, who, once he started, never stopped; and for Maya, Hana and Zachary, the next generation.

Introduction

On the first day of February, 1996, James A. Michener looked out his window and forgot momentarily that he was in Austin, Texas. The thin layer of clean white snow covering the ground reminded him of other places in other times, of Alaska and the Antarctic. When he snapped back from his Proustian revery, he remembered his promise to a local bookstore that he would appear on his eighty-ninth birthday, Saturday, February 3rd, but it just didn't seem prudent now, in such weather. He wasn't able to get around without the aid of a cane and helping hand, couldn't even lift himself from his chair without help.

When he told his aide, John Kings, that the birthday celebration might have to be cancelled, Kings reminded him that a lot of people were planning to come from as far away as New York to wish him a happy birthday.

The next day, Friday, the roads were so slick and the weather so cold that the bookstore stayed closed. Michener, however, ventured out for his dialysis treatment—part of an alternate-day routine that he could not miss. The blood cleansing was not pleasant and left him exhausted, but he had learned to accept the process. His kidney failure during a 1994 visit to the Far East had put an end to his century-long career as a world traveler. Now, confined to one city, he made the most of his situation—entertaining, watching the passing parade on CNN, reading the N.Y. Times, playing along on Jeopardy, and writing.

His latest work was a novella called Miracle in Seville, and his next book, This Noble Land, would be a series of twelve essays on problems facing America. His sonnets, which he'd been writing since the 1920s, would be published on his ninetieth birthday.

The weather was supposed to be clear and not as cold on Saturday, and Michener decided to brave it, since he didn't like to disappoint people.

The next evening when they drove to the bookstore two thousand people were waiting in a line to see him, clutching the books he had written over the last six decades.

Michener was not a man who showed much emotion, but tears came to his eyes when he saw how many people were there. He hadn't been this moved since his wife Mari died two years ago. His time as a best-selling author had passed; he accepted the smaller advances his publisher offered him now, only 10 percent of what he got when they were printing close to a million copies of his books. As he looked at the crowds on the first and second floors, he no longer felt like a weak old man who could barely walk. On this cool Texas evening in this supermarket of a bookstore he was the hero of readers who had traveled long distances just to have the chance to say they met James Michener, to show his bookplate signature inside their books. He spoke his gratitude to the crowd and shook as many hands as he could, listening with pride as people told him how much his work had meant to them. And for two and a half hours on his eighty-ninth birthday, he felt young again.

Three and a half years earlier, I drove with Michener from Brunswick, his summer home in Maine, to a local fisherman's restaurant on Bailey Island. He liked the place because it had retained the local color that was rapidly disappearing in America. The menu had two sets of prices; for the regulars, who sat at the counter, the same food was cheaper than for those at the tables. "Wait'll you see this place," he said, as he gripped his cane between the fingers of his large hand. "It's the damndest thing."

As we drove through country lanes as picturesque as when he first saw them more than half a lifetime ago when he arrived as a young researcher from Harvard, I wanted to ask him a personal question: Why, after he had already endured one marathon of my grilling more than ten years ago, had he agreed to spend so much more time with me? He was still working hard, in his ninth decade, with very little spare time. Yet whenever I wrote that I wanted to come see him, he made himself available.

He knew what he did was important. And before he put down his pencil, he wanted to make sure there was a trail, he said. That was why he agreed to talk with me over the years. It was part of the trail of one writer's journey.

I first met James Michener in the spring of '81 when I flew to Miami and then drove up the coast to Juno Beach, where I was to interview him for a national magazine. *The Covenant,* his

879-page novel about South Africa, had just been published, and he was working on another long novel, *Space*. Michener was a Quaker, and he and his third wife, Mari, lived in functional, spartan surroundings—modest furniture, shelves almost bare, with no copies of any of Michener's books. The books in his office mostly had to do with his current research. His desk consisted of a door balanced on two small metal file cabinets, and his typewriter of choice was a standard Royal. He said he bought them whenever he found them. He didn't like electric machines, just as he didn't like leaving margins on pages. Michener was from the old cut-and-paste school: after he wrote in longhand he would type his pages by himself, then add additions on yellow paper and cut and paste these to the first typed draft. On his fourth go-through he would make handwritten changes in red or blue ink, then give this eyesore to a secretary to retype. And when he wrote, he said, he worked up an athlete's sweat, smelling like a horse by the end of a long day.

We met in the evening, and he asked me how long I thought our interview would take. I said I could never predict that. He thought we could get through in a day if we began the next morning at nine and finished by dusk. I was willing to give it a try, but I had strong doubts that we could get through the fifty-seven pages of single-spaced questions I had prepared. He shrugged and said he'd see me in the morning.

Five days and fifty hours of talk later we completed what would be the first round of our talks. Most people grow tired after a few hours of conversation, but Michener never waivered. He wasn't supercilious or irreverent, and he didn't dabble in small talk, which meant he wasn't gossip-column quotable. Instead, he was thoughtful, direct, and honest. He was a serious man of curious contradictions: a man who loved sports though hated boxing; who lost a Congressional election running as a Democrat and then went to China with Richard Nixon; who personally didn't believe in abortion but nevertheless championed a woman's right to choose; who paid the college tuitions of friends' children but who gave back two adopted children of his own when his second marriage failed.

The interview, which ran in *Playboy* in September, 1981, pleased Michener. And thus began our relationship, which turned into a letter-writing friendship as, over the following years, we would correspond about matters large and small.

In early June, 1983, Michener was invited to deliver the commencement address at the California Institute of Technology in Pasadena. I stopped by to see him for an hour at the Athenaeum Inn before he attended a faculty-hosted dinner. We talked about the book he had coming out in the fall (*Poland*) and the one he was in the middle of (*Texas*). He had his doubts about the Poland book because he didn't know how it would be accepted.

But Poland was already recessed in his memory as the monumental history of Texas had taken over his current thoughts. Michener was stuck in the period just after the Civil War, which had been a disaster for Texas and its people. And the post-war reconstruction was hard for him to grasp.

He was still fascinated with Houston—the only city with a population over 30,000 that had no zoning, where Mexicans were killed and nothing was done about it.

I mentioned that I had been seeing Truman Capote and we talked about what Capote was attempting with *Answered Prayers*. He recalled that he had been in Japan after the second World War and remembered an outlandish French homosexual who dressed in red velvet and was hauled out for every social function. "You knew he represented culture," Michener said, "it didn't matter what he did. And Truman is that for us."

Norman Mailer's name came into our conversation and Michener remarked on Mailer's Harvard training. "People forget that," he said. "You sure can't find three more different writers than Norman, Capote, and me."

Before we parted he received one other visitor: an engineering graduate student who had come to meet him for the first time and thank him for his sponsorship. Michener had given the young man two scholarships after he had heard about his talent and his hardships. The student wasn't the first to receive the writer's help and wouldn't be the last. It was something Michener did in his own quiet, unheralded way.

After suffering a heart attack in 1965 Michener had forsaken a long novel about Russia and instead wrote *Iberia* because it wasn't as physically taxing on him. In the early eighties he had decided that writing novels about Alaska and the Caribbean would be remote, because the magnitude of both projects would sweep him away. But within a few years he successfully tackled both subjects. "I do not want to sit in a fine house on Sunset Avenue and look at a shelf of my old books," he told me later.

When I mentioned in one letter that I had been asked by a publisher to write a book on the art of interviewing but had turned it down because the advance was low, he chastised me: "Get the damned thing on the shelf and good things might accidentally happen."

I also once told him the quandary I was in when a certain publisher made me a lucrative offer to write a book about a movie star, someone who had become a close friend.

"Here I adopt the strategy and morality of our mutual friend Truman Capote, who wrote rather devastatingly about some of *his* friends and who riposted when they bellyached about his having betrayed confidences and friendships: 'Who in hell did they think I was? They knew I was a writer.' I believe there is a Kantian categorical imperative dictating a writer's behavior: 'Look at it. Study it. Digest it. And then objectify it as much as possible, and to hell with what the non-writers think.' My books have been banned in five or six major countries—and for just reasons—and I've been kicked around rather extensively, but I've lived to see them all retract, invite me back and say quite wonderfully: 'We still don't like your damned book, but so many visitors tell us that that's why they came here, that we have to admit it did a lot more good than harm.' I'll work for that ultimate judgment."

"I take solace from one overriding fact: 'I'm a writer. I can use words to achieve a telling effect. I can tell a story, and while we writers in the U.S. don't command much of a position in society, we can write, and the others can't.' If it were easy, everyone would do it. We're the lucky few who can, and it's worth all the headaches."

On Febuary 3, 1992, Random House threw an elegant eighty-fifth birthday party for Michener at the J. Pierpont Morgan Library in New York City. Two hundred people came from all over the country to raise a glass to this well-loved man. Former CBS news anchor, commentator, and sailing partner Walter Cronkite and baseball Hall of Famer Stan Musial led the toast, offering a few anecdotes about their good friend.

Michener and Mari went to Antarctica soon after this party and when they returned they closed down their spring home in

Austin and headed for Maine. But before departing Texas, he met with some university officials regarding the endowment he wanted to establish: a writing program which he would fund. But in the officious world of academia it isn't always easy to give money and set up a program—there are committees which must meet, approvals which must be gotten, and other universities which will try to block it. As all of this was going on, Michener left for Brunswick.

During the week I was with him in Maine he received daily calls updating the program's progress. "If the University of Texas gets all their ducks in a row," he told me, "by the end of this week I'll give them fifteen million dollars to fund a new school which will help to train writers in the creative fields of radio, television, drama, newspaper work, the novel, and poetry."

On July 17, 1992, I went with my family to say goodbye to Jim and Mari and to take some pictures. Twelve years before I had a picture taken of Michener and myself with my baby daughter sitting on my lap. Now Maya was a young woman and I thought it would be nice to take another picture. This time there was another daughter as well, Hana, who was nine. Hana had just completed writing a story about a seal, complete with thumb size drawings in a two-inch book, and she was eager to show it to Jim. Michener was impressed and treated Hana as a fellow writer, with the proper respect and enthusiasm displayed for her work. When the phone rang and he picked it up the first thing he told the caller was that he was sitting in his living room reading an original story by a young writer. Hana beamed as she sat next to him. Then the conversation got serious and Michener excused himself to take the call in his study. When he returned he seemed a slightly different man, as if some weight had been lifted from his shoulders.

"That call was from Texas . . . the program's been approved. I've just given away my last fifteen million dollars. I'm going to have to make do with what Mari's got, and with whatever I can earn from future books."

It was a moment of historic occasion for him and I felt privileged to be there to share it. He was eighty-five and one-half years old and about to start all over. He had funded a museum in Bucks County, given two major art collections to galleries in Hawaii and Texas, paid numerous college tuitions of needful students, now established this writing program. By his own estimate he had given away close to sixty million dollars. That's the way he was dealing with the last chapter of his life. Freeing himself by giving all the material things away.

Before he told Mari that they were suddenly fifteen million dollars poorer, he sat down to finish reading Hana's story about the seal. The call from Texas, the little book of Hana's, it was all part and parcel of his hopes for the future.

By the fall of 1994 the writing program was in full swing, and he had three more books published—two compilations, *Creatures of the Kingdom* and *Literary Reflections*, and a novel, *Recessional*. But then came two brutal and life changing blows: his kidneys failed, bringing his travels to an abrupt end; then cancer was discovered in Mari's lower body. She had won two previous bouts with the dreaded disease, but on September 26 she passed away. Michener was heartbroken.

He had fully expected to go first—they had arranged their wills accordingly—and now, seventeen weeks from his eighty-eighth birthday, he was alone.

On the 7th of December I flew to Austin. I expected him to be exhausted from his dialysis treatments and the grief following Mari's death. When I arrived at his door, a woman named Amelia greeted me. Jim was in the living room, sitting at his desk, cutting and pasting articles about Mari.

He had lost a lot of weight and had aged quite a bit since I last saw him in Maine, but he hadn't lost any of his vigor to converse. "I had a fantastic evening the other night," he said. "Willie Nelson was in town to give a concert. Five piece band with him as a lead guitar. Electronics like you've never seen before. After the show, we went into his traveling bus and sat around for forty minutes recalling old times, new problems."

There were plenty of new problems, not the least of which had occurred just a few hours before I arrived.

"The dialysis went bust," he told me. "The needle came out. I have to go through all that again tomorrow."

We talked for four-and-a-half hours.

Life after Mari, he said, "knocked me off dead center for a while." He took a moment, then continued. "But I don't stay off very long. I lead an active social life. I have fun."

When Amelia came into the room I looked at my watch and saw how late the hour had gotten. Michener usually went to sleep at 7:30—it was three hours past that and, worse, we hadn't eaten anything. I was supposed to take him to dinner; instead we dined on words. Amelia knew how important it was that Michener eat and she was not at all pleased that he had missed a meal. (Later Jim would tell me what his doctor had told him: that most dialysis patients die from starvation. They have no appetite and unless are reminded to eat, often don't.)

At eight the next morning I was back at Jim's house and we resumed our talks until ten, when someone came to bathe him. At eleven, on the way to the hospital for his treatment, he warned me that he could barely take the insertion of the needle. "You'll see me wince like hell when they put the bloody needles in, but three minutes later everything's working."

After his treatment we drove to a cafeteria-style restaurant where he slowly ate a meat soup and some tapioca pudding. I asked him if he was satisfied with the writing program at the university. He wasn't. "We have not solved the riddle. The school that does it best is Iowa."

Aging had created a serious problem for him, which he talked about when he got back to his house and was sitting in his easy chair where he liked to nap in front of the television before going to sleep in his bedroom.

"I have a pang of enormous regret, in things you never would have guessed," he told me. "I see advertising season for the new automobiles and they always show a couple driving along some heavenly country road out west, the lake on one side, mountains on the other. And I think, 'Oh hell, that's all finished.'"

"The other is when I see a film or ad of a cruise ship coming in to some exotic port and I can visualize the whole ship inside and outside, and I think that that day is gone."

For a man whose entire life had been one of movement, not being able to feel that the world was his home had a profound effect on him.

Before I left he asked me to bring in a large manuscript in a looseleaf binder from the living room. It was a bibliography which a scholar in Arizona had compiled and which the State House Press was going to publish.

"The bibliography will be incomplete," I commented, "since you've got three more books in the works."

"That will be next year. They're all done and edited. So I'm in an autumnal mood."

In August, 1995, Jim sent me a long letter to buoy my spirits after I had written to him detailing the doubts I was having about our profession. Editors I had worked with had either changed jobs or been fired and the people who replaced them had their own group of preferred writers. "Publishing has galloped off in directions I cannot follow," Michener wrote, "I am satisfied to be eighy-eight rather than fifty-eight.

"The specific changes that concern the writer are the wild, almost cyclonic rearrangements of publishing houses, the selling out to conglomerates, the fusions of once independent companies and, especially, the torrent of changes in the editorial staffs of the surviving companies. That's where the bite comes, that's where the beginning writer faces his greatest danger."

Three months later Michener wrote again: "I recently received a good knock on the head. A magazine had asked me some time ago to write them an article on the Caribbean: 'Use your own judgment.'

"I did, and sent them what I thought was an original and rather stylish piece. But they sent it back with the explanation: 'This is not what we hoped for. We expected you to write. . . .' and they spelled out what I had to confess was superior to what I had written, but if they knew what style of piece they wanted, they really should have shared their ideas with me. They asked if I would re-draft my own article to conform more closely to their proposal and I had to say, 'No.' I told them there was no ill will between us and that I would not expect or accept a kill-fee. As an old pro I had tried my hand on what was basically a sound idea and had flunked the course. No regrets, no bitterness."

He knew I was going to New York in a few months on some business and invited me to stop in Austin on my way and stay with him for a few days.

In January, 1996, I was back at his house on Mt. Laurel Lane, only this time with an overnight bag and a folder filled with newspaper articles dealing with the changes that had occurred in the last year.

There was a lot to talk about.

I quickly became aware that Jim had also undergone some changes over the year. He moved slower, spoke less, watched more television, and suffered new pains. Two weeks earlier I happened to be at a party with Shirley MacLaine who said, when I mentioned that I was going to be seeing Michener, "Why is he still hanging on? Why doesn't he just let go already?"

There were two other people visiting with him when I got there, a husband and wife, both orthopedists, who had brought dinner. When Michener suddenly sat upright and shouted "Jesus!" they witnessed what he had previously complained to them about—that he had been to four different doctors and none of them could determine what was causing the sharp and excruciating pain in his left elbow.

"Do either of you have any difficulty in my saying I want to consult a chiropractor?" Michener asked. He was scheduled to see an acupuncturist next and was thinking beyond that.

After they left Jim and I sat at his dining table and talked about the book of essays he'd completed that day. His editor at Random House, Kate Medina, had read the first draft and sent him back thirty pages of notes. "We haven't settled on a title yet—I'm not good at titles. I've called it *Lament for the Noble Land*. It is a lament. Things are happening that are just dreadful. They want to remake the nation a leaner, meaner society."

Part of that meaner society had hit particularly close to home for him when Amelia's nephew was gunned down in a drive-by shooting in Austin. And, of course, he paid attention to the world at large and though there were some ceasefires and peace initiatives taking place he was not optimistic about the world's future.

Though his conversation wasn't as robust as in times past, he still thought cogently. During one of our breaks he turned on *Jeopardy* and for the final round the question dealing with state capitals was: In the 1920s, the Progressive Party was headquartered in this capital. The three contestants all guessed wrong. Michener didn't guess. "Madison, Wisconsin," he whispered hoarsely. Then, with his next breath, he turned to me and said, "Amadou M'dou." That was the answer to a question I had posed a few hours earlier, wanting to know the name of the Senegalese in charge of UNESCO who had once treated him and Arthur Miller with contempt.

It was a few hours past his normal bed time and Amelia was waiting to help him move from the television room to his bedroom. The room where I slept was opposite Jim's and after his guests left I watched how she took care of him. She called him "Sweetie" and he called her "Dear."

There was a paperback of Michener's *Return to Paradise* on the shelf and I started reading his observations about the South Pacific islands which he wrote between the stories. The old man in the next room was having his teeth removed to be placed in a plastic cup, but he knew that he was about to escape the infirmities of age once he hit the pillows and traveled to all those exotic places in his dreams.

At his ninetieth birthday celebration I sat in a room filled with 357 well-wishers applauding Michener in his wheelchair next to a bronze bust in his likeness that the University of Texas had just presented to him and held high his book of sonnets, hot off the State House presses. He didn't know three-quarters of the people who were wishing him well but those he did, like Lady Bird Johnson or the presidents of three universities or the two former governors of Texas, he greeted with a firm grip. And for the next few hours he listened with graciousness and with some slight amusement as honored guests honored him.

But at his home the next day Michener was less sanguine. "I know what it was about," he said as we sat in our familiar setting, me with my tape recorder going, our knees almost touching. "People feel if they're going to get aboard the bandwagon, they'd better do it now. I'm growing older and the other guys aren't here any more."

It wasn't easy to sit with this man whose vitality had diminished so and talk about the last inning of his life, but that was part of my reason for being with Michener. I'd been coming to see him wherever he had lived and many times at airports as he traveled to and from the Far East and South Pacific. As he told the crowd the night before while proudly holding up his *Century of Sonnets*, "I was a man who stayed at the job even into his nineties." And then, with a nod to the shroud and the skull, he added, "But I think there is what the lawyers call a statute of limitations . . . and I face it."

On October 6, Amelia called from his house and said, "You asked me to let you know when it gets bad. It's got bad."

"How are you?" I asked when I got on the phone to him. Of all of our conversations, this was the toughest.

"Not too well," Jim answered. It was the first time I ever heard him say that. "They said it was terminal, which is tough news."

"Are you in any pain?"

"We're bearing up under it."

"There's not much time, is there Jim?"

"How're your daughters?" he asked. His life was already in the past, he was thinking about the future. I told him about Hana's musical progress and how Maya was beginning to apply for college. "Which ones?" he wanted to know. For the seventeen years I knew the man, education was always his greatest interest. I mentioned some of the universities being considered. He was quiet for a few moments. And then he said, "If you want to bring her here [to the U. of Texas], we'll pay her tuition for the first year."

It was the last thing James Michener said to me. He was dying and we both knew it, but his instincts were always to life, and even though he would be gone in a few days he was extending his hand once again.

He died on October 16. The news traveled fast around the world, reaching obscure and far-away places where people recognized his name. "I held nothing back," he had told me during one of our conversations. "I am not saving anything for a sequel."

**Talking with
Michener**

Have you come to grips with the legendary, almost Paul Bunyanesque stature you've achieved in American society?

My life has been, in its way, sort of a fable for our times—a portrait of the American experience—a guy starting with absolutely nothing, winding up giving away a substantial fortune.

It's more than your fortune, of course, that has given you your reputation. But, regarding financial matters: as a Quaker, you haven't been very forthcoming about discussing them.

I think you can understand my reluctance to talk about this but events have happened in the last couple of years that have thrown my life into a different perspective. My lawyer died and I had to write a new will. I am older and I worried about my wife's security from a legal point of view because our marriage was illegal in eleven states when it was contracted because of miscegenation laws. Because I don't know who my parents were, I thought that my will would be very subject to contest and decided to protect my wife by divesting all my property and income and putting it into her hands. I wound up without a nickel. It was an outright gift to her, which would have made her a moderately well-to-do widow if I died first.

Well, she very thoughtlessly died first. My will now reads almost humorously. Hardly a clause pertains to the real situation. We're unraveling it. Mari's will is a beautiful portrait of her: feisty, giving to all the good liberal causes she espoused. Curiously, thank God, she made very generous technical protections for me. It's a will that bespeaks conviction and love. She established a trust which I may not touch, but whose dividend reverts to me. It's big enough so that the interest will allow me to live pretty well. So I'm not in trouble. But it's a bizarre way to end the play.

At ninety you're still going strong. Do you worry much about dying?

Back in 1964 I had as major a heart attack as a human being can have and still survive. My EKG looked like a runaway horse. I thought I was dead. Fortunately I fell into the hands of Paul Dudley White, the great cardiologist who took care of Eisenhower and many famous men. He had a theory that was very brutal but very good. He said if you do any violent exercise before the heart has mended you were insane and would probably drop dead. But if, after surgery, you don't have all the physical exercise you had before, you are also an idiot. Then he said, of course, when you try it you may drop dead, but you were going to anyway, so give it a fling. Since then I've been around the world more than a dozen times and written everything since *Iberia*, eleven or twelve powerful novels, all the television, and everything else. I've had thirty years of a most active, creative and vigorous life, though I've had to take some time off for a quintuple coronary by-pass in 1986, a hip replacement, and because of some recurring bouts with vertigo.

Have you ever thought your life as a writer might have to cease?

I have had periods—after my heart attack and after the quintuple—when I believed without question that I would never be able to write again. I could not focus and I could not hold the reins together. It was terrifying. But fortunately, pain doesn't bother me much. So I just get on with it.

In early 1994 you had a scare on a cruise to the South Seas and had to be flown back to Texas from Hong Kong. What happened?

Another medical problem. It involved kidney failure which causes the legs to blow up the size of tree trunks and made evacuation to a state-side hospital absolutely necessary. Dialysis is now a life-time project.

You're lucky to be alive, not to mention still writing.

The way I look at it, I'm on borrowed time anyway. I survived three airplane wrecks, three bar room brawls, three marriages, a riot in Saigon, a near-goring in the streets of Pamplona, a cable car I was in was struck by lightning in Buenos Aires, and I once got hit in the face with a line drive in baseball when I thought I was dead. I figure if you live to be sixty-four, sixty-five and you're not in jail, you haven't contaminated yourself too badly, and you're not in an asylum or a poorhouse of any kind I think you've won the ball game; all the rest is gravy.

You actually once spent time in a poorhouse, didn't you?

I was in one in my youth for two extended spells—one about six weeks, one a long time. In those days, the poorhouse was the end of the line. I had very bad moments. We don't have poor-houses like that now. When you go through the kind of child-hood I had—the kind that does kids in—you harden up a bit. I was just a tough little son of a bitch. The hard years were from zero to fourteen. The easy ones came thereafter. I peddled chest-nuts at the age of ten; worked ten hours a day during the summer for the Burpee Seed Company at twelve, earning $4.50 per week, which I gave to my mother.

Your mother was obviously a significant figure, since you never knew your father.

I was raised by women. I had no men in my life at all. My mother, Mabel Michener, was a heroic woman. She made her living sewing buttonholes in a sweatshop, taking in other people's laundry. Yet she sent four kids through college and quite a few through high school. On her own. She took in abandoned chil-dren, you see. Hell, there must have been thirteen all together. And every night of my life, starting when I was five, she would read to us—Dickens, Thackeray, Sienkiewicz, Charles Reade. I suppose I owe all of my basic attitudes to her art in narration and the things she introduced us to.

Years later I was told that my mother worked for a real estate man who would move her and all of us into a rundown house which she would then clean up, renovate, and then he would sell it and we would move on. We lived in nine different houses all over Doylestown, in Bucks County. I remember each one vividly.

What opened your eyes to broader horizons as a kid?

One of our town's citizens was a famous scholar named Henry Mercer who had a lot of money and wild ideas. He imported a group of Italian artisans to build a castle right across from the house in which I then lived. I'm one of the few American writers who could speak about the building of a castle from first-hand experience. One of my first visual memories is of the winter night when I was about five years old with these workmen chop-ping down cedar trees and lugging them to the top of the castle on the parapets. At midnight he doused the trees with gasoline, threw a lantern in, and set the whole thing ablaze! The fire police came and everybody thought the place was burning down.

But Old Henry was just celebrating the completion of the castle, which was made of concrete and wouldn't burn. It lit up the whole horizon though, with Henry cackling away as his castle was in flames. That's a pretty vivid memory. Henry then moved his workers to the other side of town and built another castle, bigger and better than the first. So I lived in a town that had two castles. In the second one he put together a great museum, installing all the artifacts that workmen had used in the preceding century which he had collected. So if you want to see how dentists and doctors worked, or wood joiners or piano makers or barbers or wheelwrights, you would have to come to my hometown and go to this castle and in these rooms would be maybe two thousand examples of dental tools graded by decades, going back to about 1770. It's a record of American life that is incomparable and I grew up with this, knew them intimately as a boy, even helped set some of them up. It had a gallows that was the part we kids liked best. We would have mock hangings and when you went through that you were so terrified of jails and punishment that it had a very salutary effect.

Another boyhood memory I have is of the Boys' Brigade, sort of a rebel outfit. It wasn't the Boy Scouts; that was the quality outfit. But we had a wonderful three weeks of real camping out and canoes up and down the river and marching and rifle drills.

It sounds like something out of Mark Twain.

I have a great love for Doylestown—it gave me my education and my start. When the library first opened, the first two people to sign up for books were Margaret Mead and then me. The day a boy takes a book out of the library and takes it seriously, he starts the long decline. It can be a very grand experience, but the minute you taste knowledge you get caught up in this tremendous battle . . . which you're going to lose.

Still, there really wasn't a lot to hold me in Doylestown. I knew there was a bigger world elsewhere.

What books tickled your imagination at an early age?

I learned how to write when I was very young. I read a child's book about the Trojan War and decided that the Greeks were really a bunch of frauds with their tricky horses and the terrible things they did, stealing one another's wives. So I rewrote the ending of *The Iliad* so that the Trojans won. And Achilles and Ajax got what they wanted, believe me.

What about movies, did they have any influence?

One of the best things I learned about writing was at the movies, seeing the Saturday serials. They often ran fifteen weeks, and to get you hooked in the first episode, where you paid a nickel to get in, you'd better have something pretty exciting. They always had a hero and a villain, it was pretty clear which was which. But you didn't know whether the villain was a real villain. We'd been fooled on that a couple of times, but one time they had him do three things: he kicked his dog; he slugged his mother—both of which I could accept because I knew some dogs that were pretty obnoxious and some mothers who could stand a bit of pushing around; but then when he wanted to write a ransom note and couldn't find any paper he tore a page out of the Bible. I can still hear it, I can still see him do that. Oh my God, you are in real trouble. I was sorry for him! But I wanted to know what happened to the SOB. I remember that series very well.

Then my Aunt Laura in Detroit sent us this series of books. I read the whole bloody bunch—I've always been a sucker for a narrative, especially old foreign language novels, the great historical novels. I read all of Balzac when I was fourteen.

What, exactly, do you feel you learned from Balzac?

That there is no reason for drawing back from the major commitment. That it is not at all improper for a writer like Balzac or Tolstoy or Dickens or Joyce Carol Oates to attempt thirty-five or forty novels on a single theme. It's not ridiculous at all if your mind is of that magnitude, that character. Another thing would be the virtue of having established a milieu in which you were going to tell your story. He did that marvelously with Paris, but he wasn't bound to Paris, he could go into the provinces and see where these people came from and what their problems were there. One of his novels that I liked best was *The Quest for the Absolute*, which deals with somebody collecting Dutch paintings among other things. I don't think it involves Paris at all. The third thing would be the great value of having a continuing character to whom you relate things and through whom you see things. Rastignac is a marvelous character in that way. Better than Pere Goriot, who is himself a more interesting character. And the fourth thing was that a writer is somebody who writes. And he cannot be expected or it be demanded of him that everything be on the same level. Sometimes his mind isn't on that level, but he's the guy who does it and you have to take what he is willing or able to do at that moment and trust that when you catch up with it, you'll see that he has something to say.

That's when I began seeing life differently. I knew every house in a town of about thirty-eight hundred people because I delivered papers in the morning, walking the entire route for which I was responsible. When you do that you become involved in certain tragedies: the leading doctor, who everybody thought had it made, blows his brains out; a teacher is thrown out of school; a girl becomes pregnant and leaves home. I saw lives go awry; lawyers put in jail because they got involved in their clients' problems. At a very early age I adopted the policy of attending court, which was right next to the school house. I watched the dramas unfold.

For example?

In our high school we had an absolutely beautiful girl who had a rapscallion brother my age. One day their uncle was found dead, and then a salesman was found dead, and it was traced to her brother. I had several brushes with this brother, and he scared me because he really meant if you didn't behave that he was going to tend to it. You believed him. He was caught and tried and sentenced to be hanged. Then he broke out of the courtroom and went rampaging down the street of our town, which was thrown into terror. Somebody tackled him and he was recaptured and taken to jail and hanged. Several other people of my acquaintance were hung but this was the most dramatic case because I was involved personally with the family.

I was very close to abortion when I was a boy. The known abortionist, a trained nurse, lived in a big house at the end of town. About every four or five years they would arrest her under pressure from the public and there would be a trial, and we would sneak in to hear it, utterly fascinated by the mystery of the thing.

We were fourteen or fifteen. But I noticed that the girl involved who had had the abortion was always the daughter of a lawyer or a judge or a clergyman or school principal. It wasn't some floozy from the southern end of the county. And if the Supreme Court upsets *Roe vs. Wade*, we're going to see the same phenomenon. It's going to be the very children of the people that pass the law who are going to be in the middle of it. Of that I am quite sure, just from my experience as a boy. It was always the girl from some known family.

So you're for abortion?

I am against abortion. But I also believe that women have to have the right to decide these things.

What else influenced you as a boy?

When I worked in an amusement park I saw everything there—prostitutes, killings that were hushed up in the newspapers, drifters. I even learned to become a short-change artist, accepting a two dollar bill and claiming it was a one. We played that amusement park like an accordion, finagling the turnstiles, stealing the bloody place blind. If I could get a nun to put down a two dollar bill, con her into thinking it was a one, I was the victor. When I go to the theater now and pass money in, I watch. They're using every trick we used. It's still flourishing.

So how did these experiences fire your ambitions?

I never really had childhood ambitions. I've had reunions with people who knew me for a long time, and their testimony is overwhelmingly that they never expected much from me. They knew I was a bright guy but not very well organized.

By the time I was fourteen or fifteen, I had knocked around a decent part of the country. I rode the railroad once, it terrified me. I went all the way from Canada to Florida on the rails and hitchhiking. Sometimes I'd be bothered by men who were interested in me and I had to be pretty forceful a couple of times. I was an athlete, moderately good-looking, red hair, loose limbed, free and easy. A manly kid for better or for worse. I was always able to handle it fairly easily. I never ran into a real goon and I was completely heterosexual.

Did you ever have encounters with police?

In the South, in states like North Carolina and in Georgia, I was arrested for vagrancy several times and got my fear of mixing with the police. I was scared stiff when they showed me how their jails were run. They wanted to scare me, and the vaccination took.

The South has produced a different brand of American writer. Could you tell the difference between southern states and where you came from?

Georgia made a powerful impression on me because I knew it was different. Iowa looked just like Pennsylvania to me. I didn't know it was so different, that it had a different system of education, a whole new system of values. When I got out into the drylands, it never occurred to me that they were entirely different. They might have looked like home, but they certainly were not home. I didn't even realize Canada was a different country. But Georgia—there they had the cotton shacks, the blacks, the tough police. I knew that was not rural Bucks County.

Did your travels mature you?

Even though I was gaining experiences, I didn't have that same kind of knowledge about myself. I was really rather dumb. I was in that amusement park about a year and a half before I knew what a prostitute was. Once I knew, I'd go down to what was called Callow Hill Street where the prostitutes were in Philadelphia with some friends—we'd get some money together and borrow a car. But most of us would be afraid to go. I was pretty slow in that field. We also had the old German tradition in our town of bundling— that's where fellows and girls would go to bed together starting at about sixteen or seventeen, but with the assumption that they would get married if the girl got pregnant.

Were you a popular kid? Did you have many friends?

I went along fairly happily, though I was a very difficult child. I don't think I was very likeable. I never had any clothes that were bought for me until I was about fourteen. I never had a pair of skates or sneakers, never had a bicycle, never had a little wagon or a baseball glove. I never had an automobile or the use of an automobile. Never took vacations. And I used to get into fights. Look at my nose, it goes around a corner. That's from speaking when I should have been listening. I was clubbed up by my peers. They disciplined me. I was different and that made me very tough. I was suspended from every school I was ever in, including college. So there was a dark undercurrent. I could easily have been sent to reform school, but I avoided that. If I hadn't gone my own way I'd probably be a different person. I had such a personal agenda, it was so difficult, that unless I defended myself vigorously it was not going to hang together.

You were nine when the First World War started. What do you recall about that time?

In our little town near Philadelphia there was a succession of absolutely wonderful young men in the British military—goatees, wonderful uniforms. In 1916 they came and said there was danger and they needed us. We were not yet in. I heard them and then went down and stormed this German shoemaker's house and burned the portrait of the Kaiser. Just me.

That might have been 1917 or even '18; I would have been eleven. But that parade of British apologists talking about Belgium and France and their own trench warfare, they were very powerful. Also, all of my older friends had to go into the war. A hundred men from our town went overseas. So the First World War was very real to me.

How real was it when you got to meet President Calvin Coolidge in 1924?

It was purely capricious. The top students from different high schools went to the White House every year in the spring. Coolidge sat and talked with me.

As a top student, did you find anything about school difficult?

Education was easy for me. I have a Germanic type of mind, a bear trap. I can organize and assimilate material. I distinguish between the Germanic and the French way of thinking. The two systems are quite at odds with one another. The German process is heavily deductive, it's one of amassing data and making deductions from it. The French is inductive and intuitive, very poetic and emotional. Each has its merits and each has a flowering.

I was gifted with a marvelous high school and two very fine teachers, Miss Mathews and Miss Spencer. Miss Mathews was a remarkable woman, four feet ten with a will of Genghis Kahn, absolutely fearless in bucking the administration or the fashions of the time. Miss Spencer gave me my love for math. Maybe more of my habits were formed from her.

There was also a woman who gave me a box of carbon paper when I was a young kid. She was rather poor, didn't have much else to give, and she showed me how it should be used and how you could duplicate your writing an endless number of times and it quite enchanted me. I've always been fascinated by the reproductive miracle of either carbon paper or type or now word processing. For some of us that is what life is all about, the transmitting of ideas. First codifying them, then transmitting them.

Did you learn how to do this first as a journalist?

As a reporter for my school newspaper I found that I simply could not tell a story badly. If we won a basketball game or if we went on a camping trip, I would have to tell it in an artistic way. So I learned early on that I could do that and somebody else couldn't.

Didn't you also learn that some people in positions of power had it in for guys like you?

My high school was run by Dr. Carmon Ross—a tyrant—but his heart was in the right place educationally. He loved rich people and despised poor people and gave me a very bad time. He was a real strict disciplinarian. He was not pleasant. When I was fifteen I was apprenticed to a plumber. I got pretty far. Then my Uncle Arthur came to visit and just went up the wall. He said, "This boy is not intended to be a plumber!" He went down and took me out. Why was I there? Because the principal, Dr. Ross, had come to my mother and said, "It's time this boy prepared for a job. He would be ideal as a plumber's helper." I thought maybe he was right. College had never entered my mind. I was pretty naive.

When I got a scholarship to Swarthmore, he came to see my mother and told her that I was not college material and that she should make me turn it down because I would not be a credit to the college. It burned him up that I got that scholarship. He couldn't believe that his judgment was so faulty.

How much different was college than high school?

After being what you might call a big man on campus in high school, it took me about a month to figure out that Swarthmore was going to be a tough ball game. I was elected into one of the good fraternities but I couldn't stand the nonsense and resigned under very tense circumstances, leading the fight against them because I thought they were crap. In a conservative college in that period, to buck the fraternity system was as radical as you could be. I didn't go out for any sports; I roomed off-campus and got a job as a nightwatchman in a hotel. I don't know when I slept, but the last two years I was put in a vigorous honors program. No class had more than five students and each lasted for two and a half hours with a very bright teacher. So you were always called on and it was quite a different educational experience. I had a major and two minors and then was left on my own. I learned to write term papers, to do research, to use a library, to do comparative studies, to read more advanced books. I learned a lot about the language through the heavy writing I had to do. I had papers due every three weeks, and I excelled in British history. I knew everything that a kid my age could know about the Elizabethan period, the period of the great reforms of 1832, all of which I was encouraged to learn on my own. I never had a course in American history, philosophy, or literature. At Swarthmore you were British or you were nothing. You could be French or German, but American . . . no culture. So although I had read almost all world literature in the narrative form by the time I was twenty-five the one I missed was American. I missed Cooper, I missed Fitzgerald, and Wolfe. But I had a fantastic grounding in world literature.

Was there any one book which showed you how a writer works?

The book which first gave me a strong sense of how a novel was constructed was Arnold Bennett's *The Old Wives' Tale*. I try to fashion myself after Bennett. Then came Samuel Butler's *The Way of All Flesh*. But I'll never forget how overwhelmed I was by *Vanity Fair*. I didn't read it until I was maybe nineteen or twenty.

I can remember being so excited about it, how the characters in-tertwined and played upon one another. I have gone back to read *Vanity Fair* and find it very stylized and eighteenth-century, some of the preaching and advice quite boring. I do not find that with Dickens or Dostoevsky or Flaubert.

Many books of great merit made no impression on me at all. I didn't need Camus, but oh boy, I needed Butler, I needed the great poets, and the great Russians. If a kid doesn't stumble upon these things he's just terribly deprived. And it doesn't have to happen through books or good teachers—it could be a play or a scientific experiment. Or a Boy Scout master, a clergyman, or an uncle who was wiser than the father.

How rigorously were you tested in college?

At Swarthmore you were tested not by your professors but by four scholars they brought in from the Sorbonne, Oxford, Princeton, Harvard, Yale, the Universities of Indiana, Pennsyl-vania, or Denver. We had three-hour exams morning and after-noon for a week and then at the end you had an oral exam. The professor from Princeton who examined me in English was so as-tounded at the width and breadth of my knowledge that he got me a fellowship to Chicago.

I worked with great professors and I had great admiration and respect for them and I would feel like hell if I let them down. Maybe they were father figures.

Some time ago a group of Nobel Prize winners and a couple of other people were at the White House for a big session. I spent a good deal of the time with James Watson who cowrote *The Double Helix*. He told me two fascinating things. He said that at thirty-four he was an elder statesman in his field and not even able to keep up with the work being done by the really bright young men. I've often suspected this. If you look at the lives of Shelley, Keats, Mozart, you have this youthful effervescence in typical fields like mathematical analysis or poetry or writing a symphony.

The other thing Watson said was even more dramatic to me. I asked him about education and he said the great secret of educa-tion throughout history was when you were young to go where bright people were. Nothing is more important. He said, 'You not only need a bright person, but you need a group of bright people to bounce your ideas off and compare yourself with.' He was so adamant on that, it was really quite exciting.

You've covered your strengths; what about your weaknesses in school?

My one deficiency was in foreign languages. In all the years of my education nobody ever sat down with me and talked with me about what I should study. So I was allowed to go through high school and college without either French or German. It's been a terrible deficiency in my life that I don't have those two wonderful languages. I got Spanish because they had to put somebody in the class and I have written about Spain and things Spanish all my life.

Didn't you also have something to do with the theater at Swarthmore?

Swarthmore had a traveling Chautauqua which operated under a circus tent in the summers and brought programs of extremely high quality to the people. It was the television of its day. I worked there as a tent boy when I was ten and remembered listening to the great addresses of William Jennings Bryan, William Howard Taft, and Russell Conwell. I got to know the people and it gave me a sense of a much bigger world. Then during my senior year I joined in Chautauqua myself.

I was in a famous play called *Skidding* which was a sensation of that period. We took this play throughout the Eastern states for a long summer. I was also the puppeteer of the Chautauqua circuit and with the aid of another gifted young man we gave puppet shows all over the country.

What year were you in at Swarthmore when you found out that you had been adopted?

I was a junior when I found out that Mabel Michener wasn't my real mother. It hit me with an overwhelming force. I had to face the very difficult problem of what my parentage was and what my place in the universe was. I could be part Negro or Jewish or Irish or Russian.

I've done a lot of work on this recent move to uncover all records—a very bad idea, really. I doubt that much good will be accomplished. I've followed a hundred cases: everyone handled it a different way, all of them handled it wrong. I don't think there's a right way to do it. If you tell the kid from the beginning, I've seen that work very poorly. If you don't tell him, as in my case, you run a great risk.

Naturally you can't help but speculate. When things are going bad it would be fascinating to daydream that there was a rich somebody somewhere who was going to come in a black Buick and save you. I'm sure people who are parented divert that dream to an uncle somewhere. That's in *Death of a Salesman*. I decided I'm never going to solve that one.

One day I suddenly thought, Jesus, I'm penalyzing myself twice. I'm experiencing this unfairness and now I'm brooding and bitching about it and I'm losing double. From that moment on I never bitched about anything.

In psychological profiles on me it's been speculated that my drive to research subjects is really a search for my own parents, but I'm not wise enough to answer that. When I was unmarried I courted several girls who were going through psychoanalysis. In every instance the psychiatrist told the young lady, 'Gee, I would like to get my hands on that guy Michener, to unravel that tangle of snakes.' It quite frightened me. I felt that I had, through some exercise of character and will and intelligence, worked out a system that worked for me, that enabled me to do what I wanted to do and survive in society. I didn't want a stranger to come in and rearrange it all. The great secret that one of them had was that I would be different if there had been men in my life. Christ, I knew that at age two!

So there are questions about your life that have remained unanswered for you.

There is a great deal about me that I don't want to know. A life is an agreed-upon set of decisions, never the best ones, but pragmatically it works. I have stabilized my life. I get by. I have no belief at all that it is as good as it could be, but I sure as hell don't want somebody messing around with it when I am reaching a kind of stabilization, pitiful as it is.

**WAY AHEAD OF
MY GENERATION**

2

What did you want to be after you left Swarthmore?

I graduated from college without having a clue as to what I was going to do. But I got lucky. The Hills School, a wonderful private school in Pennsylvania teaching children of very wealthy parents, offered me a job. I became a teacher almost by accident.

How long were you there?

I was there two years, at the depth of the Depression, when I read a very powerful book about the social structure of main line Philadelphia, *Huntsman in the Sky* by Granville Toogood. He was a writer much like Edith Wharton or Louis Auchincloss today. Those people have a hell of an advantage in that they know a total aspect of a social past. Even though I had a high-paying job—more than $2,000 for the school year—I went in one day and said, "I'm resigning because I want to go to Europe." And everybody said, "You're out of your mind, look at all the people who don't have work; if you do this you will destroy your life, your chances."

Remember, everybody was out of work, selling apples, the W.P.A. started sending kids out in the country. But I didn't allow the Depression to derail me.

And did Europe turn out to be the right move for you?

It's the best thing I ever did. I never would have developed the way I did if I had not done that. No way. And when I came back two years later, all the older men who told me how I'd regret my decision were still there, with no bigger visions than the day they graduated from college.

Why Europe?

I went to Europe to find out what the score was. And whom did I run into and live with as a roommate when I got a fellowship to study at St. Andrews University in Scotland? A red-hot Nazi from Germany, Herr Wagner, who taught me everything I needed to know about fascism. And then I lived with this group of young communists who were going to try to overthrow Europe. Their economic and political analyses were quite flatulent—it had no attraction for me. I did a lot of the reading—Karl Marx, Engels, some of the English Communists—and learned what it was all about, but it was spurious from the word *go* for somebody like me who had studied the Industrial Revolution and the evil consequences of it.

Didn't you also learn to be a sailor while you were in Scotland?

Because I always loved the sea, I used to read the Sunday paper at the Union in Scotland. I was fascinated by the P & O Line, Peninsular and Oriental, the great line of British maritime history. It was the lifeline from London to Bombay and Calcutta, and later to Australia and New Zealand. I used to dream of having enough money to take a ride on one of those ships.

One summer I hooked up with a company, the Bruce Line. The Scottish ships had a wonderful program of inviting college students to come aboard and they paid you a shilling a month—twenty-five cents. You shipped aboard a tanker and you went all over the Mediterranean and the Baltic.

How fast did you travel?

These were slow, slow ships, in a day they did ninety-six knots. When you were aboard, you got a place to sleep and you ate with the officers and then you had some trivial duties. Mine was a chart corrector. I got to know the Mediterranean as few people know it.

What did the freighter carry?

We would leave Scotland with the ship hardly visible because sooty coal was all over the top deck. They would use all of it going out, so they loaded every goddamn inch, except the bathrooms, with bituminous coal. You were pretty dirty on the way out, but the ship was like a parlor coming back.

Were you allowed off the ship when you arrived at different ports?

As soon as you hit port you were free. I could then go by rail to the next port and I saw Europe that way. That's how I got to know Italy so well.

Was it on these travels that you developed your interest in bullfighting?

That was another summer when I went to Spain and joined a touring group of bullfighters. Every summer without rest scores of aficionados, many from foreign countries, follow the bullfighters of Spain from town to town. I was such a camp follower, at age twenty-four. It was not unusual, except that most such travelers are well heeled; I had minimum funds.

What got you interested in bullfighting?

Hemingway's *The Sun Also Rises*. I had a college professor who told us one day that Hemingway's short story "The Killers" had remade the narrative form, and he read it in class to justify his enthusiasm. That led me to the novel, on my own, and I was captivated by Pamplona, about which I would write in due course, and at which a famous photograph was shot of me avoiding a maddened bull who had just killed a man practically on my boot tops. I saw my first fight cold-turkey in Valencia in 1933 and I think I caught the full flavor of the spectacle immediately. This was at least a year before Hemingway wrote his excellent *Death in the Afternoon*. How was it possible? Writers are people with instantaneous reactions to dramatic situations, and in my case my first incandescent reactions often enlighten the entire experience.

Were you attracted to the symbolic aspects of the spectacle?

I see the bullfight as an exemplification of dark, mysterious power operating against the dancing pirouetting man, the bull in his primal dark coat, the man in his extravagant suit of lights. This imagery has been so potent for me that my novel *Mexico* is a retelling of that experience. I believe it is that symbolism that accounts for the fascination that many find in this arcane and almost outdated art. Other writers have written movingly of a fisherman battling with one canny trout, or a young girl reacting to her horse, or a sea captain chasing a white whale, so I stand within an honorable tradition.

What other early European memories do you treasure?

The trip I took to Barra one winter while I was studying in Scotland. It's one of the most remote of the islands in Europe, in the Outer Hebrides. It's not as remote as either Easter Island or Pitcairn, but it was where I learned to love islands and where I did a great deal of collecting the folk songs I heard there. When

I heard them I responded to them overwhelmingly. I collected the wording, bought all the records that were available, played them for scholars who have marveled at their tremendous quality. I still have them these sixty years later.

How did those two years in Europe change you?

I returned from Europe way, way ahead of my generation. As I was broke I got a job teaching English at George School in Newtown, a private school in Bucks County. I got married during that time to a wonderful girl, daughter of a minister, and could well have married one of the students there, a senior, who was an absolutely marvelous girl but she was never in my class.

Were you one of those teachers whose roving eye influenced what grade a pretty girl might get?

I did find on occasions if a girl was especially pretty and lovely she tended to get an A– rather than a B+, in my classes as well as in others. I'm not stupid! But it never got me very far.

A–, B+, those are pretty high grades. One would have thought you'd be harder on your students. Did you like teaching?

I loved it. I get letters from my students of sixty years ago constantly, saying that I did work to jolt them out of their preconceptions. I'm asked if writing can be taught. I think that any human behavior can be improved upon with thoughtful analysis or instruction or insight. I doubt that one can change internal character or make a writer, but teachers can sure as hell help one.

Including changing the way classes were taught?

When I wasn't allowed to improve upon the way English was being taught at George School I quit and moved into history. I started all over in my education to make myself a historian and became a high official in the Social Studies Society of America. The National Council for the Social Studies brought out a book in 1991 of all my educational writings, which were pretty gutsy. And I helped administer the National Youth Administration at a time when people simply did not have enough to live on. The government said it is to everybody's advantage to have the young people continue their college educations. For God's sake, don't take them out of school! And they gave $35 a month, it was like $5,000. Marvelous, marvelous rule, just like the G.I Bill after the war.

What were you most proud of as a teacher then?

One of the things I'm most proud of was I deduced a whole theory of stereophonic music and wound up building, with an electronics wizard who was also a brilliant young student, a stereo system that was as good as anything I've heard since, excepting the digitals. And this was back in 1934. It started when I went to Philadelphia and got one of those great RCA's for $35. It was a curved, monstrous machine with a gigantic generator. We took the sound track and divided it into three parts, using heavy filters: the central, the base, and the tenor. Then we got four different speakers that had different physical qualities and knocked out all the high notes in one, and all the low notes in another, and moved them all around. We had them widely spaced and it produced music so beautiful in 1934, years before anyone was doing it commercially, that people would come literally from miles around.

Wasn't it in The Drifters *where you wrote that no man whose relations with women are satisfactory would need to construct a high-fidelity system which he could dominate?*

I think there is a very powerful sexual factor involved here. I have never known a woman who enjoyed high stereo, but I've known thousands of men—all the astronauts, all the scientists— who are real big on it. It's one of the few things in our society that you can dominate. If you don't like the bass, you just take it out.

How important is music to you?

I listen to music every day of my life. I have tapes I make for any book I'm working on, with the music generic to that subject. It can be folk music as it was for *The Drifters*, rock and roll, whatever is germane. The big bands and the girl singers of my youth were saccharine and sentimental; anything that followed that was an improvement. I missed Louis Armstrong, though I see now he was very special. Liked Nat King Cole. Joan Baez is my favorite singer. I hold the best of Bob Dylan in high regard, though I was never much taken with the preachy content songs, which were sometimes pretty shabby intellectually. I thought the Beatles were authentic music voices, though I deplored their preachments on dope. I liked some of the Jefferson Airplane, Simon and Garfunkel.

I do the same thing with classical music. I listen to the Beethoven String Quartets, all of which I know almost by heart; Mahler's First Symphony—a masterpiece; some of Mozart; a lot of Palestrina. I'm very fond of Stravinsky and Brahms. I would always prefer Brahms to Mozart—I'm not much taken with light dancing music. I like Mozart in its place, but not seriously. Schoenberg is difficult but he's very necessary. If you listen only to Bach and Brahams, Beethoven, Schumann, and Mendelssohn, you fall within a pattern. That's why Sibelius was so good for me, he felt he didn't have to follow any form at all, just wrote it and it was really quite magnificent. So I could never have done what I've accomplished without the great classical rhythms, because that's what I'm trained in, in poetry, in fiction, and in music. Music gives me a sense of form and structure.

Can you be more specific with how music helped stimulate your writing?

When I was writing *The Source*, I had Stravinsky's *Symphony of the Psalms* as a reminder of what the ancient Hebrews probably were like. It was very refreshing and very clean. Beethoven's *Fourth* hit me very hard; there's a beginning and then there's a long prelude, you would not know there was any piano involved. And then when the piano does come in, it is quite majestic. I really got my idea of the start of *The Source* that way: the understated opening, rather than a big, tremendous bang! bang! say with Tchaikovsky or Beethoven's *Fifth*, the great Emperor concerto that's so wonderful, but it's boom! And sometimes that doesn't suit the individual writer or artist. Anyone who wants to be an artist is well advised to look at *all* the artists of his lifetime in popular music, dance, cinema, architecture. It's very necessary if you want to get a style of your own.

What about opera?

A major factor in my education was opera. I know probably a dozen of them by heart and could conduct them, every note, if I had a score. I know almost all the great arias and choruses. Arrigo Boito's *Mefistofele* is my favorite record of all time, though I am deeply moved by *Aida*. The closing scene of *Aida* comes very close to the heart of what human tragedy is: this young football hero, you might say, gets messed up in a bad deal and is sentenced to death for treason, and she decides to go live with him. It's as real to me as if it happened in the next town. A great deal of the storytelling quality that I have comes from this.

When I was a young man I had maybe five hundred of the major Red Seal records of all the great voices. The ones I liked most were Toti Dal Monte, Luisa Tetrazzini, Renata Tebaldi. Renata Scotto is a very good artist. Rothenberger, Calve. I knew all the tenors. I had a big regard for Gigli. Caruso, of course. Bidu Sayao. Monserrat Caballe. Leonard Warren may be the best singer America has ever produced, he was tremendous.

If I had a disappointment in the way my work is treated, it is that no movie or play came along that developed it musically in high music form. Look at Prosper Merimee, the French writer who wrote this absolutely glowing novella *Carmen*. Another man, Georges Bizet, who has never been to Spain, reads it and is swept off his feet by it. And out of this you get probably the most widely accepted opera in the world. The artistic experience is sometimes like that: you may not be the hottest thing that ever came down the pike, but you have this one vision and boom! it is forever. That is no mean accomplishment. I think if Bizet and I could have gotten together in some bar in Paris, unquestionably something would have come out of it. Maybe King David coming to the town from *The Source*.

It may not be opera, but you did get to hear South Pacific, *and more recently, wasn't* Sayonara *done as a musical?*

Yes, and it was delightful. A trio of talented young fellows started work on the book and the music and the lyrics twenty-two years ago. Year after year I extended their dramatic rights to my novel and prayed for their success. No luck. Then I heard that they'd made a deal with a light-opera company in Houston, Texas, with a backup little theater company in Seattle, Washington. I went down to Houston with my fingers crossed and saw two breathtakingly beautiful performances.

We diverted from your building stereo systems back in the thirties. How long did that continue?

I brought my stereo machine with me when I went out to Colorado and every year I would build two or three complete audio systems with Heath kits and then give it to a church or school. I did that all the time I was in Colorado.

Why did you go to Colorado?

Just as I left the security of my first teaching job to go to Europe, I did something just as dangerous when I left George School to go out West to teach at the Colorado State College of Education. But I really saw America then.

And what was it that you saw?

I was a child solely of an English type education, in a narrow eastern seaboard of the United States. Then suddenly to find out there were some thirty-six states west of where I was with their own qualities and their own values was a revelation. I went to Colorado and saw there was a Hispanic component, a French component, and, above all, a liberal free-swinging component. Colorado was amazing in that its three top jobs—Governor and two Senators—were never of the same party. In Pennsylvania if you were not a Republican, I'm not sure if it was safe to go out during hunting season. But in Colorado you could be anything that you wanted to be. If I had stayed four more years in my eastern environment, I would have been doomed. In Colorado I wound up leading the fight for Mexican rights because it was perfectly obvious it was going to happen.

Would you consider yourself an avant-garde educator at that time?

Very. And word of it circulated and I was invited to teach as a visiting professor at Harvard, where I also became editor of publications for history teachers in America. I conducted a study for them of four New England communities that were undergoing economic and social changes.

Harvard's got the reputation, but is it everything it's cracked up to be?

Harvard is a majestic place. I'm awfully glad I had the experience, even though after my two years I wasn't invited to stay. While I was at Harvard, the White House invited me down to dinner. It was a very trying time—1939—and I had dinner with Eleanor Roosevelt, who was quite charming and very interested in what I was doing. We talked a great deal about education. After dinner we met the president, who was obviously preoccupied with the war in Europe. He was in a chair when we went in to see him and I was not aware he was crippled. It never appeared in the press, there was never a photograph of him that way. They just kept it quiet.

Seems pretty fortuitous in retrospect that Harvard didn't keep you.

While I was at Harvard, Macmillan Publishing Company sent out questionnaires to all their academic people who had written text books for them, searching for someone to edit high school texts who could be trained to take over the presidency of their company, one of the great publishers in this country. Three names surfaced repeatedly. I was third on the list. The first man took the presidency of a university; the second man took a hell of a good job somewhere; so I was moved into top position. They offered me a marvelous job and three times the salary I'd ever had. So I wasn't just seduced out of teaching, I was really dragooned. And always felt a little bit guilty and always regretted that I didn't stay at Harvard, where I was also working on my doctorate. Had I finished my doctorate there I would have remained a teacher for sure. But it did lead down other paths, and I certainly can't complain.

Publishing must have seemed a whole other world.

The job at Macmillan gave me a chance to live in New York with the Metropolitan Opera and the New York Philharmonic and the plays—heady stuff for a man who loves the arts and what's going on. It also gave me a long intimate indoctrination into the book as a book until I really became an expert in production and the make-up of a book, how they ought to look, the care that's to be taken with them, the printing processes. And too, very important, the economics of the profession. I have maybe more regard for and know more about book production than almost any other writer I know because I was right in the middle of it. I learned to revere the book.

Were you more of an editor or an administrator at Macmillan?

Editing is where I really spent my time. I loved it. You learned the rules of grammar as they apply to books. You learned how to abbreviate, how to cut, how to work with the author without destroying his or her enthusiasm. And you learned how to compensate for lines, because it was very expensive to change a whole paragraph—you never made a correction at the beginning of a paragraph, only at the end. And I learned about the selling of books, about their distribution, their warehousing.

It must have saddened you to see what happened to MacMillan, first bought by Robert Maxwell, then sold to Paramount.

When I think of what Macmillan was in my day, and that it would wind up falling into the hands of that slimeball Robert Maxwell it is so awful. When I was there it was a noble company. Before, everybody used to laugh at our fall list; ten years later they all wished they had it. That's really a summary of Macmillan. Because we had books that lasted a long time and sold just as well in their seventh year as they did in the second. That came about because we had certain principles and good judgment and we had the support of the British company, which had a long honorable tradition and whose president, Harold Macmillan, became prime minister of Great Britain. So we were in the fast lane.

Some think that Maxwell didn't accidentally drown. Do you?

I followed that whole story about Maxwell's boating death, and I have a feeling that a man like him, who had made the terrific moves that he did, heading for a title I would suppose, knowing what he had done to strafe his own company and his own family and everything he had touched, when it all began to fall apart, I could see him committing suicide. Look at Donald Trump, look at Michael Milken. These guys can crash.

How far did you hope to advance when you were at Macmillan?

I was asked to go into training to be its president. Other publishers were offering me big chances to write text books. I even kicked around the idea of writing a western novel. I got moderately well into it but didn't have the skill or the courage to see it through.

And since I was on the inside of publishing I saw the operation of a great house that had the top best sellers of the decade, like *Gone With the Wind* and *Forever Amber*. I saw that a great deal of that kind of publishing was hoopla, which I wanted no part of.

What do you mean?

Every publisher has a wonderfully bright girl, about 29 years old, they still have them, they're interchangeable, always good-looking, and her job is to get those amenities which are so important to a writer, on no budget at all. Getting them on television, or in those days radio, in the newspapers, on a speaking tour. We had an editor at that time whose job was to go to the piers and meet the big six foreign writers as they came in, pick up the English author and whisk her or him down to the publicist's office. They had lunch in a paneled, stately board room, then got the author interviewed. It was quite obvious that they were paying these dear people off with hoopla and high nonsense rather than royalties. We didn't give that treatment to the writer from Sioux City, Iowa. He got the same advance without the hoopla. But the English author was *somebody*, though he was paid in a rather debased coinage, one that just turned my stomach. I wanted no part of that circus, and I've never been part of it. I know no publicists, no book reviewers, no publishers or editors other than the ones I work with.

But when you were at Macmillan you weren't yet a writer. How did you cross that bridge?

I probably would not have become a writer, except for World War Two. I have often thought that I might have been like Giuseppe Di Lampedusa, I might have written *The Leopard* when I was about 68, living on a small pension. I didn't see myself breaking out any sooner.

And then Pearl Harbor was bombed.

Exactly. I knew this was a battle to the death and that I had to respond, had to go to war. Now I don't want to cover myself with glory because I don't know whether I would have. I *think* I would have. But I could have claimed an exemption both because I was a Quaker and because I was over age at 36.

Was your religion the only factor involved in testing your decision?

There was another issue involved. When I was teaching world history and current events in Colorado, I fell into the clutches of the head of my department. When they made horses asses they broke the model with him.

He was determined that I should go into uniform, it was the only manly thing to do. And he hounded me, even after I got the job in New York with Macmillan and moved out of his jurisdiction. He succeeded, and his draft board gave me an order to report to Fort Dix, way the hell out in Colorado, on Friday. So on Thursday I cut a deal with the Navy. He was upset when he heard about it. He wanted to go to Washington to get me back in the Army.

How memorable was your indoctrination into the Navy?

I'll never forget it. They broke you down from the minute you got into the system. You sat naked in this goddamn room after your physical for maybe two hours. They asked the first four guys on my right what they did. We were all in our thirties. The guy sitting next to me was from Georgia and they asked him what he could do and he said, "I can repair diesel engines." They wanted to make him an Admiral! So I figured out what the rule was. They got to me and they were about to pass me over because it said I had been a college professor, so I said, "When I was a young man I had my papers in the British Merchant Fleet." So they took me and gave me a lieutenancy within one minute, and they sent me out to the Pacific.

And that's where your life changed?

I saw the devastation of war, the loneliness of that terrible Pacific duty. I had two complete, rather arduous tours out there.

I was in on a couple of landings and saw far more in the Pacific than almost anybody else.

When I was through with my first tour, I had orders home. Then the machinery turned up the fact that I was also an historian and had an advanced degree, and they propositioned me: would I stay over for another two or three years and take charge of the history of the area? I tried to make believe I was bitter about not getting home, but it was pretty obvious to everybody I was very happy because it was *carte blanche* to go over the whole Pacific. I was everywhere, from Hawaii to Christmas Island. In Samoa and Bora Bora it was so beautiful that when I went there as a senior lieutenant with orders for many of the men to be sent home they would come and plead with me not to go. I remember driving along this road in Samoa at six in the morning as the driver blew our van's horn, collecting the American military who had been sleeping with the beautiful girls there. The girls would come out with sarongs and wave goodby and blow kisses.

Your're making your experience sound like it was all pretty girls and beautiful islands.

Not all. For some of those men the Navy was brutal when they got caught committing the unspeakable crime, which was homosexuality. I objected, and I defended a couple of cases in a court martial. The Navy had a system then—they may deny it, but I know that when a young man was accused justly of making homosexual advances to someone else, they were shipped out immediately to Portsmouth in New Hampshire where there was a military brig and the Marine guards were invited to beat the hell out of him. Even to the point of death.

That's why I'm very apprehensive about the current moves to remodel the Navy. I would certainly not have sexual orientation as a criteria for either men or women in the Armed Forces. They exist in human life in all societies in about the same proportion everywhere and we just have to face up to that. But I would have some apprehension about a close-knit ship like a destroyer where you have all those fellows cramped into that area. We're in an area of sexuality that we're just beginning to understand. We're in the dark ages, really. The incident of Tailhook in the Navy is symbolic of the terrible confusion we're in. It's very dangerous ground because the military has always been of a certain type. I saw *South Pacific* just recently and as the play unfolded and you hear that chorus: "There is nothing like a dame"—that is an invitation to the kind of behavior that sailors have had all through history. It stems from the long perilous life at sea and the dangers. And through the years that tradition has been generated, honored, respected, and the play laughed at. But it's pure sexual harrassment and makes the play a period piece. And now we're going to change it all overnight. It may be that with the passing of men my age who have been indoctrinated the way we have been for good or bad, we'll all change.

Hold on, South Pacific *comes after your book, not before! Let's stay with how you decided to become a writer.*

One of the most profound experiences I ever had was on the island of New Caledonia during the war when I survived rather miraculously a near plane crash. Walking that night along the airfield at Tontouta I realized that I was able to tell a story and write much better than the people I had been editing or that Macmillan was publishing. And it came to me as quite a surprise. Among the men I had gotten to know almost all the ones that I liked had decided that they did not want to go back and do what they had done before; they wanted to be something else. Quite a few of them had been deeply moved by their experience and had a spiritual awakening and went into religion. Others went into politics or returned to college on the G.I. Bill. I was one of that group who said, 'Now wait, if you're ever going to change direction, let's do it now.' I didn't say, 'I'm going to be a writer,' but I decided then to spend the rest of my time in the islands writing about them. I did it because I knew the men there were bitching about the South Pacific twenty-four hours a day and I realized that twenty years from then they would look back upon this as the highlight of their lives and would want a record of it.

Did you feel Macmillan would publish it because you already worked for the company?

When I decided to submit *Tales of the South Pacific* I did it incognito, under a pseudonym, because many publishing companies have a good and reasonable rule that they do not want to publish manuscripts written by their own employees, and since I was happy at Macmillan and thought it was a prestigious publishing house, it never occurred to me to send it anywhere else. Once it was accepted, however, there was editorial work to be done and it became necessary for me to reveal myself. There was some embarrassment, but they decided that I had not actually been working with them at the time I wrote it so I was exempt from that rule.

And so, a writer was born.

It's amazing that a career like mine could start with such a modest beginning as *Tales of the South Pacific*, which did not earn a nickel. It was published in relative secrecy and it had a very fragile life. And it died, unmourned and unsung. So I did not start at the top at all, I started way down, and had grave apprehension as to whether I could make it as a freelance writer. As I was working as an editor at Macmillan I knew the figures of what writers were making in yearly royalties: John Masefield, $1,230; somebody else, $1,800. I knew that people did not make livings by writing books.

How surprising was it when you found out you'd won the Pulitzer Prize for your first book?

I didn't even know *Tales* was under consideration for a Pulitzer and was editing a book on geography at the time. I had screwed up east and west on a map and was being chewed out by my boss when someone burst in and said I'd won the Pulitzer Prize. A few people came in to congratulate me, then they left and we continued the discussion about this crazy map.

The Pulitzer came out the week that the paperback was published, so any publicity sold the paperback. The Pulitzer didn't mean anything really. I didn't get any more book contracts. But in the magazine field it meant a great deal. Young writers aren't aware of this but all the big publishing companies keep book on writers: who's doing what, who is writing for the little magazines, who's a good reporter. If word gets around that so and so is a winner, they come after him. And that happened to me with the *Saturday Evening Post, Ladies Home Journal, Holiday, Colliers, Life.*

But your life didn't really change until Rodgers and Hammerstein came along with some tunes in their head.

When the musical *South Pacific* came out, which was much later, in '49 and '50, it was a tremendous experience for me. I got enough money from that to permit me to travel and to buy books and maps. Rodgers and Hammerstein drove a very hard bargain. On the evening of the first presentation in New York they knew they had one of the all-time winners, and I certainly knew it. So they voluntarily came to me and said that they would give me a share of the show. I said I had no money and they said they would lend me the money, which was quite remarkable. It was $7,500. In effect they gave me one percent. Through the years my annual take was never great, seven or eight thousand dollars, but there it was, it paid the rent, the insurance, it made a world of difference. It gave me the freedom of a small regular income that a lot of writers don't have.

An artist is just lucky beyond words if he epitomizes his period, the way Toulouse-Lautrec did because of those peculiar posters he made. That doesn't happen to many people. I'm not too keen on his art, and there must have been fifteen painters better than he, but that son of a gun caught the world's imagination and symbolized a whole period, just as *Tales of the South Pacific* summarized what that aspect of the war was all about.

You followed Tales *with a tale of your own,* The Fires of Spring. *How was that received?*

It was semi-autobiographical and didn't do well. I had wanted the central character to be less interesting than the peripheral characters and that was a mistake. When I submitted it to Macmillan they suggested that I take it to another publisher, since I was back under their rule again. But over the years I've been very pleased with *The Fires*. I get an enormous amount of mail about it, because it does hit young people who are going through that period rather hard.

The year before Random House published *The Fires of Spring*, Ross Lockridge won the first M.G.M. prize of $100,000 for his novel *Raintree County*, which catapulted him to a fame really without parallel. And my publisher hoped that I was going to win the prize a year later for *The Fires of Spring*. I disappointed them. During that period I was constantly being compared to

Lockridge. Besides Lockridge there was Tom Heggen, who wrote the play *Mr. Roberts* and John Horne Burns, whose *The Gallery* was one of the best novels about World War Two. And within a short period of time these three men did themselves in. And I had close, intimate contacts with all three of them.

You can't imagine the excitement *Raintree County* evoked. *Life* magazine gave a wonderful summary of it, and Lockridge was the most incandescent figure of any of them. Temptations were thrown his way, and he behaved very foolishly. He milked his publicity for everything. He wrote some of the most extraordinary letters to his publisher seeking further praise, further accolades, that scared the hell out of me. He wrote to magazines about putting him on the cover. And then Tom Heggen came along with this great stage play which was a sensation, but he realized that writing it gave him trouble, because a wonderful part of his life had ended and he had a pretty clear vision that it wasn't going to happen again. He felt he wasn't up to it. Then came Burns, who was maybe the most talented of the bunch, and he couldn't get things in balance either. I think of him constantly. I wrote about the three of them and the funny thing is, Lockridge and Heggen are finished stories for me, but Burns is unfinished. He would have been extremely valuable these days when we are trying to define multisexuality, he could have been a spokesman in that jungle. He was way ahead of his time.

So these three gave me pause. I think of why I survived and have still kept active into my ninth decade when others have been stricken, either by drink or by their own lack of character or by premature senility or by lack of courage.

You've written a chapter about Burns, Lockridge, and Heggen in The World Is My Home. *Did you ever consider writing biographies?*

I've never written one because I don't think I would want to submit myself to that heavy obligation of both the research and living within it. Though if I ever did, I would contrast the great tragedies of those three men with the more contemporary trio, Norman Mailer, Truman Capote, and Gore Vidal.

After your second novel was published did you consider leaving Macmillan to write full time?

I had no illusions and no great faith in myself when I was first starting out as a writer. I stayed on at Macmillan from 1945 to '49. It was almost '50 before I felt confident, '51 even, to quit my job and try writing. But I didn't make any money in those first years.

When did you finally decide to make the break into freelancing?

Before I made the break from Macmillan, after the success of *South Pacific*, I discussed it with John Mason Brown, one of the most charismatic public speakers we've ever had. He used some of my work as the basis for one of his lectures, and when I called him on the phone I said, "I think you've been mentioning some of my books and I'm deeply appreciative." He invited me to one of the posh clubs, and he gave me about two hours of very good advice. He said, "You've got to take a shot at freelancing." So I've always been deeply indebted to him.

That's when my agent, Helen Strauss, got me a job with the *Herald Tribune*. Helen was a wonderful agent, tough as nails. Her dictum was: 'Jim, you write a good manuscript and bring it to me and I'll sell it if it can be sold. It might be in a little magazine and I'll get you $150, but I will sell it. But don't ask me how to make it better; I'm not going to buy you tickets for the theater; I'm not going to help you with your divorce; I'm not going to go to Gimbels and get you a white shirt so you can go to this meeting. None of that. You write 'em, I'll sell 'em.' And as soon as I got back from an assignment for the *Tribune*, which took me to Pakistan and Singapore, she got me a job with *Reader's Digest* and I wound up divorcing my second wife because she didn't accompany me on my travels and I was away all the time, I wasn't home at all.

So it's the Reader's Digest *which was to blame for your second divorce?*

The *Reader's Digest* suddenly saw that they were picking up my stuff fairly regularly, so they came after me. I had never spoken to them. And that has happened to me all my life. The founder, DeWitt Wallace, offered me a deal: I could go anywhere in the world at his expense and write what I wanted to write, and he would have first refusal of it. If he liked it he would then buy it, even though he already owned it. Thus, *Reader's Digest* allowed me to write almost exactly what I wanted to, although I did notice that if it had a political flavor, it somehow never got published in September or October in an election year. But those are the rules of the game. Just as the length of my manuscripts: I was a bit of a headache to them because they would ask for eleven hundred choice words and I would turn in about thirty thousand. Once, by error, I was allowed to see the front page of one of my manuscripts, and on it an editor had written: "Who the hell does he think he's writing for?" I think that's funny. Because I was writing more to explore my own mind and things that I might want to do. I didn't know what they wanted and I don't imagine they were happy with all the words I wrote, but they were always happy with the outcome, and every year since I started writing for them, *Reader's Digest* offered me a staff job with financial inducements and other things, but I always felt I was better off as a total freelance. They would hit me with ten or twelve story possibilities a year. If I did one, fine. Then I would come up with an idea and they would be very excited about it, but not one of them ever got into the damn magazine because when it got to some editor's desk there was nobody to ride herd on it, no one to champion it, since no editor had assigned it. Whereas had they thought up the idea, then it would really have to bomb for them to admit that their boy didn't do it. This is a phenomenon in magazine publishing that I just can't get over, but in truth I have never sold one of my own ideas to any magazine. Not one! Nor have I ever published in the *Atlantic Monthly* or the *New Yorker*, which deeply grieved me. I would be very proud to be published by them, but they never asked and I never offered.

It was around this time that you wrote The Bridges at Toko-Ri. *How'd you wind up in Korea?*

With the outbreak of the Korean War and my working for the *Tribune* and *Reader's Digest,* I was soon in Korea up to my ears. I was having dinner in Connecticut with Richard Rodgers and his wife when I first heard about the outbreak of fighting in Korea. I went home and started immediately making arrangements to go to Korea. And I got there in time for the retreat from the Hungnam reservoir. It was a terrible defeat for the American troops and the Marines bugged out under orders, but they did bug out.

One of the results of my time covering the war in Korea was my attempt to write a well-crafted English novel while preserving the Aristotelian unities, writing about a small group in a confined space and time span. With *The Bridges at Toko-Ri* I proved to myself that I could, and it was one of the best things I've ever done. But it gave me no satisfaction, and I took no great pride in it whatever. I suppose, quite seriously, that I could have written one of those books every year for the remainder of my life, but it didn't have the complexity that I wanted.

It wasn't big enough.

How normal is it for a person to opt for a career in the arts at the age of forty?

I don't think one would go through the agony of writing a book if he were a perfectly normal person. I doubt that a well-rounded, completely happy, rational person would want to be a writer. Or a painter. Or a musician. Any man who doesn't get a decent nine-to-five job and go off in a Chevrolet at 8:30 in the morning, getting the hell out of the house, there's something wrong with him. Artists, by and large, are deviant in one way or another. You have to have a drive, a compulsion, that is very powerful. You have to have the kind of aberration which gives you the power or the guts or the gall to go ahead with it. Anything that diminishes that is terribly risky.

How deviant are you?

I've never probed my own impulses that set me to writing. I suspect I'd not really want to know. They may be as venal as a masochistic desire for self-exposure, as James Jones has said. I've let it go as: Because I have this driving compulsion, to codify, to explain, to share the perceptive experiences I've had. I know that's true, unquestionably, but that merely begs the question: But *why* do you have that compulsion? And that question I cannot or dare not answer. My motivations could well come not from some ethereal impulse in the heavenly brain, but from some visceral drive from well below the waist. I'm content not to know. I'm getting by and I cannot risk losing everything on the gamble that I might be nine percent better than I already am, regardless of how high or low I am when I enter analysis. I do not want to be psychoanalyzed. Let the sleeping dogs of ultimate motivation lie where they are. Let me keep my fingers crossed and get on with the job at my own faulty speed and with my own muddy motivations.

Why do you suspect you have the large and dedicated readership that you do?

It isn't because I am the Charles Dickens of the twentieth century. Nothing like that. It is because I have this tremendous sense of narrative.

Throughout all of history, when people gathered around the

fire at night, they wanted to remember what had happened and reflect upon the big events of the day. The narratives in the Bible, Homer and Aeschylus—I would put Boccaccio in there, and Plutarch—they knew how to tell the story of a human life as well as the modern novelists do.

And once you set pen to paper you discovered you had this gift as a storyteller?

There is a great deal I can't do—I'm not good at humor or psychology, I'm not a stylist—but I can tell a story. If the reader will stay with me for the first hundred pages, which I often make difficult, then he or she will be hooked and want to know what's happening. That's storytelling and I prize it. A writer is prudent if he stays with what he does well and perfects it. You can't do everything. I'm one of the guys who sat around the fire and did the talking.

Do you think most of your readers actually finish your novels?

I suppose a good many readers do not get through my books because they are rather formidable. In *Centennial* it was over a hundred pages before there was any dialogue. That's pretty heavy going. I sympathize with the people that do drop out but the fact that so many don't is really quite remarkable.

How did you know there was a market for 800- or 1,000-page novels?

It was television which made me realize there was a need for the big novel. The minute I saw how it was broken up into hour segments in which the hour consisted of forty-eight minutes I realized that a lot of people would be willing to go for the longer work; would, indeed, be hungry for it.

I knew there would always be readers. If we have a population of 250 million and if only ten percent buy books and read them, that's still twenty-five million people. And if you shoot for just one percent of that, that's two hundred and fifty thousand. That is significant to the writer.

I've had only three basic ideas or concepts in my life: the brotherhood of mankind; the social wisdom of ensuring that workers receive just pay for their efforts so that wealth can circulate to the benefit of all; and the fact that in an age of television people would actually long for and seek out long books that created imaginary worlds of significant meaning.

So what you're saying is that you were in the right place at the technologically right time to write the kind of books you had in you.

I got a break chronologically by not appearing on the scene thirty years earlier, before we'd had our overseas experiences, before the world had opened up. Thirty years earlier I would have been pretty small potatoes. Because what I wanted to do, I'm afraid, would not have found a receptive audience. But thirty years later, you know, you can write about any part of the world and get a hearing. Paul Theroux and John McPhee are proving that. I've proven it. I can write about sports, about esoteric Japanese prints, about this and about that, because I have an embracing interest in things. And these two fellows are just like me, they can write about anything. Joyce Carol Oates is that way, so is Mailer. Joan Didion too; she's awfully good, though I don't think she's achieved the universality that McPhee has.

What do you aim for when you write?

It is perilous for a writer who prefers to remain a generalist as opposed to someone who has carved out a selected nook about which she or he will write continuously—say real life murders, corporation delinquencies, or travel to exotic places. Such writers sometimes do capably define and exhaust their little world, but I have never believed that was what a real writer should aim for. What do I aim for? A story which I myself would want to read.

Do you consider your books historical novels?

I never think of my books as historical novels because a good two-thirds of each book occurs in the present. But I do have wonderful respect and love for the old days. I try to figure out what they were like and where did they come from; how did they get their money? what agitated them? what was their drive? what were they after? And I get swept away by the magnitude of the thing.

If that is a formula, then I'm stuck with it. It's a formula that Dostoevsky used, that Chaucer and Dickens used.

How do you choose your subjects?

Invariably I take five arbitrary subjects which have a long vertical span and I study them as intensively as I can at my level of understanding. One would always be the geography or geology or anthropology or botany. One would be an intellectual field like religion or literature or philosophical understandings or history, something with content. The other three could be very arbitrary. In the case of *Chesapeake* it was railroads and banking and the history of a church. But if you do that vertically for four or five subjects you get a structure that is just so concrete, you know what was happening: that during the Depression corn was selling at a giveaway price; that railroads had decided not to go to Denver; that shipping was tied up because of French-British antagonism. You begin to see ramifications and structures.

In *Texas* I was deeply into the cattle industry and oil, but also border troubles.

What I followed for *Mexico* was bullfighting, mining, and the fact that at the end of the Civil War there was a lot of southerners who were fed up with the north, especially with General Grant, who was such a son of a bitch.

Never have I picked all five subjects. I don't think I have ever done better than three. But with that in place, you begin to fill in.

When I was writing about the West, what do you have? The mine, the village, the mountains are very colorful and anybody could write about them. The dramatic scenes of finding gold are cliches of the West, anybody could write about it. But you go out into the empty plains where there are only buffalo and people striving to make a buck and there are broken-down Chevrolets and you have quite a story. Because what I'm after are the great stories. Writing about a family that's partly falling apart or Chekov writing about three sisters lost in a little village out in what would be eastern Russia or Jane Austen writing about a woman trying to get her daughters married—these are great timeless themes. That is probably why Dostoevsky is a greater writer than Tolstoy. Tolstoy needed the big canvas which itself has magnitude.

So when you choose to tell the story of Alaska, which is a big canvas, how do you get it into focus?

Alaska is about race relations. It's a strong statement about the opening up of a different part of the world. The Gold Rush, and salmon fishing, and the MacKenzie River which was an unknown part of the whole Klondike experience: great subjects. I was tremendously interested with that group of photographers who had miraculously come up to Alaska in 1897 and '98. Name any subject—the gold fields, a specific Chinese who had a laundry on the corner—there will be a photograph of it. It was photographed like no other place.

I didn't think I could write *Alaska*—I was afraid I'd get swept away by the magnitude of the thing. I knew it would be an absolutely marvelous story, starting with the animals and the arrival of the Asiatic progenitor and the closing of the land bridge and the Indians.

Whenever I went to Asia I'd always stop off in Alaska. I'd be in Fairbanks and go up to Prudhoe Bay and then up to the Arctic Circle, Nome, down to the southern part. I guess you get a little more courageous when you are older. Once I decided to tackle the subject, I covered every corner of Alaska, using little boats, small airplanes. Explored the glaciers, the MacKenzie River, which was rough. But I figured, what the hell, I'm on borrowed time anyway, why baby myself?

No wonder you chose the Caribbean to cover after that. No glaciers or polar bears to deal with there.

As I prepared myself to write *Caribbean*, I looked deeply into the sugar industry, which is really basic to the Caribbean; the British experience, which is very profound to the area; and the French Islands and the French Revolution, a most extraordinary story.

How much of your histories are made up?

I make a pledge not to fake anything, not to give spurious quotes or portray a person contrary to what the facts are. And I always pin the story on fictional characters or boats or regiments or companies. In history I would never write about the *Mayflower* because it's been done so often. I would write about the third ship that came in, and I'd call it the *Thetis*. And boy, are there going to be some interesting people on that ship. I then am not adverse to bringing in historic characters, to give it authenticity and color.

My novel *The Source*, deals with the digging of this well, in a place like northern Israel. Anybody doing that would ultimately come into contact with King David. And so my boy does, and I try to show David as a troubled, worried king. As a king who, late in his life, told his prime ministers to go out into Israel and find him a couple of nice seventeen-year-old girls because he was lonely. A king who sent his prime general into the front lines so that the general would be killed so that David could inherit the general's widow. That's my David. And I'm entitled to that because I know David intimately. So I will use David to elucidate this whole period, but I will not fake him. And that's a tricky gambit, and I have fallen on my face sometimes. As in *Centennial*, when I wrote about the marriage of Winston Churchill's father to this wonderful daughter of a New York jeweler, Jenny Jerome. I have him out there looking for Jenny eight years after he married her. The book was in print for eight years, and nobody caught it until some teacher in high school nailed me. I'm ashamed of that and disgusted with myself. But I don't do it too often.

Where do you place Caravans *among your books?*

I believe *Caravans* to be a minor classic, that is, it's a book which was read by everybody who ought to have read it. I wrote it at forty-four; I hadn't hit my stride yet but I had a great feeling of competence.

You've talked about your gift for narrative, but can you be more specific about how you keep a story moving?

I have a couple of techniques that I've worked out the hard way and sort of cherish. One is I never introduce a concept without identifying it at the point of entry and unless I'm going to use it three times. For instance, some years back I was dealing with a very difficult concept of oblation, which is an offering or a sacrifice to a god. So I threw it in, but I didn't define it the first time. Then I defined it the second time when the reader wants to know what it is. Then I came back to it a hundred pages later. By the time he's through, he knows this very difficult concept as well as I know it.

Another technique I use is that I never pepper a manuscript with foreign words just for the heck of it. One might do it if one were writing light material, like S. J. Perelman. He did it to perfection. In my lifetime Perelman used the English language better by far than any other writer. He didn't use as big a vocabulary as Cousins or Styron or Updike but, boy, he used it with a precision and with an effect that is simply dazzling.

The third device that I have is that I have studied most of the fine novels that rely upon dialect, odd spellings, devices, and I have found that almost universally they have a very short life. They are praised, lauded to the skies, and three years later they're on the shelf, because this is an unnatural form and it goes against the grain. Faulkner is the best technician in that field that we have. And I suppose his readership is highly limited because of it.

But language for me is an agency. My gods are Dreiser and Zola and Dostoevsky and Multatuli and Martin Andersen Nexo. One of the most insightful things I've read about this was in Somerset Maugham's *The Summing Up*. He has a passage in which he said as a young doctor, when it dawned upon him that he might be a writer, he got a notebook and wrote down all the marvelous words of the English language that a writer should use. I remember *chalcedony* was one of them. And he had about twenty others. At the end of five years of rather successful writing he found he had never used one of these words. And I am the same way. Writing of the kind I do does not depend upon the arcane word or the forced study of a brilliant sentence construction or anything like that.

Of maximum importance in my work are what I call *carry* and *scene*, *carry* being the part of the narrative in which you set the stage and have your own reflections and justifications and development. *Scene* being the section in which something specific is happening to specific characters with a specific weight and force. *Carry* usually does not use many quotes, *scene* if it's done well can be told mostly in quotation. The proper balance between those is the great artistic problem: to have a mix of philosophical content and a mix of scenes in which it's illustrated or exemplified.

Toni Morrison's *Tar Baby* is a very good example of that. She's damn good at each of them, but does mix them beautifully. The philosophical weight and the illustrative incident. I am better at *carry* than I am at *scene* but at the end of four or five days work I will suddenly stop and think, geez, a third of that ought to be in *scene* and I'll do it all over. The balance is an intuitive one.

But how do you know what people want to read about?

I don't have a clue how I know what people want, but I do know that when I go into restaurant after restaurant across the country I can always pick out, with unfailing accuracy, what the central dish is. Because nine times out of ten they're out of it! It's because I have an absolute everyman taste. I look down at a menu for what is the most central thing there that will be well-prepared, reasonable, and apt to be good. And that's what everybody wants. It's never anything exotic, just the best dish on the menu. And quite frequently I'll go for the best three things and they'll be out of all of them. Then I lose my appetite and I'll sit there and have a cracker and fume. This happens so often that I can only judge it's a portrait of me, that I have a central tendency that I'm not even aware of. And I think I know that about human concerns.

Since your stories are often so encompassing, how do you know when you're done?

I once roomed in the house of a marvelous woman in New York named Nancy Shore. She wrote for the women's magazines, and it was always about a young girl taking a job and falling in love with a married man, then finding true love with the honest guy in the shipping office. She did this again and again, and she was damned good at it. I remember one time a group of very aspiring and wonderful young people from N.Y.U. and Columbia and Fordham assembled in her living room in Greenwich Village and we talked about some pretty high stuff—Camus, Sartre, Faulkner, Fitzgerald. And Nancy was off, she was a rather heavy drinker, a wonderful blousy woman, a real Midwesterner come to New York and gone to seed. After she had listened to this twaddle for about half an hour she suddenly plopped her glass down and said, 'Listen, you sons of bitches, I sit at a typewriter in a little room with a quart of milk on one side and a pint of gin on the other. Now, when they're both empty, the story is done.' Whenever I get pontificating too much about this, I think of Nancy.

What kind of room-with-a-view do you need to work?

I need a quiet room. The view is of no concern whatever. The temperature is of no concern; I've worked in the Arctic and in the tropics. I need a big work space. I long ago formed the habit of buying either two small filing cases or a pile of bricks or cement blocks, putting a door across them, and that has been my desk. I have written all of my good books on the top of a door.

What's the best time of day for you?

I work every day, Saturday, Sunday, holidays. But I only work in the mornings. I get out of bed, and within five minutes I'm at the typewriter. I don't eat much breakfast and by noon I'm very hungry. I never write in the afternoon, very rarely in the evening. For years I refused to answer the phone before 1:00 P.M. Now I'm so nosey as to what's happening that I will say hello, but hang up after about one minute no matter how important the call. When I work with aspiring writers I find myself often asking, as I look into their bright, brimming faces: has she the courage to stay with it, day after day after lonely day? And the unspoken answer is usually no. Most successful writers do their first three books at about four o'clock in the morning or ten-thirty at night, in conjunction with a full day's work, and if they have not the discipline to do that they'll perish along the way . . . unless they marry someone with a lot of money.

Do you write in longhand, typewriter, or computer?

The typewriter dominates me. I can't think sequentially in an outlined form without a typewriter. I can think creatively, and some of my best passages are handwritten, but I'm not satisfied with them until they've been typewritten because it doesn't count with me. I type with two fingers and a thumb. The mind cannot keep up with ten-finger typing. I am almost too fast with two fingers.

I am terribly irritated with the $8\frac{1}{2} \times 11$ inch page. It's a prison for me. I just wish I could solve it. Coming to the end of the page I frequently feel very irritated. I type to the last quarter inch to avoid changing it.

What about names for your characters, how do you find them?

When I work on a novel I will probably have fifty names for every character. I will use them, reuse them, substitute and reject. It's essential that the name be usable and memorable. Dickens was known to have kept a catalog of names and I am very much like him in that respect. I will go through newspapers, phone books, or catalogs when the time comes to find a name, even for a throwaway character, because you want to keep the book moving.

Abner Hale, the missionary in *Hawaii*, was a most happy invention. I can't tell you how hard it was to get that name, but I'm rather pleased about it because the church in Hawaii had so many requests by tourists to see where Abner Hale was buried that they had to print a little pamphlet which said, 'Dear Reader, you must understand, this is a novel. There was never any Abner Hale. This is a made-up name.' People read that and say, 'This is very interesting, but where is he buried?'

Was Hawaii *the book that opened you up?*

I never had great faith in my capacity until *Hawaii*, really. And I didn't have it on that while I was doing it, I was by no means sure that it would be published. It wasn't a hot item at that time, with the length and the vast number of characters, that opening chapter which everyone advised me to drop. When the paperback came out they printed it in italic, with the implication that if you really wanted to get on with the story you could just skip it. But it's now held to be maybe the best thing I've ever written. Writing *Hawaii* was certainly the greatest risk I'd taken as a writer, but after it was over, with the tremendous reception it received and the vitality it showed, I realized I could handle things, big themes, jeepers creepers!

Before *Hawaii* I had done *Toko-Ri*, *Sayonara*, two short books. Then *The Bridge at Andau*. I really hadn't hit my stride yet but I had a great feeling of competence.

How long do you ruminate about a subject before you tackle it?

Almost every book I've done has had a long period of gestation, many of them go back ten, fifteen, twenty years. It isn't that one day you decide to write a book about Africa or Asia or the Middle East. Even *The Bridge at Andau*, which I did on the spur of the moment, went back a long time because I was always interested in the Balkans.

Do you choose all of the areas you write about or do you get inspired by letters or requests?

Ever since the publication of *Tales of the South Pacific* I have received at least a dozen letters a year—oh, that's *way* too low!—begging me to write about other parts of this country. It reached a head when I published *Centennial*. The typical letter was: 'If you could make the dry lands of Colorado important, think what you could do with the Masabe range in Minnesota.' Same with Nebraska, Michigan, California. As I mentioned, I got probably a hundred letters about going to Alaska: 'You've done the South Pacific, why not do the North Pacific?' Also an enormous number of appeals to write about Northern Ireland, but what's going on there is so terrible I decided I'm not going to write about it.

I had been affiliated with Texas since 1936. It was forty years before I wrote the book, but I had been down there many times.

Is it possible to pinpoint specific inspiration for your books?

It comes at the end of a long winnowing-out period.

Centennial was the impact of the West on me, very powerful. I had started collecting material for such a novel in 1936, didn't get around to it until 1976. It's a long process of germination. With *The Novel*, I started thinking about it thirty years ago. I had that notebook and it was lost in the transit from Maine, but there it was. And I modified it, changed from first person to third person and back to first person. But the outline and the target never varied. I wanted to write about India—I had the exact same impulses, but I never wrote it. I was scared of it, I think.

It seems curious that you wound up writing about Israel rather than a Muslim country.

The Source is one of my most widely received books. I have lived in all the countries in the world that had Islam as its major religion, except Arabia. I was never allowed into Arabia. I had intended writing about Istanbul through the centuries. I knew the Islamic world far better than I did the Hebraic world. Then I went to Israel with Leonard Lyons and Harpo Marx and I began to see that what I was really after was the conflict between the Arabs and Christians, with the Jews playing almost no role at all in that period. We went to see a crusader castle on the shores of the Mediterranean. We went through the dungeons and in the semi-darkness, within the flash of a second, I saw that the novel ought to be transferred there. I saw everything that I had done regarding the Muslim world and Istanbul focused exactly in that world. I borrowed a matchbook cover from Harpo and wrote down the whole novel, fourteen chapters. Of the fourteen things that I noted, thirteen of them stood exactly as I put them down.

I thought it should have been done from a Jewish background, but there was nobody available. It was my most difficult book to research because I was working in three different languages that I didn't speak, Russian, German, and Hebrew. And I wound up going to synagogue every Friday night for two years. I was so faithful I was allowed to perform part of the minion.

The Source was enormously popular, but you've also written a number of books which have had a limited audience, including some about Japanese art. How does a popular writer deal with writing semi-popular books?

The five books I did on Japanese art were all books that I had to fight to get published, and even had to pay for a few of them myself. Like my book on sports and the one on the electoral process, I wondered if anyone would want books on Japanese prints, but I didn't care, because I wanted them. As it turned out, people didn't want to read about the electoral process, but they agreed with me about the others.

How did the Japanese books come about?

The Japanese art came in a roundabout fashion. I fell in love with the Siennese paintings and was going to write a history of Siennese art, when a Boston art professor did a marvelous book. It superseded anything I might have done. So I transferred all of my enthusiasm to the field of the Japanese print. I knew that the Japanese print had to come to the surface, because it was such a superb art form. World War II had put a damper on it, and un-derstandably so, but I knew it wasn't going to stay down long. I slowly built up my expertise and then going to Japan crystallized the whole thing.

I not only learned about Japanese prints, but began collecting them. As a result, two things: the five Japanese books that I wrote are all in print, they have gone all over the world, in edition after edition, in different languages. And, secondly, a portion of the prints I collected, which cost me no more than $100,000, are now valued at nine million dollars!

Isn't there a story about some musicians who got you to write Legacy, *one of your smaller books?*

A group of very fine musicians in Sitka wanted me to write a text for 1987, to celebrate the two hundredth anniversary of the Constitutional Convention, which they would set to music. We got into it and it would have been bloody good, but it didn't get off the ground. I did all the work for that music group and then I did it in another form for the *New York Times*. When they changed their mind I did it in a third form, and that's the book. But it goes way back to when I was a student in Scotland and a pageant about Scots who participated in the American Revolution and they wanted me to play James Wilson, an intellectual leader in the Constitutional Convention, who later became a justice of the Supreme Court. I became very deeply involved with Wilson. I really could have written a biography of him and always wanted to write about him. So I had been kicking that one around for a long time and then the Iran/Contra affair happened and that was the impetus, because that was a real constitutional crisis. I was sick about that.

Sometimes a single incident erupts that has a tremendous dramatic impact and anybody who is bright enough can see it's crucial. That's what happened with *Kent State*, which, besides the Hungarian one, is the only book I've ever done in a hurry.

You also took some flak about that, didn't you?

When those National Guardsmen fired on the students in the spring of 1970, killing four of them and wounding nine, I felt compelled to understand what happened. I think we all saw that this was a kind of watershed point, that we were heading in a direction that nobody really wanted to go.

One of the things I'm proudest about in my professional life is that I went into a very complex situation after the shootings at Kent State with only my own resources, and not very extensive ones, and by patient legwork and by talking with a huge number of people and listening and putting things together, I covered it about as well as the FBI did with five hundred agents and all the police powers and subpoena powers at their disposal.

It was a dreadful period. The people of Ohio were not unhappy that Governor James Rhodes called the troops in and gunned the students down, not at all. They reelected him. When I got there, people were riding around in pickup trucks with shotguns just waiting for some student to make a move. They were going to gun them right down. They told me so.

You had some research help for Kent State. *How often do you employ others to dig out facts for you?*

I'm often asked about all the researchers I must employ before I start writing my books. My staff is me. I do all the research myself. There are several exceptions to that. Like *Kent State*, because we were doing it under the hammer; for *Centennial* the *Reader's Digest* turned loose an editor when I was about fifty percent done; and for *The Covenant* I sought help, but the whole body had been laid out. In all the other books, nobody.

How do you compare what you do with writers who rely more on their imagination than on research?

The best books are written by people who don't do a great deal of research, who just sit down in a little room with a typewriter or word processor, some maps, and write a great book out of their own experiences. That's what Jane Austen did, what the Brontë sisters did, Emily Dickinson, Tennessee Williams, Truman Capote. I doubt if Eugene O'Neill ever opened a research book in his life. Then there are the writers like Gore Vidal and Herman Wouk and me, and the great classicists who are greater than any of us. Balzac and Tolstoy needed data, they did research.

For me the research is a joy. It's just as exciting as reading Shakespeare. Before I start writing I do so much reading pertaining to that subject it's staggering. Thousands of books! Really arcane material. In the latter years of my life I find that I really live with indexes because I don't get a chance to do as much reading as I used to. So if I have to read three hundred books on a subject, I'd better be good at reading indexes to see what in that book is what I really want.

Why have you preferred fiction to nonfiction?

What makes my job as a novelist easier than a nonfiction writer's job is that when I come across a block or an area I'm not all that interested in, I say the hell with it and go on to another avenue. That's where the personality of the writer comes in. In *Poland*, for instance, I simply decided I was not going to fuss around with the Saxon kings and queens. Boy, that takes out a hell of a bit of Polish history! They were not rewarding, they weren't bad enough to be villains, and they weren't bright enough to be heroes. You make those choices all the time.

How important is it for you to write fiction as if it were nonfiction?

I'm a teller of stories. I've learned how to do that, and I can do it so that people get a feeling of meaning out of it. That's a matter of research. But to make it palatable, and to make it usable, is the role of the artist.

How hard is what you do?

Writing is very hard work. When I'm through with a day's work I have to take a shower, I smell like a horse. The nervous tension on top of that typewriter every inch of the way is terribly taxing. I perspire more sitting at my desk for five hours then I do when I take a ten mile walk. I don't believe for a minute that John Updike can write an easy short story. It's just as tough now as when he started. I have never believed in inspiration. Insight, yes. Flashes of clear thinking, yes. But the vaunted inspiration that makes everything easy, no. Not with me, at least. The way I like to write, for better or for worse, is to give a portrait in great detail of what has happened and to indicate what the moral values are and what the complications are and then let the reader come to grips with it and solve it.

Do you usually know your endings before you begin?

Before I start I have the last thirty pages written in my mind with great clarity. All that means is that I have a target and the trick is how do you get there? I cannot actually write the final pages at the beginning but rather when I'm about a third of the way through. With the shorter pieces I've done, I invariably write the end at the beginning. I notice that that's the difference between a novelist and a symphony composer. The musicians start with such great themes, immortal ones, really, but by the time they reach the conclusion I can hear them muttering: 'Let's get this damned thing over with.' And that happens time after time with whole pages of pedestrian stuff and great crescendos. The glowing exception is Beethoven's *Ninth*. There it's some of the front stuff that could be dispensed with.

How often do you rewrite a manuscript?

I rewrite almost everything three times. The first time it's really, I suppose, drafting, rather than writing. It's brutal, distasteful drudgery. Probably a third of it is usable. Then I rewrite it. The second version, when you have assurance that the job can be and will be done in high style, when I have it all down and realize that it's viable, is sheer joy. Sometimes working on that second draft I get a feeling of real power that I never do with the first draft. I can hardly wait to get to the typewriter in the morning. Then comes the third draft. By the time my publisher gets to it the manuscript looks like it's been turned in by a college kid, it's been corrected on every page.

Do you take criticism well?

Writers divide into two classes: ones who will take criticism and those who will not. I seek criticism when a book is done. I think that it has accounted for the fact that all my books are still in print, going into different languages all the time. I circulate the manuscript among very wise people and pay them to read it and kick it to pieces. I want the most severe criticism, but I sure don't want it while I'm in the process of writing, not at chapter three, say, because bright as you might be, you couldn't guess what I'm driving at for chapter eleven. When I get through with that and I think it's my finished manuscript, then it goes to New York where it's kicked around like a football. The editors at Random House go over it with a fine tooth comb. I insist upon it. The copy editor, the outside editor . . . it's the most meticulous editing for fact and grammatical accuracy and propriety. Fact is very important. We go over every line of it. Then Albert Erskine, who was a damn good editor and a brilliant man, was very good at suggesting cuts. He had a very strong sense of what the reader would tolerate and I don't. He said, 'I don't like any of this, nor will the reader. But if you stop it here, at least it isn't going to be offensive, he isn't going to gag on it.'

In *The Covenant* I had a very good forty page passage and he felt it wasn't necessary at all! He said, 'This does nothing.' I was in a bit of a shock. Upon reflection I had to admit that maybe he was right. Now, on another passage an editor might say that and I'll come back saying that without that I don't want to publish the book. Then the question is what can we do about it. We'll talk it over and maybe I'll take out a character or tighten a fifty page passage down to thirty pages. They baby me and I think they're very prudent to do so. But boy, the amount of criticism I will get might be a few inches thick.

Bennett Cerf said that John O'Hara was the finest writer in American letters; he's so good at a manuscript, it could go right to the typesetter. If you sent one of mine to the typesetter, the editor ought to be arrested. Do I envy O'Hara? When I see my end product, I have to say no. I think one can profit from another eye, another intellect.

How long is the process from completed manuscript to published book?

From the time I finish a manuscript and I've had outsiders hack it up and I feel it's in perfect form and I'm ready to send it in, it's fourteen months before the book appears. Normally I would be keyed into the next job, or speculating on it. At the end of that time I'll have fifteen or twenty notebooks on each group I want to tackle, maybe sixty books altogether.

You've collaborated twice, with your assistant John Kings on Six Days in Havana *and with A. Grove Day on* Rascals in Paradise. *How did those projects come about?*

I had a great idea and it germinated for a long time and I suddenly realized one day that I was never going to take the time out to do it unless I had somebody riding herd on me. Whenever I have worked with another person it's been at my suggestion and my insistence that they will get half the royalty. I wouldn't do it any other way. My agents have usually raised hell about it, but there it is. I wrote *Rascals in Paradise* with A. Grove Day, who seems to come out with a new book every six months. I had all the data for some of the stories and meeting Grove I found that he, by the most wonderful accident, had all the data on another group of stories that I hadn't even heard about. So we each wrote what we highly specialized in and then passed it back and forth and read it and thought about it. I hadn't even heard of Will Mariner, the young English boy who, a hundred and eighty years ago, went to sea at the age of thirteen, survived the massacre of his ship's crew, was taken in by a Tongan chief and at sixteen became a chief himself. It was a splendid story. So our collaboration was a very happy relationship.

You also had a collaboration of another sort that was not as happy with a man who later wound up in prison for bank fraud. Your readers might be surprised at this story.

Thirty years ago the *Reader's Digest* had decided to launch a campaign against child pornography and wanted me to write the article. They introduced me to a tall, lean man in his mid-thirties—very handsome, well-dressed, well-spoken. He carried with him a briefcase—the filthiest, most awful collection of smut I had ever seen. I remember that whenever we met he talked about family values and how the United States could go down the tubes if family values were in any way diminished or denigrated. I worked with him on two articles. At the end of the second article I backed off. I think my collaborator's constant sanctimoniousness got the better of me. About six years ago, I saw him coming out of the front page of the newspaper, right at me. It was Charles Keating—the man who was given a twelve-year prison sentence for looting Lincoln Savings & Loan and defrauding investors of more than $250 million.

He had got his start by leading an anti-pornography drive in Cincinnati. He was my boy!

Did your pieces on pornography generate a big response?

The two articles I wrote about pornography received a lot of attention, but nothing like the one I did for the *Digest* on American women, where I called them the hardest-working women in the world. I wrote about the burden placed on young American wives who couldn't afford hired help. In other countries servants are common. In America it wasn't unusual for my wife Mari to do all the preparations for a sit-down dinner party of five or six couples. She'd do the pre-cleaning, the cooking, the baking, the table arrangement, and the serving. When the party would be over she and I would stay up until three washing the dishes. If we were in Asia or the Orient, most of that work would be done by a corps of servants. I wrote this in 1959, before there was such an influx of illegal immigrants who began filling the need for this service. When my article appeared, I suggested that we launch a campaign to convince young grandmothers and able widows to volunteer—for good wages—to help younger women. I called for a new occupation—household helper—removing the stigma of being a servant and making it something more glamorous. The *Digest* got so many letters it was extraordinary.

So you're a spokesperson for the plight of American women.

I think American women have been shafted. I sit in my hotel room in a bleak town in southern Alabama listening to some charismatic television minister shouting that God said that just as the husband is to revere Jesus, so the wife is to revere the husband, for he is the Lord and Master. To think that doctrine can be preached in this generation and taken seriously and embraced by the women, more than the men, is appalling.

Let's talk about relationships. How crucial is the choosing of a mate?

It's probably the biggest decision that anybody will ever make, and we do it so haphazardly. It's just a grab bag.

You're obviously no stranger to marriage . . .

I've had three, been divorced twice. Any person who has been divorced is a monument to failure.

What went wrong the first time?

We were separated for four years during the war. She was in the Army in Europe, and I was in the Navy in the South Pacific. She came back and we were together for maybe three weeks, and it was primarily her decision to split up. I was very unhappy about it, but we were so changed that any reconciliation was just impossible.

And the second one?

I was away in Asia, in Korea, most of the time, and she didn't come with me. I put my work first and that relationship just faded away.

Did you ever try to have children?

I had always thought that my not having children was my deficiency: I had a savage case of mumps when I was a boy, and that often produces sterility. My second wife and I had adopted two children, but when we separated she made the decision to turn them back to the orphanage. At the divorce the courts gave the children to the mother and the adoption was voided. I pleaded with the court not to do it, but that's the way they wanted it.

Did you ever find out what happened to them?

When Mari and I decided to get married, we talked about re-adopting them, but there was some concern that my ex-wife would make it unpleasant and we didn't want to hurt the children, so we decided not to reopen a potential can of worms.

Still, you must have had some regrets.

We had regrets, but we didn't belabor that. We usually had children living with us, and we assumed the responsibility for the education of a few kids, so we'd been in touch with children all along.

Your marriage to Mari was obviously the most successful of the three. How did you meet?

I met Mari when I was doing an article for *Life* magazine on Japanese war brides. They sent me to Chicago, where they had some very good research people, gave a lunch, and invited this very bright Japanese girl who worked for the American Library Association and knew more about the problem than any of them. We met that way. Then we corresponded for about a year while I was in Afghanistan and Indonesia. After that year we got married, in 1955. Perhaps the most important decision we made was that we would not separate, and that was a pretty good decision.

Wasn't Mari put in a California detention camp during World War II?

Yes, and it's the main reason why I have never lived in California or written about it. She had some bad experiences there, but she became very philosophical about it and objected when I used the word *concentration* camp because she said it was not like a German concentration camp at all. But she was treated abominably, thrown into stables fifteen to a room.

Was she bitter?

She wasn't bitter at all, although economically it was extremely difficult. They lost everything and they were never compensated for it. I remember how totally offensive it was when Senator Hayakawa from California said that the people who were asking for compensation didn't suffer and it wasn't half as bad as they said it was. He didn't know a damn thing about it. In California, where the Japanese could not possibly have been a threat, they were treated this way because people wanted the land and good valleys that they had. In Hawaii, where they might conceivably have been a problem, especially if the Imperial troops had landed—which they damn near did—they weren't treated this way at all, because their work was needed in the sugar and pineapple fields.

Did anything positive come out of that experience?

It did move the Japanese around. From California Mari was moved to Colorado and was never shot at, never starved, never beaten, never barb-wired. She was offered scholarships to three of our finest universities and went to Antioch College and later entered a graduate sociology program at the University of Chicago. So it was a mixed experience. A very harsh one for a young girl. She was born in 1920, so she was just twenty.

Did she ever become a sociologist?

Mari was very knowledgeable in human relations and the racial construction of society, which was her field. She did a lot of work in that, took one of her degrees in that, and she had been on the firing line.

How difficult was it marrying a Japanese-American when you did?

Marrying an Oriental woman was very difficult in general in the early fifties, but in the case of a writer people were willing to grant concessions that they might not somebody else. At the country club we said we would attend no more meetings because they wouldn't allow any Japanese to play on the golf course. Mari was very forceful about this.

Are women stonger than men?

In my books I often write of strong women, many of them stronger than the men. I find that in life. When you live in a primitive society like the island of Barra in Scotland or in the jungles of Sumatra, if the woman is not stronger than the man it all falls apart. It's true in many aspects of natural history. Female lions, for example, behave pretty much as the human women in my life behaved.

In America the average married woman must look forward to something like ten years of widowhood. I was reading some statistics from the census bureau that showed that men tend to marry women three years younger than they are and women tend to live four years longer then men. In many instances when the man dies the income stops, the house is sold, the children are gone. She better be well-coordinated and able to handle it. And I've seen this all my life, in all societies. The boy babies die much easier and quicker than the girls. So there really is this inherent imbalance.

Norman Mailer has said that men basically hate women. Do you agree?

There is a basic hatred that many men feel towards women, which perplexes me. I have done a great deal of work in Islam where women are not even allowed in the mosques. I'm a Quaker, where even when I was a boy all the men sat on one side and the women on the other. When I wrote *The Source*, I went to synagogue every Friday night for two years, and the men sat downstairs and the women sat up behind a curtain, not even on the same floor. As I've said, I was even allowed to perform part of the minion, but the women, who are real Jews, they're not even allowed to look at the thing. And certainly the Catholic Church, under St. Paul, was viciously anti-women. They do have women saints, but women are forbidden to the priesthood and forbidden participation in the government of the Church. Then take India, where I lived, where if you were to die tomorrow, your wife is supposed to commit suicide and is encouraged to do so by the whole community. Or look at what they were doing to "witches" in Salem. Now what conclusion am I supposed to come to from that?

Good question.

Man's hostility runs very deep. It may have something to do with menstruation, which vividly says "You are different." It certainly has to do with childbearing and the viciousness with which pregnant women are attacked in backward cultures. In most societies I know, including Hebrew and Muslim and certainly the South Pacific, a woman who had borne a child was considered unclean for thirty or fifty days. In the primitive societies I know so well, the women were not allowed to go near a canoe or hunting instrument because they were thought to be contaminated. So I can only conclude there has been a primordial enmity between the two sexes.

Do you think this enmity is reflected in our language?

The vocabulary that writers use stems largely from the Bible, which is incredibly male-centered and anti-female. Everything strong and constructive and forward-moving is given a '*he*' pronoun. Everything that is destructive, seductive, and negative in the biblical sense a '*she*' pronoun. This has bothered me a good deal. To my shame, when I write I write always with a masculine pronoun if the attributes are noble and fine and good. Then, in a moment's common sense, in revision I correct it. But when you get to a sentence like: *If a man wants to protect his property he had better be sure that his boundaries are well- drawn*, then I cannot say '*he or she*' or '*his or hers*' The grammar is all against women.

You were a supporter of the Equal Rights Amendment. Were you surprised when it was defeated?

It was one of the biggest surprises of my life. It never occurred to me that the women's rights law would fail. I assumed that the E.R.A., which was so very innocuous and so very necessary for the proper balance between men and women, would have passed easily. And it almost did—it came within two or three states of passing. Then the backfire was started and it was defeated by women, who sometimes really hate one another.

I became aware of it by two accidents, one in Florida and one in South Carolina, when I happened to be there with nothing to do and decided to drop in on the anti-E.R.A. meetings which were being held in my hotel. I often do that to find out what people are doing. I was just shattered by the vehemence of the speakers and the dedication that they were applying to this.

In South Carolina a roving television reporter was asking people about it, and the opinion against it was unanimous. So they came to me, not knowing who I was. I acknowledged that I was not from South Carolina, I was a visitor. And I said, "I'm against it completely." The reporter asked why. I said, "Well, I think that women really ought to stay in the home. I don't think they ought to be on juries. As a matter of fact, I doubt seriously if they ought to have the vote." I went the whole hog. I was glad they didn't discover me, I would have been in trouble.

Who was more vociferous about woman's rights, you or Mari?

I am a very strong women's libber. Much more so than my wife was. She came from a conservative Japanese background and it has taken a while for the movement to hit that group. Also, it's a difference in personality. My wife had a more early-twentieth-century attitude, but I looked more toward the future, and I was probably the more adventurous.

My wife and I had a fair and complete distribution of responsibilities. She decided where we lived, how much we paid for the house, whether we had new furniture or not. And I decided what our policy should be toward Egypt and Abyssinia.

She was a pretty tough cookie, wasn't she?

She was such a tiger. She had unbelievable energy, in spite of the fact that she lost a breast to cancer twenty-five years ago and had to have surgery on the other side more recently.

She really controlled things. She handled all our money; I have not been in a bank in the last fifteen years. She handled all our travels and made all the arrangements. I frequently had Mari clue me in on what was happening on any particular day. More often at night before I went to bed I asked her, 'What's the drill for tomorrow?'

How great a shock was Mari's death in September of '94?

The chemotherapy had hit her with such terrible force. But she was a fighter. She was in her own home, surrounded by her friends, she had six or eight or ten visitors a day sitting around telling war stories. On the last day, a Sunday, she really outdid herself. She had friends from all over. It was a lovely spring day in late September. And at 7:30 she just disappeared.

We understood what was happening. I, because I had just written this bloody book [*Recessional*], knew as much about the subject as anybody who came here. And I'm sophisticated about these things. But I was *totally* unprepared for her death. It was a shattering experience.

In Recessional you have a character, Muley Duggan, say "There's an overriding knowledge that death is growing closer . . . Judicious men don't brood about death, but it does creep into their thoughts."

I didn't will that her death would hit me so hard. That's the way it happened.

Were you an easy person to live with?

There's a great problem with being married to someone like me. One is that I work at home and there I am, day after day, right in the middle of things. She must often have felt that she wished the hell I had a nine-to-five job and got out of the house.

When did you first discover how different women and men were?

A very brilliant southern girl was working as my assistant. I was driving and she had the map, and we were trying to find a house of a very radical young professor at Penn State. And she froze, her hand started to tremble. The map was upside down—south was going north and north was going south—and she was absolutely incapable of transposing. I pointed it out to her and she said, "Oh, is it?" And for the first time I realized that she didn't have a clue what a map was. Nor did Mari. It drove me crazy.

After Mari's passing, did you find out anything about her that you didn't know before?

She had about eleven lock boxes. We can't locate them all, nor do we have keys for any of them. She had something like sixty suitcases, most of them never unpacked—in them we found $34,000 worth of American currency and traveler's cheques. I think it was a Japanese peasant fixation: that there was never enough rice in the bin, and bad years are sure to come.

The relationship between the sexes have drastically changed since you married Mari in the fifties. Where do you think it's going?

The radical changes in the relationship in just the last twenty years have been so staggering that if I were younger I would concentrate all my writing on that, I'm sure. They are so radical that we're really not facing up to them. The dreadful plague of AIDS, the sexual harrassment at Tailhook in the Navy and the issue of gays in the military are perfect examples of what I'm talking about.

When did you become aware of how serious a problem AIDS was?

Beverly Sills wrote a fabulous article in the *New York Times* in which she said that in the last two weeks she had been asked to attend the funerals of five brilliant young men who worked with her in the theater. In wonderfully effective and heart-rending phrases she told about burying these five guys and said, 'I don't want any more talk about the fact that AIDS is hitting only the end-of-the-worlders or anything like that. It's hitting our sons and some of the best ones we have.' It was an overpowering article which was widely read and which ended there. She would not discuss it any further. But she did say she expected to continue attending these funerals almost indefinitely. In *Leviticus* the Israelites faced up to the terrible plague of leprosy that affected them. It had exactly the same impact as AIDS has today. What they came up with is to burn the clothes and get the blood of a white turtle dove. In over a hundred verses you realize that they'd come up with something infinitely bigger than they'd been able to handle, and they were not going to find an answer to it for three thousand years. They fought it, they lived with it . . . we'll do the same.

Didn't you once blame the women's movement, in a women's magazine, for scaring a lot of young men away from marriage?

Yes, and I feel that strongly. We're going through a period which is very hard on young men and a lot of them are opting out. Some are moving into homosexuality, which has the sad result that there will be a lot of young women who will not find husbands, and maybe not even partners. Homosexuality isn't the basic problem, it's the change. I don't really blame women, I blame society.

How do you feel about gay school teachers?

I don't think that is any greater risk than heterosexual teachers in schools. Most of the schools I've been acquainted with, male professors have had emotional relationships with their girl students, and female professors with their male students.

So where do you stand on homosexuality?

I believe that human beings are all scaled along so-called feminine and so-called masculine traits, from zero to a hundred and from a hundred down to zero. I think most of us come in at a component of, let's say, 63–37.

You touch on this towards the end of Recessional *when you write about how people who function with the greatest efficiency have a proper mixture of male and female characteristics. What about people who are all male or female?*

My experience has been that I do not respond at all to the female who has 100 percent female traits. She's apt to be a nymphomaniac or terribly aggressive or can't keep things in balance. I have very little rapport with a man who is 100 percent masculine, if there is such a thing. I find them gross and brutish and not to my liking at all. I don't want to bother with either extreme.

Where do you think you come in?

I would suppose about 65–35 on the masculine side. I think I have had perceptions both ways and have, from a very early age, always been aware of that division.

What do you think your feminine traits account for?

My aesthetics. For instance, I can identify very easily with the dispossessed. I have an outgoing attitude toward people in trouble. I have a wider sympathy than I would otherwise have had. It may account for my love of art and chamber music. But I don't believe that aesthetics are equivalent to the feminine characteristics, not at all. I think the 35 percent can modify it very admirably.

The willingness to project oneself into the life of another is a very rare attribute which most of us don't have. I do not begin to have it to the degree that Mailer or Capote has. Or John Cheever or even Updike. I see things a different way. But to see the total structure requires a certain kind of insight and a willingness to surrender one's own personality that I think comes from the 35 percent part of me.

How important is the family in modern society?

I am a very strong believer in the family. If I were a young Jew in Israel, I would surely be in a kibbutz. The idea of the nuclear family with everybody having a kitchen and preparing three meals a day is one that is just ridiculous. In our society we don't have kibbutzes, so I would opt for some kind of group living until about the age of thirty. Then, because I am strongly attracted to the opposite sex, I would want to settle down with someone and establish a home of some kind. At about the age of fifty-five I would want to get away from that as far and as fast as possible and return to some kind of group living.

If this is how you feel, why haven't you done it?

Because my wife was a total recluse. We had a long discussion with some extremely bright people—talking about retirement homes under topflight auspices—and all the men wanted to go and none of the women did.

But in effect I live in a kibbutz anyway. The government gets most of my money right away. I live very simply. I would just as soon have all my contracts in the hands of someone else as long as I get an honest living out of it.

What do you think about when you think about love?

Love relationships are so damn complex that a lifetime of analysis doesn't solve it. I remain bewildered. The love one feels for other people is one of the best parts of life. I think a lot of older people realize this, that by and large the triumphs of life are terribly temporary and they're often illusionary. As a younger man I wrote in *The Fires of Spring* that love could not be defined. It remains more mysterious as I grow older. In recent years I've had a great deal to do with Alzheimer's disease and it absolutely bowls me over. It makes me wonder if what I wrote in *Fires* about old men forgetting what it was to be young and wholly in love is true.

I've had the feeling that older people do forget. I suspect that the virgin love of a fifteen-year-old boy is something rather more cataclysmic than I would now remember it to be.

Why do you suppose that is?

I suppose it's the loss of courage as much as anything else. Youth and love are components of that.

Does sex change as you get older?

At various periods in your life you figure that you have this problem knocked. That now you're forty-one and you see what the ballgame is all about. Then some forty-two-year-old man at the desk next to you runs off with an absolutely adorable waitress and it perplexes you deeply and you sort of wish you were he. So, at forty-one you don't quite have it knocked. But by forty-eight this is all settled. And then something erupts with such passion and power that you suddenly realize that the definition of sex that you had isn't quite the one that the guy in the next apartment has had. But at fifty-six, it's pretty well all put to sleep. But they've been saving the big guns for the latter part of the play. You say to yourself, Jesus, I wasn't even in the ballpark. So when you hit seventy-four, you figure you have it solved. When it hit me so did the coming of the administration of Ronald Reagan. The preachers took over and promised to square away everything. And what did we find? Two of the staunchest Republican Congressmen, rightwingers, defenders of family decency, members of the new party that was going to revolutionize everything and take care of magazines like *Playboy*, movies like *The Devil in Miss Jones*, were caught in the men's toilets soliciting sex within almost a shadow of one of the most sacred institutions of the government. So at seventy-four I was just as bewildered as I was at sixteen, really. And the same holds true for me today, at ninety-eight. I would hate to reach a point when I could pass a tennis court, where young girls are playing, with impunity. That's when the game is over.

**EATING YOUR ENEMY
FOR MANNA & OTHER TALES
OF THE QUITE SPECIFIC**

5

Do the sixties seem distant and innocent to you now?

When I was in Spain once I remember seeing this beautiful girl, I mean really ravishing, and she was meeting with these two guys for the first time. She'd never seen them before, but somebody she had met had recommended them as possible traveling companions. The first thing she did when they came in was look at their arms to see if they were all scarred up. When she saw they weren't drug addicts, she got in their car that afternoon, and goddamn it, they drove to Yugoslavia. That just blew my mind! There was just this innate trust that existed at that time, in the mid-sixties, when there was a freedom in the world.

With terrorists blowing up buildings and shooting at tourists in airports, do you still recommend that youth should travel to broaden their horizons?

I'm very much in favor of young people traveling. One of the most innovative things we've done in our society is the Peace Corps. That and the GI Bill of Rights for a college education were some of the finest investments this nation has made. The government will probably get back ten dollars for every buck spent. In taxation! And where are you going to find people with imagination if they haven't gone out and had these experiences when they were young? They're not going to do it when they're forty—their arteries are usually too hardened by then.

You promote travel as a way of gaining experience, but what are some of the negatives you've seen?

Of course sometimes these young travelers have a rough time—they get sick, they run out of money, they have no means to get back home. I remember once this kid in Torremolinos who was showing off a check for one hundred dollars that Hemingway had given him three weeks before. He had gone up to Hemingway in the bar where we were sitting and had given him a sad pitch about being short on dough and Hemingway wrote him the check. This is the sort of thing that happened all the time with me. I was once told about a poor English girl who was dying in Tangier and would I go and collect money to ship her back to London? So I went to Tangier to save this poor child and when I got there she was dead, so we buried her there.

Then I went on down to Marrakesh with some of the kids, where they were living, often in abject poverty. The filth and hovels were pretty dreadful. But out of that comes appreciation that you would not get otherwise.

Do young people recognize you abroad?

While I was knocking around the great square in Marrakesh, looking at the snake charmers, this very pretty American girl came up and said, "Is it true that you are James Michener?" I said I was. She gave this squeal and said, "Oh wow!" Then, "Are you staying here? Oh wow! Could we see you tonight?" Then I found that she and her friends said "Oh wow!" to everything. They were having Coca-Cola and it was "Oh wow!" And they had a couple of hashish cigarettes. "Oh wow!"

What about drugs? While researching The Drifters *did you get high?*

I was fed some LSD without my knowledge while I was there and even a little was pretty frightening. It terrified me because I'm very high strung to begin with, it doesn't take much to trigger my imagination. I can get high on a Delacroix print, so I don't need LSD. But I have tried most everything. I smoked opium when I was a newsman in Asia. I was in Phnom Penh and the houses there were run just like drugstores. It's inevitable that you would want to know what it was about.

I was in very good physical condition at that time and the casual experiences I had were not strong enough to induce anything.

Is marijuana dangerous?

I have had great difficulty in believing that it is the evil drug that people said. But I've never been much impressed by the product of the societies which give it free passage in the Near East. Though it's fatuous to say it's a totally destructive drug because the people have been using it for two thousand years with no great destruction. The harsh sentences by the Texas courts are way out of proportion.

What about heroin?

Heroin is another matter. I've seen some bad results with cocaine, but not nearly as bad as from heroin. I have never seen, in the forty or fifty cases in my own experience, anybody retreat from heroin.

Speaking of escape, how does the average American do traveling abroad?

People from the most ordinary towns in America will travel to Europe and intuitively know that they ought to look at the architecture, see where the great writers lived, see some plays, listen to some music. Otherwise, how do you establish any taste?

You feel that Spain is an essential destination for any traveler, don't you?

If you're going to look at Europe . . . or the world . . . then you have to come to grips with Spain. Spain ruled the world. Spain is in the league with Greece and Italy. It produced wonderful artists and words and music and painting and architecture. But Spain also initiated the Inquisition, so you have to wrestle with it. That's why *Iberia* was so fascinating to write.

Many of the letters I get from people who have read that book are about the trip I took as a pilgrim across northern Spain, which was about as rewarding as anything one can do.

Is there anywhere you haven't been?

I've been everywhere on the face of the earth that I've wanted to be except Charleston, South Carolina. I'm extremely grateful that I've lived into the period of these great explorations when it was possible to get anywhere. Mari and I always had our bags ready to go, and we often packed for a trip around the world in fifteen minutes. If I could get to the moon, I'd go. If an alien spacecraft landed tomorrow and invited me aboard, I wouldn't hesitate.

What are the essentials you have pre-packed?

I have my Ghurka traveling bag packed with my shaving gear, a couple of extra pairs of glasses, a slide ruler, a pocket computer, some medicine, a spare tooth, some nasal spray, a few notepads, my passport, some traveler's checks, my vaccination/health record. I keep a tight list of everything I need to take, about thirty items which I check off, throw them in my bag, and off I go. As for clothing: two dress suits, a pair of slacks, a casual coat, underwear, two shirts, a couple of sport shirts, a spare set of shoes. I travel very light and go great distances with it. I buy things en route and give them away. I would judge I have given away twenty typewriters.

Are there any rules you travel by?

Philip Knowlton, an editor at Macmillan to whom I was so indebted, gave me five rules of travel which represented the accumulated wisdom of that period: Get your laundry done at every chance. Never eat at a restaurant called *Mom's*. Never play poker with a guy called Doc. Eat, no matter where you are, any meal on the menu that has wild rice. And never pass up an opportunity for sex. I don't know five better rules.

Knowlton had one other rule. "There's just one rule of successful management: Never have sex with a girl in the first postal zone. Meaning in your immediate vicinity."

How facile are you in languages?

I speak Spanish and can read Italian and French fairly easily. I have no German, to my sorrow, and none of the Oriental languages. I have often lived with primitive people who had no English whatever and I had none of their language, but it never bothered us a bit.

How do you get by?

I manage by participating in the total life of the village—hunting with them, carrying water, tilling the fields with their cows or oxen, tending the cattle, going to a wedding if there was one.

What are your most memorable travel experiences?

Probably the most extraordinary experience I had was in India, when I went up from Calcutta to a district called Twenty-four Perghanas, in the Sunderbans. Nobody spoke English there and life was about as primitive as you could imagine. I also once lived for a while among the Sakai, a really primitive aborigine group in the jungles of Malaya. I was the only American—a correspondent with a regiment that did a lot of jungle patrolling. I never carried a gun myself, but we found a nest of communist guerillas, a Viet Cong group, and had a running battle with them, capturing them all, including the group leader.

The Sakai took hot coals and put them in their mouths, closed their mouths and stood there looking at us. Then they'd spit out the coals and there would be no strange steam and they weren't burned. It's a phenomenon I'm not sure I understand.

In Singapore I was startled by the fire walkers. I was right at the scene where it was too hot for me to stand, touching the cigarette paper to the coals and watching it go up in a second. A minute later an Indian, in an obvious state of frenzy and catatonia, walked right through these glowing coals. One guy, who should never have been allowed to go because he obviously hadn't reached that state of self-control, went screaming in mortal terror as he tried to walk across and didn't make it. He went under.

Indian mystics would take a skewer and just stick it through parts of their face. And they don't bleed. They don't feel pain.

Who are the most primitive people you've studied?

The Big Nambas of Malekula, in the New Hebrides, were maybe the most primitive people I've ever worked with. I had the privilege of walking across Malekula during the War, which very few people, black or white, have ever done. They were cannibals and were, I suppose, as primitive as there were on earth, even more so than the people in New Guinea. They were delightful. I mean, if they're not eating you, they're a very pleasant people.

Most cannibalism in the last two hundred years has been ritual. That is, you eat a powerful enemy for manna, not for anything else. Of course, we have adopted this totally in the Christian religion. You eat the body of Christ every time you go to mass.

Did you ever encounter any other cannibals?

I was with the cannibals in Malaita when I was in the Navy. It was most dramatic— getting cannibals right out of the Stone Age and bringing them to Guadalcanal, giving them a pair of shorts and a T-shirt, and three weeks later they were driving Mack trucks and servicing the airplanes along the Henderson airfield. I've seen this three times: once in Malaita, once in the New Hebrides, and once in Afghanistan, where the most primitive people on earth can learn to drive a gasoline engine with joy and expertise in weeks.

Care to go through a best and worst list?

In all my travels I am often asked to list the 'best' and 'worst' places I've been. I've written that Afghanistan was my most memorable land, the Na Pali cliff in Hawaii the most beautiful view, Bora Bora the loveliest spot, the basilica of Santa Maria Maggiore in Rome the finest building, Angkor Wat the most compelling sight.

That's what you've written—let's add to it.

The Grand Canyon, the European Alps, the Himalayas—they were pretty important to me. So, too, the Pacific Ocean, as it's the largest single item on the entire earth.

What about sights like Niagara Falls or Murchison Falls in Uganda?

The great waterfalls don't move me very much; I don't get much intellectual content from them.

What does stimulate you intellectually then?

The tremendous memorials of ancient Egypt—Karnak, Thebes, the pyramids. Edfu, a little temple town about a half-day up river from Karnac, is just a gem; it's as great as Chartres Cathedral in its own brutal way.

What are the ugliest buildings you've seen?

The ugliest architecture is in Nebraska.

Favorite markets?

The best marketplaces would be the great market of Barcelona and the souk of Istanbul.

Best beach?

I don't know that it has a name, but it's on the north side of Oahu.

Most exotic place?

The road from Colombo to Galle Face in Ceylon would be the most exotic place I've been.

Most erotic?

Tahiti on the fourteenth of July.

Most incomprehensible?

Borobudur, one of the world's greatest Buddhist monuments, built in central Java about 800. Angkor Wat would be another. And Easter Island would also rank very high.

What most people don't understand about Easter Island is that there are these great inscrutable statues, but there are also the quarries from which they were dug. There are more than one hundred and fifty statues in various stages of completion. There's one area where five are all parallel down the side of a hill, they were cutting them out from the top to the bottom, there's no question to *how* it was done, but there's never been a good solution for *why* they did it, and *who* did it.

What's the most repressive place you've seen?

The town of Portadown in Northern Ireland on a Sunday in February. That's the bleak bottom. I was with a group of pretty tough American newsmen and we witnessed two terrible bombings and real horror.

The worst place?

It was in Trengganu on Malaya. Rough river, incredible bugs and heat, skin disease, poor food. There was a Catholic missionary there, an English trader, and a Chinese man. We had one of the most wonderful colloquies extending over four days that I've ever engaged in. If you could find four utterly delightful men, it didn't matter where you were. It was a marvelous lesson.

Have you ever been stuck with someone who made your skin crawl?

The most boring person in the world has got to be an Englishman who has served in India and doesn't have enough money to go back to England and has settled in the shadow of Gibraltar.

Who are the best travelers?

The Germans. They're intelligent, they're daring, they're adventurous, they spend their money wisely, and they wrote the best guidebooks there ever were on this earth.

The Germans are superior and they are destined to rule the world. They're destined to, because they're tough, they're well organized, they write far better music than we do, Goethe is better than Walt Whitman, and so on right down the line. The only thing that saves us is that they go ape every four or five decades.

The best looking people?

The Burmese, though the most beautiful women are Sophia Loren and the late Audrey Hepburn. The most handsome men would be the Samoans.

The worst looking?

The native tribes in Africa with the enormous buttocks.

What people throughout history most fascinate you?

John Knox. If I were to write about him, I'd want to portray him for the tremendous man he was, and also for the monster he turned out to be. I was once attracted to Prince Rupert in the 1630–50 period and his relationship with Cromwell. I found myself always siding with Rupert and very glad to see Cromwell done in. Thomas Jefferson is a tremendous challenge to any intellectual understanding of America, partly because of the wonderful counterfoil of Alexander Hamilton and the relationship to Washington and Adams. Jefferson had a vision of the people that is a nice mixture of extreme intellectual brilliance and compassion and understanding. I was always greatly attracted to Calhoun of South Carolina, a man who lost all his battles and came out looking awfully well. Maybe Grover Cleveland. Some of the artists and musicians might attract me. Handel, who had such a tremendous career in five different countries. Flaubert. Bizet. I feel as close to Bizet—and Stendhal—as any artist, even though they're both French and I tend to be more Germanic.

And if you were to give a time-warp dinner party, would these be the people you'd invite?

I'd probably go with Balzac; Mozart, just to see what the hell this kid was up to; Marco Polo, for having the guts to do what he did; Jefferson; and Michelangelo. I'd choose Michelangelo over Da Vinci because Da Vinci didn't do a hell of a lot, except shine like an evening planet. But I see great forts that Michelangelo built and cities that he designed, I see the sculpture, the beautiful paintings, the things he wrote—he's my type of boy. Two others might get invited for dessert: Alexander the Great and Winston Churchill. Getting all the way to the five rivers of India from Mesopotamia, my God! If you had a caravan of camels it would be a magnificent accomplishment. To do it with an army and fight battles every step of the way, I don't see how he did it. And Churchill is a mixed bag. At Gallipoli he almost destroyed the British Navy and the Armed Forces there. Then he survived that debacle and became the savior of the nation thirty years later. Incredible!

Churchill was a great talker, which is what you want at your table. But most great writers—forget it. I suspect Homer might have been a damned dull guy to talk with, and you'd not have gotten far with John Keats, that shy, hesitant, retiring young man who could nevertheless write like an angel. We know that Herman Melville was a stumble-tongue who saved his fiery visions for his pen, and James Joyce certainly did not move through Ireland, Italy, and England mouthing his arcane sentences, nor did William Faulkner come even close to talking the way he wrote. I would judge the overall score among the great writers of fiction would be Writers 93 percent, Talkers 7 percent, and the latter the windiest.

What period of history has most interested you?

The years 1520–1540, with that fantastic constellation of great men who operated in the world in India, Japan; the Incas; Charles V, Suleiman, St. Francis, Henry VIII, Calvin, Luther. So much was happening, so many decisions were being made.

In modern times, what's most stimulated your imagination?

The most exciting experience intellectually has been the series of photographs from Mars. Not only the content, but the way it was done and the implications for society.

What's your most disappointing experience?

The failure of the Semites—Jews and Arabs alike—to work out some *modus vivendi* in the Jerusalem area. The two groups are destined to work together. With the richness and the wonderful capacity of the Arabs and the organizing, educational, and scientific abilities of the Jews, it's a natural relationship. It will come to pass, probably about 2025.

What's the strangest spot in the world?

Fatehpur Sikri. It's about twenty miles from Agra, the site of the Taj Mahal. Around 1500 or 1520 a really great city was built there of red sandstone. They had a great central square and on it, in huge size, was a chess board. The emperors used to sit in their balconies and their knights would be the chessmen. There is zero humidity in that area, also zero water supply. So after a very brief occupancy they realized it was a no-show and they left it. And it's preserved as one of the wonders of the world, just as if they left yesterday. A city of maybe 20,000. Unbelievable.

India is truly a mind-bending country, isn't it?

I was stuck in Calcutta once, which is a terrible experience. I went up north into the real backwoods of India, right on the border of Bangladesh, where the land is so flat that any water comes in and floods everything. People there spoke of the next village . . . and the next village was about a quarter of a mile away! You walked through a grove of trees and there's another village of nine hundred people, and then beyond that another. This was the boondocks of the world!

How come you've never written about India?

Because it's too frightening, too big, and I was never sympathetic. I found the Indians so difficult, overbearing. They can't run their own country, but they're always free to tell you how you should run yours.

And China?

In China what you really have to come to grips with is the enormous number of people and the great antiquity of the society. And the fact that it was a very able, clever society. When I was stranded in China at one time, with a lot of very learned people, we discussed often at night whether if we were young men we would rather be in India or China. Universally we felt that it would be China, because China taken in toto had more significance to us. Now, there is a cultural difference. It may be that what China has is easier for us to grasp; what India has is somewhat forbidding.

The people, too, are quite different.

The Indians, God, they know everything! They sign their letters in the newspaper with their name and then their schooling: 'M.A. Oxford, failed.' The letters I get from India, about four a year, want me to finance them for a year or get them a scholarship at Harvard. I've had to draft a form letter where I said I just don't have any more money. But the ones from India, they are something. You would want to help all of them, except that you know if they did come you would find them insufferable; they would be here one day, and they would be telling you how you should have done it.

Is there any one country that stands out dramatically in your experience?

Perhaps the most dramatic country where I've spent time is Afghanistan, which is so imbued with history. Alexander the Great was there 2500 years ago. You see his ruins, you go to places where he had great capitals. Go down into the desert and find a city a hundred miles long with the most beautiful architecture. Look up at the immense night sky.

Afghanistan is also where you witnessed a rather bizarre sport.

Goat-dragging. The wildest thing I've ever seen in sports. About a hundred and fifty Afghan horsemen are divided into two teams. You take a goat and put him in the middle of the field. At the signal, the two teams dash in and somebody grabs the goat. He gets hold of one leg and the other team gets hold of the other leg and they fight about it. If it looks as if your team is going to score an early goal and the game will be over, you tackle your own man and just beat the hell out of him until he lets go of the goat. After about twelve minutes the goat has been torn apart. It isn't always identifiable as to which part really represents the ball in this affair. It gets rather messy and everybody gets bloody. After about eighty minutes, with bodies all over the field and horses with broken legs and the goat torn into six pieces, somebody gallops up to the goal and scores the glorious victory. It's some ballgame!

Is there any individual whose behavior struck you as personally admirable?

The bravest and most memorable woman I ever knew was a freelance photographer named Dickey Chapelle. I worked with her in Hungary, during a considerably dangerous time when we were trying to get these people visas or entry papers.

We went behind Russian lines again and again, for maybe thirty nights, but I would always counsel caution, checking to see how we were going to get out and where the bridges were and where the Russians might be. But Dickey threw caution to the wind.

One night she went out by herself against my advice and she was picked up and disappeared. We launched interrogations to Budapest, Warsaw, Moscow. Under duress the Russians admitted they had her. Then we started a rescue operation. When we got her out, she came and lived with us for six weeks until she recovered. Then she went on and served with the French Marines in Algeria, where she did some parachute jumping. Then she went on to Saigon, walked right into a land mine, and was blown to pieces.

You've had a few near-death experiences yourself, haven't you?

I've had my share. I crashed a car into a wall in Afghanistan and cracked up another one in Turkey. In Rio Mari and I were in a cable car going to Sugar Loaf Mountain when lightning struck us as we were right over the deepest part of the chasm. There were about thirty of us in the cabin and it teetered there, no lights, no power, it was a heavy wind. Several people fainted through sheer terror.

Even more terrifying were the three plane crashes I walked away from. One, in 1944, was a plane which sank on landing. I was upstairs and survived; the people down below didn't. Another was an overturn at a field in Samoa a year later, no loss of life. There must have been about twenty of us in that C-47. I was seated in the side that was going to turn over, and a colonel was sitting opposite me. We were the only ones who were aware of what was happening. I looked at him with some apprehension and he nodded very bravely. Christ, it was terrible! After the hospital and dinner at the Officer's Club, we were sort of kidding about how brave we were. It was a horrible dark night in the tropics. I went out to go to my quarters and as I walked, the war hit me. I told myself that when it's over, I'm not going to be the same guy. I didn't know if I could be a great man, but I was determined to live as if I were. I would deal with big subjects, associate with people brighter than myself. It was as clear to me as if a voice were telling me that this was a choosing-up point. I knew that my capacities were limited and that I had only so much to spend, but I wanted to do it in a big way.

As I'm thinking all of this I fell into a great, deep ditch and just collapsed. I just had had it. I lost all control. I wasn't aware of it but it was more than I could take. I thought I couldn't get out and screamed. The medics came and sedated me. The next day I went to see how far I had fallen and it wasn't that deep. Thereafter I was very careful about making fun of anybody who had battleshock, because you can reach a point where you just opt out. I think you do so for profound psychological reasons.

The third plane crash was a ditching in the middle of the Pacific the day that Sputnik went off, October 4, 1957. The pilot was masterful, he took it right in by the book. Everybody was stone silent. We went in just like a ten-ton truck. We were in deep waves, and the plane disintegrated in three minutes. I went forward and helped the pilot out. I was the last man out of the plane. But then I couldn't get into the life raft. They kept yelling at me and finally someone dived in and got behind me; he gave me a heck of a shove and I somersaulted in, and was immediately sick. Within ten minutes ten of us became deathly seasick. In those big waves and in a collapsible raft you get four or five motions at the same time. Oh my God, were we seasick! We were in about eighteen hours before planes got to us and vectored in a Japanese fishing boat.

Was that the flight where you lost the manuscript for your book on Hokusai and the outline for Hawaii?

That's the one. It was a terrible, terrible loss. I was so determined not to lose that Hokusai book that when I got to Japan I sat at a typewriter and worked around the clock for two weeks rewriting it.

You also tickled death running with the bulls in Pamplona, didn't you?

Right. There are six bulls and maybe fifteen oxen when the gun goes off at seven in the morning and the corral gates are opened. I was in the street when the bulls were passing and stood in a doorway to avoid them. There happened to be a group of cameramen there, shooting blindly, when this happened, and a series of really remarkable photographs tell the story. The maddened bull stands with his horn three inches from my belly. The guy at my feet is dead. I remained extremely rigid, and the bull passed on.

When did you run with the bulls?

Just before the astronauts first landed on the moon. I remember because after that close call in Pamplona I went to Seville to recuperate and we saw it on television. But at least three times during the program the announcer came on and said: "I want to assure you that the Pope knows all about this and he has said that it's all right." Then when Armstrong got on the moon the announcer said: "I want to remind you that the Pope has been informed of this and he's given approval." It was very important, because people were terrified. There was a strong opinion that when you stepped on the moon you would go down about eighteen feet in the dust. The third time the announcer came on to say that they had succeeded because the Pope's prayers had guided them.

You could have used prayers in the '50s Saigon riot.

That was the closest I've come to death. Rioters came right down the hall of the hotel I was staying in and threw people out the windows, killing some, maiming others. When they got to me, they burst into my room, and for some crazy reason I stood with my typewriter over my chest shouting, "You can't do it! Press, press, press!" Somebody knew the word, and they backed off. I was scared to death, scared to death. The others were killed; I was next in line.

You've written at great lengths about geology and geography—what land mass interests you more, Africa or Asia?

Africa is a beautiful unit physically, Asia is a hell of a hodge-podge—you can't really tell where it begins and ends.

Where should the next James Michener—looking to dig his or her teeth into the world—venture?

Either Africa or South America. Learn the languages, travel endlessly, live with the Indians, read about three hundred books, and spend nine years perfecting their skills and knowledge. That's all.

Why didn't you take on South America yourself?

Because Latin America has never gotten its act together—never figured a way to govern itself, oscillated between one dictatorship or another, knocked in the head any progressive movements, and festered in its own arrogance. That's not good enough for me. I don't want to waste my time on the second rate.

In Caribbean you wrote about all of those islands. For the general traveler, which island would you most recommend?

Barbados. It's a beautiful island, very British. Jamaica is the most beautiful of the islands because it has lovely mountains and heavenly valleys, good people. But it's suffered from the demise of its three great industries: sugar, fruit, and aluminum. For a spell of years Jamaica was hostile to American and other tourists. The present government is striving to improve relationships.

How often do you get invitations to live in a foreign land?

I have been invited to live in many of the countries of the world—alluring invitations. For a while, if someone like me lived overseas for 501 days, you would be excused from taxes. Then you could move to Ireland where there are no taxes at all for creative artists. That was always a great temptation.

But . . . ?

I wouldn't want to live with any permanence outside the American flag. I do have a primordial feeling about my land and the mountains that I grew up with and the waterways that I have lived with.

Is there any country that remotely resembles the U.S.?

I remember once talking with a great geographer who had a map of Australia and one of the United States. He pointed out that the two countries are the exact same size, but the difference between the two was the Mississippi River. If you rip the Mississippi and all its tributaries—the Ohio, the Tennessee, the Missouri, the Nebraska, about fifty rivers—out of the United States, you have Australia. A desert. And you don't have enough people to support the industries on the two coasts. The difference is in the land. We have that fantastic river system and Australia doesn't.

So exile was never an option for you?

I have watched a lot of men go into exile when things went sour in their own country. I have drawn more tolerant of those who left.

If America didn't exist or you had to go into exile where would you go?

Probably to Great Britain or Argentina. I used to think I might go to Thailand, but they are falling upon evil days.

Great Britain has been a refuge for a lot of people in the last 150 years. Victor Hugo fled there, people from all over Europe fled there, and an enormous number of Americans who felt disenfranchised at home went there. So there is a tradition of hospitality and refuge. I wouldn't go to Ireland. I don't want to get caught up in that.

Argentina is harder to explain. I like the bigness of it, the fact that it's still unpopulated and it's a frontier. I would have gone there for many of the same reasons that the 1848 group in Europe came to the United States.

A number of states in this country lay claim to you. How have you chosen the areas you live in?

I have chosen to live four months of each year in three different areas of the country: Texas, Maine, and Florida. My residency, though, I still keep in Pennsylvania, which is where I pay my taxes and vote. I had seriously considered changing that residency to Florida but decided not to because I don't want to live in a state which refuses to have an income tax. For me it would be quite dishonorable.

I will keep my refuge home in Florida because when you're my age you have to think about these things.

Is Florida really the best place for old people?

Southern Florida is not hospitable to older people, they treat us abominably.

But I love nature and I live in Florida on a waterway, see the manatees, the birds. And the communal living there is very attractive and tempting. Austin, on the other hand, is a center of medical excellence. And you have the great hospitals in Houston. I have a nice house, a wide circle of friends who look after me, take me out to dinner. My affiliation with the university here is very rewarding. I teach at the university for no fee. But what I want is the library and the telephone and maybe a secretary, contact with young people, being in the mix. On the campus of the University of Texas there are twenty-three major libraries, and they have the greatest collection of manuscripts of the English-speaking world in the world—original Chaucer, Milton, the Shakespeare portfolios. The way I work, I don't need a book on Cuba, I need *three* books on Cuba, two of them within the last eight years. So it's awesome.

How do you deal with the demands of your time?

I've recently toured the Caribbean to renew old acquaintances; traveled back to the South Pacific to touch base with my people there; flew to Hawaii at the invitation of the State Department commemorating the fiftieth anniversary of the bombing of Pearl Harbor; been to Hungary and Poland for ceremonies honoring my work there and joining their celebration of their independence from Russia; retraced Columbus's discovery of America—going from Genoa across the Mediterranean to Spain, then voyaging across the Atlantic to San Salvador and then to Ft. Lauderdale; and trekked into the Antarctic, a place I never thought I'd get to. I was also honored in New York with the Continental Magellan Society of the World award as a well-known traveler.

Anything that happens in the Pacific they say, 'Let's get Jim Michener.' I get at least six invitations a year, so I have to be selective.

You said earlier that you've visited every area of the world but didn't you miss Machu Picchu?

I received a letter from the Peruvian government saying I could not close out my life as a traveler without visiting Machu Picchu. I had always avoided it because of its altitude, but they say they have another route in and you don't get higher than six thousand feet. Then I've been invited to go around the world with each of two different ships. And there will probably be an excursion to Mexico City to have a reunion with the bullfighters with whom I once toured. It just never ends. I just have to decide what I can do.

Would you say you've been in more oceans and seas than most ship crew members?

Probably. The P & O, in recent years, has quietly let it be known that I could ride anywhere in the world on their ships at any time. I give a talk or two and it's a wonderful experience.

Now, at any time, I have six or eight of these invitations from Cunard, to go to Finland and travel back across the Atlantic, or go to the Antarctic.

What was the Antarctic like?

It was painful to get there—you have to go through the Great Passage, and goddamn, that is frightening! When you get there you go ashore about eight times, wading into the water each time. You have hip boots which you put on and take off twice a day, after first putting on twenty-four pieces of clothing until you look like a little sausage. That was the strenuous part, putting your clothes on and off, especially three pairs of socks and four pairs of underwear and three different kinds of shoes and then the heavy boots. It was maybe forty pounds of gear.

But it was worth it, because the Antarctic is beyond your imagination. In all the history of the world there has never been any habitation or anyone living south of sixty degrees latitude. North of sixty degrees you have a hell of a lot of Alaska, enormous amounts of Canada, much of Scandinavia, a great deal of what was the Soviet Union.

In Alaska you have Glacier Bay, which is world famous, and you have two great glaciers coming down, one from the northwest and one from northeast. They come down, maybe three football fields wide, and you go within a quarter of a mile of them, and they're impressive. In Antarctica, everywhere you go, into any bay, you are surrounded by 360 degrees of glaciers, some of them a mile wide. And the icebergs are staggeringly beautiful. You don't see them in Alaska. The first iceberg we saw was as we left Drake Passage, it was as big as a small village, with turrets, towers, fields, a village center . . . it was unbelievable. And you're only seeing twenty percent of it!

My wife had said she didn't want to make the trip unless she was assured of seeing some penguins. We must have seen 800,000. There are six breeds of them, and they all have their tuxedos on. There would be islands where you couldn't see the soil for the penguins, it would be a blanket of penguins. You also see a lot of sea birds, gulls and cormorants, and seals and whales. About ninety-five percent of all the krill in the world are there, so the whales and seals feed on them.

Still, you wonder how the penguins happened to settle there. There is no vegetation of any kind and there are only two things growing in the entire area: one is lichen, and the other is a moss. The winters are so devastating that anything like a tree would have no chance whatever. But the magnitude of the Antarctic is just unreal.

Since I've never been to the moon, except in spirit, it will have to do.

Do you mostly write about what you know best?

It's the damndest thing that I have never written about the two things that I know best: Scotland and the Tudor period. I know them better than all those things I've written about.

What about books you've begun but haven't finished—have there been many of those?

I went very far in writing a great biography of the Mexican revolutionary Emiliano Zapata. I wrote three hundred pages of a novel about Russia. There was a book about India I never wrote; then there was my book about Islam, which is a deep regret.

Why is that one such a deep regret?

I am as conversant with Islam as I am with anything that I have ever written about. I wrote a very daring essay some years ago called "Islam, the Misunderstood Religion." It was widely printed in the Muslim countries, and, when I went there I was a kind of a minor hero. At five or six different intervals I planned to do a big summary book on Islam, like *Iberia*. I feel the same way about South America and about Central Africa. I feel those missed opportunities very painfully.

Islam seems like such a volatile religion—what is it that so strikes you about it?

Islam is a wonderfully pragmatic religion suited to its climate and its people. The Muslim world includes Indonesia, Malaysia, Pakistan, Afghanistan, and India. I had the great privilege of living in all parts of it except in Riyadh. I find it a working man's religion and of pretty high quality. If you think of it, it certainly was more successful than Christianity in certain of its periods. A great deal of Western culture derives from Islam sources, like astronomy and mathematics.

The great weakness of Islam is in linguistics. It does not prize precise statement. The word becomes a substitute for the act. When I lived in Haifa almost every week some high official in an Islamic state would announce that they were going to bomb Haifa off the map. I asked about this. "We didn't mean that, we were just saying it." It took me a long time to get that into focus.

But I am not sure what Islam is anymore these days. It isn't the Islam as we know it, it's something else.

Have you ever tackled a big subject without prior knowledge of it?

I would not consider writing a big book unless I had a background of knowledge. When I've been asked to write about Minnesota, I couldn't even consider it because I didn't have that background. In Maine I am heckled every week about writing a book about Maine. I have no capacity to write such a book, and furthermore Kenneth Roberts has done it. California, though, is another story. I have a terrific knowledge of California. So California is eligible but because of Mari's experiences there during the War, it was just out of the question.

So your marriage kept you from putting the Michener touch on California?

Yes. And saying that, it's still a sadness in my life.

Can we analyze how you start your research once you decide on a subject?

With the knowledge that I already have, I would move there, very quietly, not telling anybody. We would take a house somewhere for about six months. In Maryland, when I was researching *Chesapeake*, I said, "I'm making a study of crab cakes." In that six months, Mari would begin to know everybody in town. And she would say, "Jim, you ought to talk to this woman I met at the store today." She would bring her around and it would not be until the end of six months that I would even remotely admit that I was there thinking about doing a book.

Let's take California as a hypothetical example of how you would proceed.

I would invite people to tell me what they know and I would begin to compile their stories and try to get an honest view of North and South. When I started to become unbalanced I would work out in Bakersfield, which is sort of neutral to the two areas. You do that for three years, you learn something.

In narrowing down the areas I would focus on, two would be

obligatory: the Chinese building the railroad, because it deals with modern values; and the water rights.

What else would be mandatory?

I suspect that I would deal with the Modoc revolution of the late 1800s. So it would be the Modoc and the Chinese and the water rights.

Then I would people my book with different families. I would have to have a Mexican and the building of the great missions, Juniper Sierra, or somebody like him. I would go back to the earliest Spanish ship that came up the coast, maybe 1530.

Really come to grips with the land, the St. Andreas fault, the great beauty, the Gold Rush, the building of the railroads, the ships coming around the horn, the Hispanic adventures, the Russian adventures where they almost had the west coast—I'm surprised nobody's done a novel like that for California.

It would certainly be quite a challenge. Do such complexities ever frighten you?

California's a big subject, but Alaska is three times the size of California, with just as many interesting people and stories, and historically maybe five hundred times older. It doesn't overwhelm me. Magnitude doesn't scare me at all. Of all the inquiries I've received, the two most persistent ones were to write about Alaska and California. I managed one of the two. And regret not having done the other.

What else as a writer do you regret?

Not having a body of short stories, which most writers have, that I did not start writing in my twenties and have that under my belt. Because wonderful things happen in short stories. They are anthologized, they are used in dramatic form, they serve a wonderful role in college teaching. All of that I missed.

Once a book is written, do you put it out of mind or retain it?

Sometimes people, with great excitement, come up to talk to me about one of my books, and I realize I wrote it thirty years ago and I don't remember it. They know it far better than I do.

What about rereading your books? Do you have the time?

I don't read my former work very often. It's a very sad, exceedingly painful experience, because on the first page I see something that could be better, or a passage so inept that I wonder how I ever released it, or plain error, and I'm ashamed. Three pages later there will be a passage that's a flawless beauty, so exactly what it should have been, that I can't remember having written it; nor do I believe that I *could* have written it. Oscillating between those two responses, I am content to hand the book back to its owner.

How traumatic is it to wait for the critical and popular results of what you write?

By and large we write books and throw them out there. It's a very murderous process of sink or swim, and the publishers are even more murderous than the writers because they give the book only about six weeks. If it doesn't show any legs, that's it. Murderous. Even with a guy like me, with my track record, my publisher has to worry, and they should with a guy my age. But if it can get tough for me, for first-time novelists it can be brutal.

Publishing seems to be going through a lot of changes lately. How brutal will it get for new writers?

I'm not at all happy about publishing these days. When a union of two publishers is effected, you wind up losing half the staff. And those are the people that agents deal with: the bright young new editors who hope to latch on to some bright new young writers and they'll both go up together. My agent, Owen Laster, tells me that every year there are fewer people to whom he can send a first novel.

I am more concerned about the novel now than I was fifty years ago. The novel runs the risk of going the way poetry did, of becoming a dialogue between the elite. The breakthrough of the black writer is good, just look at the reception that Toni Morrison and James Baldwin have met. That breakthrough woman's novel hasn't been written yet. Nor has the Hispanic experience been captured.

Is the novel a dying art?

My whole evidence is exactly the contrary. I have bucked the system in every respect—against television, against the apparent domination of pop culture and Gothic romantic novels, against new systems of distribution, against the establishment, against the university domination—and I have turned out to be one of the most widely-read writers of modern times. I haven't had to use violence or wild sex, kookiness or anything else. I've simply laid out a great story and let it fall where it will. I don't think an art form is ever dead.

There is some clown out in western Idaho who is going to come out with a volume of sonnets one of these days that will just blow the mind of this country. If I were a young poet and had the capacity and wanted to do a sequence of eighty-one sonnets about the present world, I wouldn't hesitate a minute. Because these art forms don't die. They fall into disuse or go out of fashion.

Poetry seems to have fallen on particularly hard times.

I love books and this very honorable profession, and I have tried to do everything I can to treat it with decency. Every year I get a garland of letters from poets who I have managed to help get printed in book form, because I've given quite a few of my royalties to the publication of poetry. I put up funds and Daniel Halpern devised a way of going to the little presses and subsidizing them. We got it up to about $250,000 and that yields a lot of interest. When a poet is able to get his poems into print and circulated, then things happen for her or for him. That's the virtue of it.

Do you think we basically don't care about our artists?

The acceptance of the artist in society is far poorer in the United States than almost anywhere else. He does not begin to have the value that he has in foreign countries, especially in countries like Russia, Spain, Argentina, France.

When I served with General MacArthur's occupation forces in Japan shortly after World War II, Tokyo was filled with American generals and colonels, often of the most aggressive behavior and limited education background. When they gave evening soirees to which the bewildered Japanese were invited, these military leaders instinctively knew that they ought to parade before their conquered guests not only evidences of America's military might but also some indication that we were a civilized society which paid attention to the niceties of life like art, string quartets, and good wine.

Fortunately, there was living in Tokyo at that time a French woodblock artist who had come to Japan in the early 1930s, liked it and stayed, winning a modest success as an artist. On a scale of ten for the tops I would have rated him about a 2.3. His drawing was only so-so, his color sense deficient, and his capacity to design a given space only passable.

On the other hand, if I were giving him marks for looking like an artist, he would win something like a 13.7 on that same basis of ten. He wore his hair long. He had especially long fingernails which he colored. He wore a velvet suit with a flowing tie. On his feet he had big, floppy shoes of his own design, and his gestures were similarly extravagant. He peppered his amusing English with references to his atelier, the commission he was doing for the emperor, his latest exhibition at the Salon des Refuses, and his projected one-man exhibition in the major museums of South America.

In short, this character looked like an artist, he acted like one, and he spoke like one. Within three minutes of joining any American party where he was present the Japanese guests could be assured that the host took art seriously, for here was a visible artist as one of the guests.

The only artist that is allowed to appear as a sympathetic character in the bulk of American fiction is an architect. Never a poet or a songwriter or a man who writes operas or short stories. We accept architects because they're also practical men. And we abhor and are frightened of novelists like Truman Capote or Saul Bellow. America would be embarrassed to have a homosexual poet like Thornton Wilder in a government position, or a gruff Southern original like Robert Penn Warren as an ambassador. Unthinkable.

The lowered role of the artist hurts us, it hurts society. To give all this accolade to football players and juvenile singers, it's just so out of proportion that it's pitiful. I'm free to speak about it because I have not been treated poorly—I've had maybe more than my share of acceptance.

Do you have any theory on why it's like that for artists in America?

It goes back to a frontier tradition, that the only measure of a man is his macho capacity. They got off on that wrong track in the early part of the eighteenth century, and because we're a frontier society that still is the dominant factor. It's broken down a bit in the South, and that is why you're beginning to get a better body of writing from the South than you are from the North. There is beginning to be that kind of symbiosis between the society and the writer that we don't get elsewhere: Faulkner and Walker Percy and Flannery O'Conner and Carson McCullers and Eudora Welty. But within the nation as a whole, I see no evidence of its changing.

How do you feel about being an artist in such a society?

My attitude is simple: it's us against them. And writers should never forget that. The actor, the opera singer, the composer, the painter, the *artist*: it's us against them. And goddamn it, the world does not want us, they don't know they need us!

In the American system artists have a fearful time trying to make a decent living; most do not succeed, and the list of great names who have had to eke out their livelihood by teaching or other work is shocking. The average income from the two years of hard work even a small novel requires is something like $3,000, if the book is successful, and most are not. A young man could earn vastly more driving a bus than he will earn with the typical novel.

How does a beginning writer get his or her work into the public consciousness without being a serial murderer on the side?

Because my books have sold well I have avoided talk shows and—after the first very difficult years—public appearances, but if I were a beginning writer trying to establish a reputation for solid writing, I'd be out on the podiums five nights a week.

I do not dismiss an artist for self-promotion; making a living in the American scene as an artist is cruelly difficult, and I tell young people: 'Any procedure that will keep you alive until you can earn a living is defensible. If you are a writer, accept anything if it keeps you going . . . public relations for some big firm . . . instruction manuals for industry . . . articles for trade journals . . . columns for the local newspaper . . . teaching in a community college. . . . I draw the line only at pornography, and I sometimes fear I reject that only because I know I wouldn't do it very well.'

With the electronic revolution at hand, are we to give thanks that there are any readers at all out there?

I know there are people out there who take books seriously. I get mail from all over the world from people who say that my books have made a big difference in their lives. But they are fewer and fewer.

Are there any books which bear your name which you're ashamed of?

There was a book published called *James Michener's America*. Beautiful format, but a total fake from start to finish. I had nothing to do with it. Three guys named Elmer whomped it together and they tricked me into signing a piece of paper, not a contract, so that they could photograph my signature and use it under the preface which they wrote. Through the years those sons of bitches must have been the most ingenious people you ever saw in peddling those bloody things. They gave them as a corporate gift at Thanksgiving instead of a turkey. They still must have a warehouse full of them. I hope they strangle on them.

Is that the only one?

Another book has my name on it for an introduction—*Facing East*, a boxed edition of drawings and prints by the artist Jack Levine. Levine asked me to write the introduction and I agreed under the condition that I would take no money for it but he would give me one of his paintings. It was not a success, because he didn't have a big enough name to make it so. Unilaterally he decided that he did not have to fulfill his part of our deal. He said, 'Well, I will give Michener one of my etchings,' about three-by-five. I wrote him and said, 'If that etching ever finds its way into my house I will kick it all the way to the Perdenales and have the cows of Lyndon Johnson crap on it.' It was a terrible, terrible performance from one artist to another. I just . . . I couldn't believe it.

Have your books gone into pirated editions?

Once, when I was a guest of the Turkish government, this publisher wanted to have lunch with me. He was a marvelous, charming guy who said I was one of the best authors he had plagiarized and he showed me four books that he had published of mine without my receiving any royalties at all. The purpose of our lunch was to ask me what I would like him to plagiarize next! I looked at the books he had done and asked, 'What is this?' He said, 'That's *The Drifters*.' I said, 'Jesus, that's quite a cover!' I couldn't figure out where that came from. He said, 'Lesbianism was the hottest literary subject and we didn't have anything on it so we got a good writer and rewrote your book. It's a very good novel, we've had great success with it.' From the illustrations I guess it got pretty seamy. I was very big in Turkey for a while.

Speaking of plagiarism, has anyone ever stolen anything from you?

I had a fascinating case dealing with a book called *Saskatchewan*, about the great Indian who went with Lewis and Clark. A dozen pages of *Saskatchewan* and some pages from my *Hawaii*—it was word-for-word. It just threw me. I called Random House and I said under no circumstances do I want a lawsuit but I do think the question should be raised with the author. Actually, when I looked at the book I saw she had stolen even more from Jack London, and that further upset me—that she had taken *more* from London than from me. Random House made the proper inquiries and we got back one of the great letters of literary history from her lawyer in which he said that the author had never heard of me, never heard of *Hawaii*, and never read the book, so he can only conclude that we both stole from the same original source! When I read it I just exploded with laughter.

Alex Haley suffered through something similar when he was accused of plagiarizing material from a book called The Africans. *It wound up costing him.*

I knew Haley when we worked on a commission together that supervised the celebration of the Bicentennial. I was also close to Haley during the period before *Roots* was published. When I was working on the set of the mini-series for my novel *Centennial* the director came to me with a problem. He said that he had been working with producer David Wolper on an episode for *Roots* and the writer realized that what Haley had written in his manuscript wasn't working dramatically. They wanted something more upbeat so the audience would want to watch the next week. Wolper told the writer to go back and see what he could do. Out of the blue he constructs a hell of an upbeat ending. When Haley's book was published, it was en total, just as this writer had written it. And he wanted to know whether he should sue Haley. I counseled against it because I think literary lawsuits aren't good for the profession and they are usually inconclusive, though what I am saying is ironclad, no question about it. I read the script and thought Haley should settle the next afternoon because it was so powerful that it was heartbreaking. It was just straight plagiarism. I was very surprised.

How often does it happen, as was the case of the Castenada books about Don Juan, when the line between fiction and non-fiction gets blurred?

There are things that go on in publishing that can make you either laugh or cry. At the end of World War II Bennett Cerf got a marvelous manuscript from a guy in Utah, a great spy thriller, a first-person account of his derring-do in the war. It was a heroic thing, beautifully done, and created great excitement. It was titled something like *The Spy Who Was Never Afraid*. Random House published it and the *Reader's Digest* bought it for their condensed books. And one of their editors began to have serious doubts about this manuscript. The author supposedly had been in the military and maybe even in the Secret Service. So this editor went to Utah to check this guy out, found out the writer had never been out of Utah. Then he checked the library and saw all the books he'd taken out to build this marvelous story. It was a scandal which the author finally admitted. And Bennett Cerf won my affection by handling it for Random House by sending out a personal telegram to all the booksellers in the United States. He said, 'Regarding our best-seller *The Spy Who Was Never Afraid*. I suggest you shift it from your non-fiction shelf to the fiction shelf.' It saved the day, everybody laughed.

What about sequels? Have you ever thought about that?

When I am through with a book, I have said everything I will conceivably want to say on that subject for at least ten, maybe fifteen years. I hold nothing back. I am not saving anything for a sequel.

Do you feel that once you've covered a subject, it's definitive?

No, I had always thought that anything I did ought to be re-done about twenty years later by somebody who knew a hell of a lot more than I did.

Are there any novels you've completed which are still in a drawer?

There are two novels I've completed that I did not intend to publish in my lifetime, although I changed my mind about one, submitted it to Knopf, and they lost it.

You're saying a responsible publisher like Knopf was so careless as to lose the only copy of this novel? What did the world lose?

I am much impressed by the way the press plays up the predictions of people because I used to be a professional fortune teller and made a lot of money at it for charity. The secret was to tell somebody forty things of which two come true. Then you're a sensational seer. They forget that thirty-eight didn't come true.

I was known as Mich-the-Witch and played it for comedy, except that when I was in Egypt I had picked up a system of fortune-telling that was really quite extraordinary. I would answer any question very specifically, in considerable detail. It was fraudulent from start to finish. But I would hit so close that it really became quite frightening.

I had a most dramatic situation where I became sort of famous. This girl came in and the cards were such-and-such. I said, 'How did the operation go?' She said, 'What operation?' I said, 'Your sex change operation.' Just out of the blue. And it was a guy in drag. It went all over the country.

The manuscript I sent to Knopf, it's about how it was done and my relation with the woman who taught me the system. It shows the roots of this mania and how it can be manipulated.

Judging from my own experience there is a desire to believe, and there's a lot of cleverness in the world.

I was reluctant at first to publish this manuscript while I was alive because it's a little undignified. Now it may be a moot point because no one knows where it is. But this is not the first time a publisher has lost one of my manuscripts.

Who lost another?

Random House once lost *The Drifters* for four weeks. They tore the place apart to find it. What happened was it had landed on the desk of an editor of one of their subsidiaries and had gotten into the bottom of a pile. I had made a copy of the original work, but by the time it was submitted to the typist it was so modified that it was hardly recognizable. I have always worked under the assumption that I could reconstruct it if I had to, though it would never be the same.

What's the other novel you've written that's not ready for publication?

The other manuscript is about the last election and will probably have to wait until I'm gone. In it a broken-down senator and his financial advisor visit seven or eight American cities to line up some money. They go to Minneapolis, where they first see the homeless people. And Detroit, where they have the black riots. And San Francisco, where he finds his grandson having been in touch with a young man from New Zealand who has contracted AIDS and is dying. It deals with the doctor who is bucking the establishment and a charismatic woman who is willing to take these terribly unfortunate people in. And it deals with the two older men who try to come to some understanding of this and with the young doomed New Zealander himself. That one is a long, powerful chapter and could stand by itself with just a little attention.

We've talked a good deal about your life as a writer, but have you ever contemplated where your life might have gone had you not worked in publishing or become a writer?

I have always felt that I would have gotten a job—probably moved to Philadelphia and been an active union man. I think I would have progressed in the field very rapidly and been a real tough leader. I can't imagine banking the fires and dropping out of the race. Not my style. I would have been fighting for something.

Do you think you'd be the same kind of writer you are if you were just starting out today?

Someone like me coming along today would try new forms, bold new concepts. Someone like me today might very well veer over into film. The young people I meet who seem to be like me tend to be far more interested in film than they are in the novel.

As a number of your works have been made into movies, are you held in special esteem among actors?

One night during Madrid's San Isidro festivities after the seventh or eighth bullfight, I left a party at which Orson Welles was holding forth, and he was never in better form, trying to convince me that his favorite matador, Curro Romero (who continued for decades afterwards giving his appalling performances from which the police had to rescue him lest the fans kill him in disgust) was one of the best ever. He did not succeed and dismissed me as beyond salvation.

A troupe of us then trailed off, without Welles, to a gala party graced by Ava Gardner, who was delicately inebriated, marvelously amusing, and attentive like the rest of us to the two beautiful female flamenco dancers who danced nude, to the accompaniment of a dazzling guitarist with a whiskey voice admirably suited to his music and the clacking of the castanets.

Ava was extremely beautiful, a real-life Contessa, and yet hurtfully wounded in ways I could not fathom. She was grand but she was fading and the combination was haunting, one of the veritable items in a shifting, shadowy world.

She had been getting some bad press and when I had the opportunity I presented myself to her as an American writer who thought she had been unfairly treated and that she had handled herself magnificently. She looked at me through misty eyes and asked who I was. "James Michener," I said.

"And what do your friends call you, James?" she asked.

"Jim."

"Well, fuck off, Jim."

How did you react?

I laughed then, and I laugh now, because I forgive actors any excesses since theirs is a tougher ballgame than I have to play. It's the most grueling profession in the world.

Have you ever acted yourself?

When the television series of *Centennial* was made, I was asked to do a bit part. I flew out to Wyoming and the company brought in thirty-three people from Hawaii to shoot a thirty-second spot. It took three days. It was harrowing.

Did you leave right after that or stay to see how your novel was being transformed into film?

We stayed to see some filming. David Jansen and Robert Vaughn were the two principal actors and after three hours of shooting we didn't have an inch of film that could be used. The camerawoman said 'I've never had an experience like this. I cannot photograph these men. I focus on Jansen and I lose him.' And the director burst in and said, 'Don't you know what's happening? They were out roaring drunk until five this morning and if they allowed you to photograph them, all you would get would be two fried eggs. So we're just gonna keep them here and go over and over and over it and Monday morning they'll come in and they'll do this in about five minutes.' And on Monday, sure enough, they came in and they were both sober and handsome and fresh.

Are there any actors you're particularly fond of?

I have a great affection for Rod Steiger, Robert Redford, Steve McQueen and Tuesday Weld in *The Cincinatti Kid*, Brando in *On the Waterfront*, Al Pacino in *Serpico*. I'm a sucker for Audrey Hepburn, Meryl Streep, Glenn Close. Yvette Mimieux has done very good work. The best performance I've ever seen was Barbara Stanwyck in *Double Indemnity*, also one of the finest films I've ever seen. I thought John Travolta was damn good in *Saturday Night Fever* and in *Urban Cowboy*.

You're obviously somewhat of a movie buff, aren't you?

I love movies. I gave a series of four lectures a few years ago in Texas on four films that had meant a great deal to me as a writer. The first one was *The Passion of St. Joan of Arc*, a French film made in 1928 with the greatest actress, Falconetti, as St. Joan. Overwhelming.

The second film was *Les Enfants du Paradis*, which is a gorgeous film held by many to be the finest film ever made.

The third one was called *We Are All Murderers*, a magnificent film by a French director. And the fourth was Robert Altman's *McCabe and Mrs. Miller*. That's a story we've seen fifty times, but this time you get to see what an artist does with his special vision.

What other films have deeply moved you?

Stagecoach, The Informer, The Long Journey Home, The Hustler. I loved *The Great Gatsby* with Redford and was quite distressed it did so poorly. And *Ryan's Daughter*, which was as good as a film could be, yet it fell on its face. I liked that one because they were trying to do what I try to do, and it's very perilous. And in dramatic form it runs great risks. *Far From the Madding Crowd* was a beautiful film. So was *The Collector*, which is better than John Fowles's book. *Star Wars*, which is a remake of *Stagecoach* and *Gunfight at the OK Corral*, is a brilliant film, fable at its best. Mel Brooks's *The Twelve Chairs* was stunning, a real classic in humorist development and exploitation. I would be happy if I could have written the screenplay for *E.T.* or *Death of a Salesman* or the material from which the television miniseries *Lonesome Dove* had been made. And one of the films that I am forever grateful that I saw was *I Was A Teenage Werewolf.* The idea of a boy being perfectly natural and a fine boy in school, loved, except he had this one small defect. He now and then turned into a werewolf.

What about films which have disturbed you?

There are films that have given me trouble. *Bonnie & Clyde* was extraordinarily made, a splendid movie, but it was also immoral. Gene Wilder is a very funny actor and in the scene where they steal his car and then they order sandwiches and he says, "Wait a minute, I ordered mine without mustard," nobody ever acted any better than he did. And after the showing of *The Godfather* the Italian mob gangs began to act like the actors in the picture. They began to genuflect, they began to kiss the hand of their leader, because it reminded them of how they should act. No picture has given me more trouble than *A Clockwork Orange*, which cut so close to the raw harm of society that it was frightening. I'm not sure that it should have been made.

The heavy philosophizing of *Close Encounters of the Third Kind* was quite distasteful. *Star Trek, The Movie* had some wonderful things in it but the story line let it down badly. *The Black Hole* was really quite trivial and not worth the effort. *Saturn 3* with Farrah Fawcett and Kirk Douglas I would put very high on the list of the worst films ever made. Anybody interested in film should go some distance to see it, because it's an absolutely brilliant example of what happens when you figure that on a 30 percent budget you can horn in on the big movies. It's a film without a single redeeming feature.

But in recent years the film that has been most meaningful to me is *New York, New York*. Anybody who wants to write or to work in the arts should travel fifty miles to see it and ask themselves why was it such a colossal failure? What went wrong? All that money, all that talent, down the drain.

Do you have any idea why it was such a bust?

They had no writer. One scene just broke my heart, where Liza Minnelli and Robert De Niro had eloped. It was as nothing as anything I've ever seen. It sent nothing forward, gave you no vision of anybody. If I taught a writing class I would probably run it twice.

Had you gone into films rather than write books, what kind of screenwriter would you have been?

I would probably have gone more towards producing than writing. I would have gone the René Clair or George Stevens route of telling my writers that every scene had to be a goody with some quirk to it, some utilization of the actor's tremendous ability, so that it was a sequence of delights. The best films tend to do that, where nothing is irrelevant.

Have you ever written a script?

I once tried my hand at screenplays. I was taken out to Hollywood. I was not successful. I was offered some very dazzling inducements but my own judgment told me that there were a lot better people around.

Novelists are not often pleased with how their works are adapted to film. . . .

Hemingway once told me that he didn't like what Hollywood did to his books. I remember reading where he said he always went to one of his movies with apprehension and a bottle of gin. And he always got through the gin before he got through the movie, and left.

What about yourself?

I've had a dozen major motion pictures made from things I've written. Some have been superb. They've won Oscars, they've received nominations. I've had a fabulous good run. Of those, I thought *The Bridges at Toko-Ri* was the best, almost better than the book.

And Sayonara?

I was delighted when Marlon Brando was chosen for *Sayonara*, even though we paid a very high price for him. I didn't agree with Brando's happy ending to *Sayonara*. The ending he forced upon us was his decision. Mari was outraged, but I wasn't. I couldn't care one way or the other. And it worked.

Wasn't Hawaii *originally being considered for an epic six-hour movie?*

The Mirisch brothers wanted to do a movie in two parts that would run on two successive nights, and at a time of great euphoria they bought the rights for what was then the highest figure ever paid, something like $750,000. They hired Fred Zinnemann to direct and wanted it to star Alec Guiness and Audrey Hepburn. It was terribly exciting. Then along came the movies *Cleopatra* and the remake of *Mutiny on the Bounty* which were colossal failures and it just scared the hell out of Hollywood. So that never happened.

Hawaii *was finally filmed though.*

A fine movie was eventually made with Julie Andrews and Max Von Sydow which George Roy Hill directed in 1966, and four years later the second half, called *The Hawaiians*, with Charlton Heston, but they could not match the proposed original project.

What about your experiences in television?

They've been good. When ABC aired the series *Adventures in Paradise* it helped keep the network alive for two years. It went on for 118 episodes and in the end was a great money-maker.

What is your opinion of TV today?

Television today is almost the equivalent of what the Romans put on long ago: bread and circuses. With all the new cable stations it's possible that it can be used positively. You could go to Antartica, to Africa, to the Met for an opera, to a theater for *Hamlet*. It's there to be used, but I doubt that it ever will be.

You spoke about watching Centennial *being made into a miniseries. Did you like the results?*

Centennial was a roaring success as a book and I was very pleased when it was bought by NBC. There were twenty-five hours of film of very high quality when it was done. But it came into competition in its own house with *Battlestar Galactica*. And with the success of *Star Wars* in the theaters, they decided on *Battlestar Galactica*. I didn't object. It was prime time and a hell of a lot was riding on it. Furthermore, *Battlestar* could be spun off into a regular series if it worked, and ours was a one-time show.

And Space?

I enjoyed what they did.

You didn't enjoy what was done to Texas—*the miniseries went first to video before it was released on network TV. How did that deal come about?*

It's a story so unbelievable that it makes anything in the writing profession that we've talked about extraneous. I wrote *Texas* and had a fantastic sale, 900,000 first printing. Everybody wanted it. And company A bought it for an option with a heavy fee and a sure title. They sent a guy out, a Hollywood hack writer. He didn't have a clue. To nobody's surprise, company A off-loaded it.

The writers of company B were a very sensible pair and had a good idea. But the home office would not go for over fifteen episodes. So they off-loaded, to company C. They got it for an option price of maybe $5,000. And company C hired John Wilder to do the screenplay in about twelve episodes. John worked like a dog and produced a very good script. But at that point, the powers in company C said, 'We're not going anymore for blockbusters.' Paid John modestly, I'm told, and put the property up for grabs.

Then maybe three years later my agent said, 'Jim, I want to talk to you about *Texas* again. We've had a fascinating offer.' He said, 'Blockbuster Video has money galore at the moment, and it wants to try something radically new. They will publish the work as a video, no previous theater of any kind, it's a silver disc video. And then subsequently they will publish it as a paperback, and if it catches on they will publish it as a hardback.'

I have always been willing to gamble on new methods. I was the first one to give the Pocket Book people a clear range to shoot the works with *Hawaii*. I gambled on talking books. I was approached recently to be the first guy with any name to turn a short story over to the internet highway. I gave them permission.

They spent something like $18–20 million on making *Texas*, and in all of that time they never said a word to me, and when they shot it here in Texas they never told me a thing about it. They did the same with John Wilder. John got paid for his script, of which they used absolutely nothing. They put three Hollywood regulars on it and they whipped up a mishmash. He knew nothing about it.

It comes out under my name, with a big blurb that the skilled writer with a big track record, John Wilder, had done the script. And in the first two hours I saw one scene of fifteen seconds that bore *any* relation to anything I had written. And in the last half I didn't see anything!

I read that 150,000 units were sold at $50 each, which seems like a lot.

It's done well. My attitude is to take my lumps and let it go.

How many of your works have been filmed?

Some time ago I calculated that I had fifteen of my works translated into other media. There's another fifteen works that have never been touched by anybody. *The Bridge at Andau*, *The Source*, *Chesapeake*, *Poland*, *The Drifters*, *Sports in America*, *The Covenant*, *Journey*, *Caribbean*. These would make marvelous movies or miniseries, but they are very difficult things to do.

Why are they so difficult?

In about six months they're going to come back and say, 'Jim, there's no story line here. There's nothing we can get hold of. Who's the principal character?'

Still, all of these things are under option all the time. At any time I will have six or seven projects in the works and most of them will come to nothing.

For one of them to jell it requires about four years. And television and movie contracts are maybe fifty pages long. There's a lot of money involved and it can be very time-consuming.

How closely do you oversee the money transactions relating to your work?

I have always left financial matters to other people.

When I first enjoyed a surplus of income at the end of the fiscal year, I spent many months studying the intricacies of the stock market, did comparative studies and all that, at the end of which I concluded: 'You're bright enough, and you know enough math, to be a capable operator in this field, but if you spend the same amount of time writing one good novel, you'll be infinitely farther ahead on all accounts.' I've handled the money problem about as poorly as any other writer. I have lived my life as if the bottom was going to drop out two years from now and I would be a regional director for a federal writing project. I now live my life as if I had retired at age 65 with a small pension from a corporation.

You do have a reputation of being thrifty.

As I'm a Quaker, I don't spend money easily. I am a low-key, cautious guy. I have invested money prudently. If I splurge on anything it would be pineapple juice.

Is it true you don't take advances against royalties for your books?

I don't, because they can damage a writer. He feels the pressing demand to publish something that will earn back the advance, and then he stumbles. I did once, on a nonfiction book, and it didn't earn out. I am embarrassed if the book doesn't sell enough to pay off.

How closely do you follow your contract negotiations?

I have never entered into any financial negotiation, I never know what the terms of my contracts have been, I never bother with the details, I've never spoken to Random House about a nickel, nor have I plumbed for the top dollar. I try to keep away from that as much as possible.

What about subsidiary rights, auctions? Any interest?

In the discussion of collateral sales, book clubs, foreign rights, whatever, I don't want to know about it. The auctions for these rights are the process by which the big companies do business, and I never get involved in that. I haven't even known when certain auctions were taking place, and I have never allowed an auction on my own personal contracts. So in the sale of subsidiary rights, I never have a clue as to what is happening in Germany or England or Spain or France.

Since you put a lot of trust in your agent, you must feel good about him.

There's a saying in the business that you don't need an agent 'til you reach the point where you don't need one. And that is true. It's a Catch-22. I have been very well treated by my agents and I should be. All the money they've made off me has been fantastic.

You're a big supporter of the arts but you haven't spoken much about it. Think it's time?

I take so seriously writing as a profession that I would like to help young people get into it. Because society needs writers. It needs books like *Bonfire of the Vanities*, and the works of James Baldwin, Joyce Carol Oates. I have given away about $60 million, mostly to schools and museums. The United States has a very good rule that people like me who owe the government a great deal of money are allowed to give money away to educational institutions. It's a way that the person can pay his taxes in his own way, as it were. My wife and I have always done this. Sometimes the I.R.S. argues about the way we allocate and they review me every year with a fine-tooth comb, but they never find any misbehavior of any kind.

But didn't they once claim you owed a substantial sum of money?

In 1967 they issued a big release saying I owed $390,000 in

Cornelia Otis Skinner, Arnold Toynbee, and Michener at a book and author luncheon, New York, April 12, 1949. (Library of Congress, James A. Michener Collection)

After Michener won the Pulitzer Prize in 1948 for *Tales of the South Pacific*, he was sought out by the media. Here he appears in an early NBC broadcast. (Library of Congress, James A. Michener Collection)

Leland Hayward, producer of *South Pacific*, and Michener, in Honolulu.
(Library of Congress, James A. Michener Collection)

Michener talks to a Korean soldier, December 1950. (Library of Congress, James A. Michener Collection)

Michener, researching *The Bridges of Toko-Ri*, talks to a soldier stationed in Korea, July 22, 1952. (Library of Congress, James A. Michener Collection)

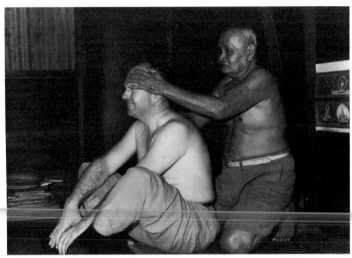

Michener with Nai Yok Nuyphakoi, a doctor known for his ability to cure nervous trouble. Michener would write about his treatment. (Library of Congress, James A. Michener Collection)

Organizing meeting of the Fund for Asia, Inc., New York City, December 16, 1954. Left to right: Ambassador Henry F. Grady, vice president; Manly Fleischmann, treasurer; James A. Michener, president; John Farrar, vice president; J. D. Zellerbach, director. (Library of Congress, James A. Michener Collection)

Meticulous in his research, Michener surrounded himself with the kind of performers on which he would base Hana-ogi, one of the lead characters in *Sayonara*. (Library of Congress, James A. Michener Collection)

Michener with his third wife, Mari Subusawa. When they married in 1955, they agreed to always travel together, and they did. (Library of Congress, James A. Michener Collection)

Michener in Yemenite village, Israel, 1963. Michener got the inspiration to write *The Source* on a visit to Israel with Harpo Marx and Leonard Lyons. (Library of Congress, James A. Michener Collection)

Michener, on his eighty-fifth birthday, with Mari; New York, February 1992. (Photo by Lawrence Grobel)

Michener and Hana Grobel, 1992. (Photo by Lawerence Grobel)

Michener, at age eighty-nine, 1996. (Photo by Lawrence Grobel)

James A. Michener Art Museum, Bucks County, PA. (Photo by Lawrence Grobel)

back taxes, but that was a ploy on their part. We had already paid $360,000 and it was really an argument over how to apportion a part of this. I got a great deal of adverse publicity about it. The I.R.S. likes to have a big headline story three weeks before taxes are due. They do it year after year.

Are you often asked for money from friends and acquaintances?

I get maybe ten letters a week begging me for money that is not institutional. Three times in my life friends have said that they would have to commit suicide if I didn't give them some money. They were not close personal friends, but under those circumstances what option do you have? It's a crisis in a human life, and the proper thing to do is to get the crisis over with and say the hell with it. You shouldn't expect to get the money back, and in every instance I never did.

You say you aren't concerned about money, but isn't it true that most professional writers write for just that?

Samuel Johnson once said that any man who didn't write for money was a fool, and there's a great deal of truth to that. I will not write for free, but I'll give away a great deal of money that I do write for to educational institutions, or turn it back to the libraries with the insistence that they buy books with it.

You've also given away your art collections, haven't you?

We've given all the art we've collected away because we couldn't afford to run the risk of one of us dying and having enormous taxes on its value. The twentieth-century American painters are now at the University of Texas at Austin and the Japanese prints are at the University of Hawaii.

How did you become a collector in the first place?

Before we began collecting American art, we looked at it very seriously. We studied, we talked, we met with people, I read a hundred and sixty books on paintings. It never occurred to me that Stuart Davis was so highly prized; Jack Tworkov was another one. One of the best paintings we had was a Tworkov.

The traditional painter was overwhelmed in the 1950s and '60s by the avant-garde, where all the accolades went. But it was a godsend to us because it allowed Mari and me to pick up the great canvases of the social realists.

Besides the satisfaction of owning works of art that you like, are there any other benefits to being a collector?

One of the fringe benefits of our collecting was that it gave me a chance to spend a marvelous day with Harry Truman, who was a friend and drinking companion of the social realist painter Thomas Hart Benton. There was no one whose reputation was lower when I started collecting than Benton, but I was convinced that he would be one of the signal artists of that period. We went out of the way to visit him in Kansas City and bought one of his finest paintings, which is now down in Texas. He said, 'Why don't you stay over tomorrow and we'll go see Harry Truman.' Benton had done in art pretty much what Truman had done in politics. We went over and had one of the most joyous days. A lot of whiskey drinking. I'm not a big drinker but it never bothers me, and I figured that if I was in the companionship of these two noble men, I'd better at least try to hold up my end of it.

Overall, how much would you estimate you spent on your collection of American art?

I doubt we spent a million dollars on the whole American collection because we did it so cautiously. There are any number of paintings in our collection that aren't worth fifty bucks now, but they were to us and they are some of the ones I like the most. And there are another great number that were a thousand dollars and are now worth $250,000. The experts who advised us said it was probably the finest collection in private hands anywhere. And it's been evaluated at $24 million.

Has money been important to you?

Up to now I've never been interested in the financial aspects of my career. I have never paid much attention to the recent radical changes in publishing: The talking book, videos. It happened when I was overseas and I didn't even know it. I'd get maybe $1,850 at the end of a time period for my books on tape. Last year, my God, these royalties were up in the respectable five figures, $25,000, $35,000. I was aware I was in a great revolution, which happened under my nose while I was looking elsewhere. Amazing.

But now I have literally given away all of my funds—all my savings *and* future income—and am living on the half that Mari accumulated and to which she had been entitled. For the first time I find myself in the position of not being really in charge. My only concern is that I have enough to fulfill certain obligations to colleges and museums which I have undertaken.

And what did Mari think of your philanthropy?

Mari was supportive, within reason. But the idea of giving back cuts very deep with me. Perhaps that is why I've been so concerned of late with leaving behind as full and accurate account of my record as a writer and why, in spite of some of my health problems, the heart attack, the quintuple bypass, the hip surgery, the dialysis, none of that has touched me one-tenth of one percent. I just wouldn't allow it.

Still, with each passing year you must be a little concerned that time is running out.

Mari had had two big cancer operations; it didn't touch her one-tenth of one percent. We found out what we could do and we did it. My own interest never flags. I can hardly wait to get up in the morning.

Do you ever get up and wonder what to do?

I've got four or five urgent requests: an art book, a book on sports, one on political trends. When you reach my age with a reasonably good reputation, people suddenly say, 'He'll be gone soon, let's see what we can get aboard this freight train.' The biographer Leon Edel said a writer shouldn't expect to work much after seventy, but I don't agree with that. People like me grow bolder as they grow older. Past performance is a very dangerous thing to rely upon.

Do you see your most current work as documentation, both in fiction and nonfiction, of your profession?

The books that I have written in the last few years are all part of the same structure—a portrait of a professional writer at work.

Six Days in Havana, *Pilgrimage*, and *The Novel* are all part of that portrait. So, obviously, is the memoir, *The World Is My Home*. The Canadian publication of *Journey* deals with the retrieval of a manuscript that had been cut. So does the introduction to *The Eagle and the Raven*. The *Writer's Handbook* is about the editing of two manuscripts, one fiction, the other nonfiction, and follows them from initiation to publication—I think it's a damn good book.

Then there has been the Texas State House Press publication of the salvation of my *Mexico* manuscript, *My Lost Mexico, The Making of a Novel*. It really deals with the creative process. It's a curious assembly, but it has all been driving toward the purpose of: let's get it on the record. Because I think it has real merit and can be a very rewarding experience for future writers.

You actually wrote most of Mexico *in your fifties, didn't finish it, and then lost it. How can that happen?*

That this manuscript should have been totally lost for thirty-one years and then to have surfaced with all the notes, three big notebooks, ten finished chapters—it's incredible.

The fact is it was a damn good manuscript, but I had lost interest in completing it. When something hasn't gone exactly right you're not afraid to kill it. I had both my original typed script and the print-out and parceled it up and directed it to the Library of Congress.

In my mind I had mailed it. But they never picked it up. What I'd forgotten was that Random House had a contract for the book. So from time to time they would say, 'Gee, let's get that book on Mexico, you had it two-thirds done.' But it was lost. When we wanted to do the memoir, there was a keen desire to have some photographs. My cousin, who lived with us, was always wondering where the photographs were. She finally found the photographs in the back of a filing cabinet. And when she did she also found behind the cabinet the lost manuscript about Mexico.

How did you feel when the manuscript was discovered?

I was excited. And it surfaced just as Mari went into this long treatment for cancer, so there I was with nothing to do but to work on the manuscript. I put in about eighteen hours a day for four months rewriting it, then three more months to correct it. It was hard work. I believe very strongly in finishing projects, in getting the books on the shelf so they can find their own lives.

With the life you've led, how did you decide what belonged in your memoirs and what was best left untold?

I pondered what should be included and what not—from the point of view of mere compilation I found it a delightful exercise. It sort of wrote itself. There was no heavy breathing.

Which was one of the criticisms of it.

I know it was criticized for lacking emotion, but I knew how to imply it, how to set up emotional situations where you either got it or you didn't.

Your critics often complain that you're a bit distant in your writing.

It's true, but I have seen emotion so abused that I don't want to go down that route. I've got a short fuse, for instance, and have had a hard battle in my life to control it. But I am much better than I used to be. And so it is with my writing. With me, the emotion, the passion, is all implied. The reader has to do his part of the work also.

Does criticism bother you?

What Michiko Kakitani [N.Y. Times] has to say about my work is her opinion to a certain group, but if you're a survivor you supersede that. The answer to a bad review is to admit the sick feeling in the stomach, invite it, then say, 'Screw you.' [N.Y. Times critic] Christopher Lehmann-Haupt is a Swarthmore man like myself and he's got to prove his independence by blasting the hell out of me. He said my novels are like Rice Krispies, they are junk food, but they *are* rather tasty. Well, you can't read my mail and say that. I once kept track of a list of all the books the *Times* and *Time* magazine said were superb and they all died prematurely and most of the writers were never heard from again. The challenge in being a writer is not to do it once, but to do it six or seven times, with increasing power; that's the trick, not to write a good afternoon book.

So you're saying you take criticism well?

All of my books have been poorly received by certain segments of the population upon which they were focused. I received scathing reviews and have been thrown out of Hawaii, Indonesia, Burma. I was banned totally in Spain and South Africa. In Israel many scholars felt it was arrogant and quite improper for someone like me to even attempt to write *The Source*. But it turns out to be one of the best books ever done about Israel. The government issued an ad that the best advertisement Israel has is the Old Testament or a copy of *The Source*.

Iberia was banned in Spain because I was too harsh on the regime. Then I got a gold medal from the Spanish Society for having written the best book in a decade on Spain.

Same thing with *The Covenant*. It was savagely attacked in South Africa. They did a very sensible thing. They banned it and it got all the publicity with the right wing that they needed, and then they unbanned it and let it circulate because they knew it was good.

I took a lot of flack on *Poland* from every quarter. With the proper passing of time I was invited back and given honors that nobody else has had, dances in my honor, because everybody said that although we don't like it, it's still the best book on the subject.

When *Texas* came out, I was vilified by the newspapers and magazines in both Dallas and Austin. So I have not had a clear run at all. I've had a tough shot. But I have always written with an absolutely firm belief that people would come to see it my way. And they have, again and again. The books survive. I've lived to see it all reevaluated, fortunately.

You didn't include your latest novel, Recessional, *among the works that have been vilified. Because the book deals with old age, diseases, and retirement homes it must have been of some concern to your publisher about who might buy it?*

Everybody I worked with advised me against writing it. Then the Franklin Mint came along and wanted to pick up a Michener book and they took it if I would autograph 2,300 fly sheets. I was so eager to get a hearing that I said yes. And then the Book-of-the-Month-Club took it. Then it was picked up by foreign publishers. It's sold 183,000 copies—ten times better than I had anticipated. But *nobody* had faith in this book.

Can you weigh the distinctions between your books?

I don't evaluate my own books. I'm just thankful, almost on my knees, that I've been able to get through one of them and get it published.

So what accounts for your drive?

I have not thought of myself as being unduly ambitious. But I do have powerful compulsions to do well and I do have a tremendous capacity for identification with other people's problems and other patterns of life.

Does writing popular novels adversely affect how you are judged among the literati?

Naturally, anybody who has a book which stays at the top of the best-seller list week after week has to be suspect. There is some validity to the supposition that anything that is distributed in those large numbers can't be very good. I obviously don't think it applies in my case. If it's Nabokov's *Lolita* or Philip Roth's *Portnoy's Complaint* you have to suspect that it's because it's salacious. But they're also a heck of a lot more. I don't use sex or violence or sadism. There's a hardness in my books, a toughness. There's a tension and an indication that life is a pretty seamy mess. I would never get far away from that because that's how I see it.

Who among artists in other fields would you compare yourself to?

If I were to compare myself to a composer, I'd choose Haydn, who built a niche for himself by being a real good solid producer and staying at it. Or if I were to look at a contemporary painter I'd say someone like John Marin, who was an extremely good workman and quietly stayed at it year after year after year, and was acknowledged for what he did.

So you're satisfied just being acknowledged for what you've done, even if some of that acknowledgement is negative?

If a man has written over forty books and each of these has been reviewed by, say, a hundred critics, you've had some four thousand critical articles. So one is accustomed to a pretty heavy barrage of both positive and negative criticism. By and large one takes it philosophically.

But I'm not deluding myself. I know my deficiencies better than most of the critics.

They are . . . ?

I am not very good at dialogue. I don't use words as well as Philip Roth, whom I admire tremendously. I don't use social structures as well as Joyce Carol Oates. I don't have the quality of touch that Robert Penn Warren has. I do not begin to project myself into the life of another to the degree of somebody like Mailer or Capote, John Cheever, or even Updike. I am not very competent in dealing with sexuality. I'm good at it but other people are so much better. And I am not very good at plotting; it doesn't interest me at all. I could end my books anywhere and start anywhere. I am giving a kaleidoscopic view, not a psychological one.

Have you ever cannibalized your own experiences for your work?

I have certainly cannibalized my experiences and the life experiences of others, without question. That's the job of the artist. Someone told me that Cynthia Ozick said at the Jerusalem book fair: 'Being a writer, I know what kind of people we writers are— and I don't trust us.' I agree. I don't really want to know what motivates me to work so assiduously over so many years. I'm not at all sure my motives were the kind we extol in Sunday school.

Do you feel that way about other writers as well?

Sylvia Plath in *The Bell Jar* has a passage in which she excoriates one of these three-name women writers. She uses a fake name and it's a terribly funny passage. Later, I found that this was a close parody of a woman who gave her the scholarship which allowed her to go to Smith College. Then, a few pages on, you have a very mordant portrait of a mother who's lousing things up. This is Sylvia's mother.

Now, I know William Faulkner's great statement that the novelist is completely amoral and would rob, beg, borrow, or steal from anybody to get the work done—a statement I believe is true—but nothing brought me up more sharply than the relation to his statement and this illustration of a sensitive girl who really had a very poetic quality, who would cannibalize two people who had been so important to her. You can understand kids cannibalizing their mothers, because that's happened in literature a great deal, none better than Philip Roth. But to cannibalize a benefactor who was the agency by which you went to college and had your whole life opened up for you is an act of aggression that I find pretty hard to swallow. Yet I know that Plath was right, and Faulkner was right in what he says. I still plan to write about this in a short book I want to do.

How much of art is really sleight-of-hand?

I think of the great portraits of Van Gogh—the Postmaster, the Little Servant Girl, his own room, the Starry Night, all of that—in relation to what the proper observation should have been, they are just as fake as a seven-dollar bill. But all art is trickery. I have a running debate with an extremely pragmatic man who is outraged by Picasso. He shouts at me, 'Can't you see that the son of a bitch is just all trickery?' And I respond, 'What do you think art is?'

Are you saying you're nothing more than a good magician?

I never thought what I did was that unique, but maybe it is more rare than I used to think. I am pretty powerfully grounded in the American system. I suppose you can project that internationally. I know what makes countries tick and I write from that background. But my success can't be because of the sheer brilliance of my writing. I suppose the bottom line is that I do know what narration is.

How concerned are you by the sales of your books?

I am by no means in the blockbuster syndrome. I've produced a lot of them, but I've produced more that fell outside that pattern. But I'm also aware that my books don't sell as many now as they did ten years ago and I have reluctantly concluded that I would not know if my mental capacity was deteriorating. I had the difficult job once of reviewing Sinclair Lewis's last books. He was leaving the scene just as I was coming on. They were disasters and he apparently did not know it. But I had enormous respect for Lewis, that miserable, ugly, repulsive person who said, 'Okay, my job is writing books and I was very good at it and I'm still pretty good and here we go again.'

Certain writers have compared themselves to great fighters, they seem to have a need to rank themselves among the heavyweights. Do you?

Because a writer deals with so many imaginary people and so many imaginary problems, he is almost driven to assess his own life and his own position on this constellation. Anybody with my experience could kid himself that having his book adopted by the Book-of-the-Month Club was the hottest thing in the universe.

I live in a small town, in a medium-sized state, in a medium-sized country, on a medium-sized planet. Our sun is one of the smallest stars in the galaxy, and our galaxy is not the biggest one in the sky. We're probably doomed in another ten billion years. So I cannot believe that I am the hottest thing in the universe.

Nonetheless, as long as we're here, I think you stay in it right to the bitter end. You do what Hokusai did, what Titian did, you keep going until you're eighty or ninety if you're allowed. Hokusai did marvelously imaginative work and great art right through his eighties. He said: "At ninety I shall penetrate the mystery of things; at 110 everything I do will be alive." That is my commitment. Not fatuously, either, because I have really some things to say.

So did Hemingway, until he put the barrel of a rifle into his mouth.

Hemingway's suicide gives me infinite problems. He gave an interview two years before his death, saying that he was as good as he ever was and his juices were still flowing and all of this monstrous nonsense. Then when the going got hard, he blew his brains out. Anyone interested in art has to come to grips with this: That it was maybe the most Hemingway thing he ever did and confirms the great legend, or it was a complete refutation of the legend and leaves you totally perplexed.

That's how it left me: I don't think it was the right exit for him.

And I loved the guy. He really was the Daddy of us all. I never fell prey to his machoism; I saw that as fake. His desire to be incognito and yet adopting a costume which was at least as flamboyant as Tolstoy's. He was so shameless. Yet look at the majesty of his sentence structure, his paragraphing, the use of words. I would be very happy to stand in his shadow.

Didn't Hemingway give you your credo?

When I met him he said that I wrote about people as if they had to earn a living and he tried to do that as well. And he said, "It's not enough to be known as a good Philadelphia writer, you want to go up against the champions, Pio Baroja, Turgenev, Flaubert." And that became my credo. I don't want to be known as a good Philadelphia writer, as a good South Pacific writer. Hemingway gave me my attitude.

8

Weren't you one of the first people to promote Hemingway's The Old Man and the Sea?

I was the first person to review *The Old Man and the Sea*, which *Life* magazine was about to publish in a single issue before it appeared in book form. After the great disaster of Hemingway's preceding book, *Across the River and Into the Trees*, they knew they had to do something to give this venture an upward lift. They settled upon me, for reasons I don't know. Maybe Hemingway suggested it. We liked one another.

I got the manuscript and on first sight I saw the real joy and delight of this thing. And I gave it a fantastic statement which *Life* used as the basis for their whole presentation. Hemingway told me that he appreciated it in a very gruff and easy way. We never mentioned it again, because you don't ingratiate yourself with a person by doing that. It's expected that you will give an honest statement and let it ride. But I think he was grateful.

What was it about Hemingway's work that made it so influential?

Hemingway had a mastery of central structure that very few of us have ever had. He had a motif, which I have not had—the macho image, the grace under pressure—and that is not a bad thing to have. I don't want it. Nor do I have a need to be number one, as he did.

Why not?

Early in my life I decided I never wanted to be first in anything. I don't want to waste my time in that pursuit.

Remember, there are ten places on most best-seller lists, sometimes fifteen. The first time I ever became aware of a best-seller was in the 1920s when we had Hemingway writing and Dreiser, Sinclair Lewis, Ellen Glasgow, Edith Wharton, Fitzgerald, Faulkner. That's a pretty startling group. But the book that was at the top of the best-seller list for about a year was *The Specialist* by Chick Sale. It was a hilariously funny reminiscence of a guy in Oklahoma or Arkansas who dug outdoor privies. Every decade you'll have something like it. It has nothing to do with literature, it does no harm, it's fun, and in three years it's totally forgotten. I would never be in competition with that.

Working with a Hollywood producer I heard that on cross-country trips Truman Capote liked to make the driver take him to the library in some rural county seat and wait while he, Capote, ran inside. I asked, "Truman, what in hell are you doing in these libraries?" and he explained with childish delight, "Checking the card catalogues. In this one Mailer had seven cards. Vidal had eight. And I had eleven."

Why do you suppose you've been spared this competitive spirit?

I've operated well off to one side, never in the mainstream, so I have not really been in competition with my peers. I don't like competition in the arts. The greater artists I know, painters particularly, they let the other artists go their way. But I have experienced inadvertent pangs of regret when I've watched some newcomer not yet thirty-three edge me off the lists, unceremoniously, and I wonder: "Where does he get the nerve, the swine?" But then I remember the large number whom I, in my day, also nudged off the lists. Small compensation.

In the days when my novels, year after year, stood at the top of the list I'd pass a bookstore window and see maybe fifty copies of my latest on display, and I'd think: 'Now that's the way to run a book store.' When the glory days were over and I'd see only one or none of my books on display I'd mutter: 'Why aren't they attending to their business?' Bennett Cerf instructed me on how to cooperate with book stores: "When you enter a city, go directly to the book stores. Be nice to the owners, tell them how much you appreciate their help. Then autograph every book of yours they have in stock, because if your name is written on the flyleaf, they can't send it back to us and ask for a rebate."

In spite of what you've said about coming in second, you seem to have a healthy ego. How necessary is that for a writer?

In the most extraordinary literary interview John Gardner in the *Washington Post* said that he was the only able writer working today; that he could write anything and there was nobody else around who could. He castigated some dozen major writers from Chaucer to Milton to Hemingway to Nabokov as being essentially trivial. He went on and on until you had to say either he was drunk or the reporter was drunk. It was comparable to John O'Hara's review in the *New York Times* stating that Hemingway was the greatest writer of English since Chaucer.

Well, that arena is so different that someone like me is hardly able to comment on it. In my drunken stupor sometime I might consider myself superior to Hemingway and Arnold Bennett and Samuel Butler and a half-dozen others. But when I reach out and include Milton, Chaucer, Shakespeare, Goethe, and Dostoevsky, somebody better blow a whistle and call me back to sanity.

So what do you think of Gardner as a writer?

Gardner's *Grendel* was gorgeous: I read it with the greatest pleasure. It's the kind of imaginative thing that I would never do. But that interview of his, I'm still staggered by it! I guess it was his way of bolstering up his own courage.

What modern writer has the best chance of surviving the centuries?

The writer of my generation who will probably be remembered longest is Nabokov. He's not like anybody else. You can't say he's like Joseph Conrad at mastering a new language at a late date because he bears no resemblance to Conrad. He bears more resemblance to Edmund Wilson than he does to any novelist. Maybe the two of them will go hand in hand. His place is very secure.

You also held high hopes for Truman Capote, didn't you?

Before Truman Capote died and left it unfinished, I thought that his *Answered Prayers* could be the Toulouse-Lautrec of this period. I found the two sections that *Esquire* published quite corrupt and venal, really quite awful . . . and quite wonderful. If he could have completed it, a hundred years from now I don't know whether people will be writing dissertations on Saul Bellow or Issac Bashevis Singer, but I'm quite sure they would have on Capote and that book, because it was a *roman 'a clef* summarizing a period. He had a better chance of being the central figure of our time than any of the rest of us may have.

I had great warmth for Truman. When asked his opinion of Jack Kerouac's lava-flow effusions he said: "That's not writing. That's typewriting." (In its later version this often appeared as "That's not writing. That's typing." Which, of course, loses the wonderful poetry, rhythm and impeccable use of words in the original. I once asked Capote about this and he confirmed the *typewriting.*) Society, especially the puritanical, rather drab society like ours, needs someone who looks and behaves like an artist. Myself, I've never been taken for a writer. The image of a writer is probably a cross between Hemingway and Fitzgerald. The majority of us don't fall into that category. Today the prototype would be Norman Mailer, whom I'm very strong on.

Do you know many other writers?

I know very few American writers. I knew Pearl Buck because she was a next-door neighbor and we worked together to rescue children. I've stayed away from the literary establishment. I've always had a real fear that literary hoopla does a lot of writers in.

I remember when I was in Spain and I met a couple of red-hot young men who were astounded when they heard that I didn't know who William Burroughs was. They said, "Oh Michener, he is the new word, the greatest writer America has produced, and what you are doing is totally passé. There is no place for it anymore." They gave me *Naked Lunch,* and I read it with absolute delight. It was a jolter. It was a frolic. But did it mean that work like Robert Penn Warren's or Camus's or Günter Grass's or what I was trying to do was outmoded? Not at all. It really meant that a wonderful new voice had come on the scene to sort of wake us up, jack us up a bit.

How important are such new voices?

Talent, of course, is quite common, and outstanding talent is probably distributed equally among all the peoples of the world. In the worlds of New Guinea among headhunters I met men who could create art as capably as anyone practicing in Paris or New York, and to my delight I listened to aboriginal women who could narrate a yarn at least as well as I could, using all the devices adopted by Balzac or Dickens. Any college class in America or Nigeria is likely to have five or six young people of unquestioned talent. Disciplined talent, especially in the arts, is rare, and when a young person like Truman Capote, Gore Vidal, Emily Brontë, or Françoise Sagan comes along, the world takes notice.

Societies need writers who are penetrating the frontier—people like Robert Lowell in poetry or Walt Whitman in his day, Proust, Joyce, Beckett, Robbe-Grillet, Günther Grass, Kafka. In more recent times it would be someone like Thomas Pynchon, whose behavior is oddball and peculiar, but he's especially essential for young college people.

Joyce and Proust are often touted as the outstanding writers of the twentieth century. Did either of them speak to you?

Joyce did not have much influence on me. I realized with great respect that he was into something that I just wasn't. Proust, who is awfully good, didn't touch me very deeply, because he was preempted by Balzac and Flaubert and Zola. I remember F. R. Leavis's great statement that if you really wanted to understand English literature there are only four Englishmen that you need to read—George Eliot, Jane Austen, Joseph Conrad, and Henry James—and two of them are not men, and two of them are not English. This is a kind of aphorism that gets more credit than it merits, perhaps, but it still merits attention. If one wanted to be a fine writer, he certainly should read those four novelists with great attention. And against that quartet I would put Dickens and Hardy.

Because?

Dickens, over the long run, will be seen to have been quite a magnificent figure. He has been in a little bit of obscurity during my lifetime, but I think there will be a reassessment there. As there will be for Thomas Hardy, who was in eclipse when I came along. Hardy is so good I could hardly believe it. The opening chapter of *The Mayor of Casterbridge* should be read by every would-be novelist. That, and *Far From the Madding Crowd* and *Return of the Native*, and the two great ones—*Tess of the D'Urbervilles* and *Jude the Obscure*—are creations that just reverberate on every damn page.

What about Cervantes?

I revere Cervantes. It just staggers you that a nation should so adopt a man as its total image—a nation which wouldn't, at many points, have tolerated the son of a bitch. He would have been in jail in Franco's Spain, in Bourbon Spain, in jail nine-tenths of the time, as he *was*. It's somewhat like America and Walt Whitman—we all now agree that he was probably our greatest poet, yet at no point would we have wanted him walking down the main street of Philadelphia or Denver. Cervantes is the great example of the fact that you cannot write these stupendous books in an armchair in a bleak room. You might do something else, but not *Don Quixote*.

In your own lifetime, who have been the writers who have most touched you?

Of the writers alive during my lifetime, Thomas Mann had more influence on me than anybody else. *Magic Mountain* is as fine a philosophical novel as could be written. The character Settembrini lives in my memory as much as any modern character. *Buddenbrooks* taught me how a family could be utilized as the hero of a novel. I didn't like Mann's *Joseph and His Brethren* as much, though I read it with avid attention. *Death in Venice* is as fine a short novel as you can write. I like Henry James's *Aspern Papers* and Edith Wharton's *Ethan Frome* very much. When young people come to see me about writing, especially young women, I ask them whether they've read *Death Comes For the Archbishop*, *Death in Venice*, and *Ethan Frome*. If they can't write better than that, we don't really need you.

As a teacher and as someone who has been interviewed often, are you stimulated by the questions asked you about literature?

Almost without exception I have had no one come to me who was prepared to talk about literature or writing. It got so bad that I typed out a letter at one time, making a list of about twelve really fine books that I thought those who approached me should have been familiar with—*Chicken Every Sunday*, about the life of a rural minister, and *Cheaper by the Dozen*, the life of a girl and her family of twelve, and so on. They hadn't even heard of any of them. They had got an A in English and they simply wanted to write.

But then, what do I know? I saw a study done by the *Wilson Quarterly* of thirty-three writers who were worth attention and I didn't even know the names of about ten of them. This seemed to me a very arrogant judgment because it ignored the reading habits of three decades of our society. They had very high praise for a young man who had written a book in which none of the pages were numbered because it didn't matter where in the book you started or ended. To say that he was infinitely superior to Saul Bellow or Herman Wouk or Somerset Maugham was simply nonsense.

You've praised Mann and James and Wharton as influential writers. Who else among your contemporaries do you like?

Though I don't think of them as great frontier groundbreakers, I'm very impressed with the works of Walker Percy, Donald Barthelme, Camus, Sartre, John Le Carré, Joan Didion, John Barth. Barth is a major figure and when he's good, he's fabulously good. And when he over-reaches himself, he loses the reader. A young writer who wanted to find out what writing was all about could read three books on the Chesapeake: Barth's *The Sot-Weed Factor; Beautiful Swimmers*, a stunning little thing written by a scientist, William W. Warner, which won a Pulitzer Prize; and my book, *Chesapeake*. These are three radically different views so wide apart that his mind would have to do some focusing the way the eye does. Of the three, *The Sot-Weed Factor* is the best, because it has this high humor and wonderful attitude toward life. And then he ought to read Barth's *Letters*. And if he could get those four books in balance, he would have a very good basis upon which to approach his own career and his own talent.

Barth's book *Letters* was almost an American equivalent of Joyce's *Finnegans Wake*. A frolic, a cannibalistic thing, a perimeter beyond which writing cannot go. It's very good indeed, with a potential readership of only a few thousand who could make heads or tails of it. It isn't writing, it's something else; he's into games-playing, into triple illusion. But I don't think I would want to do a book like that. My ambition is somewhere else.

Where else?

I believe that the novelist portrays in great detail what has happened and indicates what the moral values and the complications are and then lets the reader come to grips with it and solve it. That's the way I like to write, for better or for worse. I think Herman Wouk and I fall in the same category. I'm very proud to be there with him. He has been underevaluated by critics. His books will be read for a long time, especially *Caine Mutiny* and *Winds of War*.

But writing is a very fragile profession. What, for instance, happened to James Gould Cozzens, who was maybe the most talented writer I remember? And Herman Hesse, who was the kind of writer that college juniors went ape over but who didn't add up to very much in the long run. John Dos Passos remains a tremendous enigma, maybe the most difficult of the good American writers to get into focus. *Manhattan Transfer* was a powerful experience to all of us who were in college at that time. And *42nd Parallel*, which is the larger work, seemed to me a most happy literary device and one that I might have come upon myself. So I was much taken by Dos Passos. And then to find him degenerating into a very confused, right-wing apologist left me bewildered.

Where do you stand on J.D. Salinger?

I wasn't at all taken by J.D. Salinger's *The Catcher in the Rye*. I guess I was a little older and missed that whole thing. But then one day I picked up that very beautiful body of short stories and *Franny and Zooey*, and I was really struck by the easy way in which he created a mood and a set of characters. He displayed a talent for elusive writing which is dang near incredible. "For Esmé—With Love and Squalor" is better than *Catcher*.

Mark Twain?

Mark Twain gives me a great deal of trouble. He is very important in my life. *Huckleberry Finn* is probably our finest American novel. I prefer it to *Moby Dick* because there is more humanity in it, it's more easily comprehensible. As a traveler Twain was despicable. Whenever I want to write about a foreign country I read Twain to be sure that I don't do the things he did—the easy wisecracks, laughing at everything that was not Anglo-Saxon, playing the boob. I find it just repulsive.

Nathaniel Hawthorne?

I don't particularly like Nathaniel Hawthorne—I find his reputation over-inflated—but he brings me up short now and then. He's a real writer.

Herman Melville?

Herman Melville is wonderful, though I'm a little perplexed by his South Pacific book. Because I've been in that area sometimes

I feel that he wasn't and is writing out of his imagination. He had a powerful imagination. I respect him very highly as a poet. He has a poem called "Billy in the Darbies," which is just as good a poem of the sea that has ever been written.

Jack London?

I have always disliked and distrusted Jack London because he was a real fascist and a Hitler racist. Then I read Irving Stone's biography of him which portrayed him as a socialist liberal that I had not known. That was a beautiful, passionate piece of work, probably the best account of London that there is. When you read it you see London not the way I was thinking of him at all, or the way the general public thought of him, but as a guy who was trying to pick his way through the America of 1910 to 1920.

Solzhenitsyn?

Alexander Solzhenitsyn is also a fascist. He's far more communist than he is a follower of our form of government. I was in Russia at a great conference when the government was having a very hard time with him. I had by then read *One Day in the Life of Ivan Denisovich* and was quite awed by it. And every morning on the table outside of our door would be a new set of pamphlets proving that the guy was a complete SOB and he was a liar and a fraud. I wondered why they would bother with this when they just could have taken him out and shot him. But apparently they felt that he had slipped over into the Western consciousness and they were not free to shoot him. I read all these pamphlets with the greatest attention, because it was character assassination of the highest order. But he's an authentic, a real voice. Brilliant people will be listened to, whether they are Mussolini or Solzhenitsyn or Günther Grass.

Salman Rushdie is beginning to come out from hiding, promoting his novel The Moor's Last Sigh. *Are you surprised he's still alive?*

Yes. I think he's still in danger.

T.S. Eliot?

He had a tremendously compact form of expression. But he was such a strong anti-Semite and such a fascist and such a bloody slob that I had the same problem with him that I had with Knut Hamsun and Ezra Pound. Pound was totally objectionable, a horrible, illiterate human being. I just have a higher standard of behavior than that. Some things are forgivable, but not the annihilation of one's fellow people.

Do the well-known British writers seem to you to get a different respect than their American counterparts?

I am much impressed by the fact that the British run a kind of factory in which Clive Bell writes about Virginia Woolf and Virginia Woolf writes about T.S. Eliot and T.S. Eliot writes about Clive Bell; they go around and around and build up one another until rather fragile reputations suddenly loom gigantic. There must have been two dozen books on this circle recently and it gives you the impression that these people were of a magnitude of grandeur that nobody in America has ever reached. All I can say is they've got a damn good thing going. The poor American writer suffers because he is not seen as part of a movement bigger than he was. He doesn't have this infinite back-scratching and accolading up and down the aisles. Sinclair Lewis is an equal to any of them. But Sinclair Lewis didn't marry somebody who was a cousin of Theodore Dreiser who was an uncle of Edmund Wilson who was a nephew of Knopf. So when you read about Lewis, this poor, miserable son of a bitch, in isolation, he's just Lewis. He's not a member of this great coterie, all of whom are going to write their own books about Lewis indicating what a fantastic guy he was. If Lewis had been a part of a membership like that his reputation would be infinitely greater than it was.

Did a writer like Christopher Isherwood over-inflate himself with the kind of fictional biography he perfected?

Christopher Isherwood, W.H. Auden, Stephen Spender are part of another English circle whose members wrote about how great each of them was. One of the strangest experiences I've ever had in writing came when Barnaby Conrad conned me, in his marvelous and irresistible way, into speaking at one of his writing conferences. Isherwood, who made an enviable reputation on a rather small body of work, was there and in front of this rather large conservative audience he stood in his frail and handsome way at the edge of the podium, and his opening words were,

"I am a practicing homosexual who writes books." Then he told us that Somerset Maugham's marvelous novel *Of Human Bondage* about the doctor with the club foot, Philip, who falls in love with a waitress, was originally written with Philip falling in love with a waiter, but the general editorial opinion was that England was not ready for this so Maugham reluctantly recast it. I sat transfixed by Isherwood's performance. He was brilliant, congenial, conciliatory. Most of the time he handled questions from the audience, and the audience was often antagonistic. It was about as bravura a performance as I have ever seen.

You distinguish between authors and writers, don't you?

Yes. I think authors are essentially poseurs who are playing the part. And writers are guys like Theodore Dreiser, just sitting down and writing and having no pretense of playing a part and probably no desire to do so. I don't like to be called an author. That's for somebody far more pompous than I am.

You don't consider yourself a graceful writer, do you?

When it comes to graceful writing, I'm more like a pachyderm than a hummingbird. Dreiser was the prince of the pachyderms. A more graceless writer rarely lived yet his books have a power that is awesome. I would love to have written *An American Tragedy*. F. Scott Fitzgerald was a graceful writer, but he's a problem to me. He wrote about Princeton young men, Parisian expatriates, the flotsom and jetsom of Hollywood. That's good, but not for me. So between Fitzgerald and Dreiser, I would always take Dreiser.

As a lover of poetry, what's your opinion of Byron and Shelley?

Reading about Shelley and Byron I get awfully fed up, realizing that these men never did a day's work in their lives; they lived off the system, were free to travel all around Europe with entourages if necessary, never wrote about a guy earning a living. That is not the world I knew, that is not the world I want to be a part of, and by and large it's not a world I'm interested in.

How much poetry do you actually read?

I keep upon my desk several volumes of poetry anthologies. I read in it at least three days a week. They tend to be the great classic poets, the nineteenth-century poets. I know all of Shelley, Keats, especially Matthew Arnold. I'm addicted to Arnold and Wordsworth and Milton, Chaucer and the Elizabethans. I have sometimes felt that the highest form of verbal art is the poem. That's the reason I gave most of the royalties from one of my long novels to the publication of poetry. Maybe some girl at the University of Michigan is writing a sonnet which will summarize totally anything I've had to say in a book of a thousand pages.

If Shakespeare was alive today would he be writing those plays and sonnets?

He would probably be in television since his plays are so episodic.

Who are your favorite modern poets?

Yeats hit me pretty hard. Eliot I must say I missed. And Auden had no effect whatever. Poe I find dreary, a Johnny-One-Note, though a wonderful note. Pound was a wordsmith, and his impact on other poets was profound. Wallace Stevens is a break-even point. He is so difficult he's a paradigm of what happened in poetry. Even with my background and the attention I've paid to this all of my life, I cannot read his poems. It's like Allen Ginsberg: if I can accept Walt Whitman, why can't I accept Allen Ginsberg? It's merely an extension of rules and values. Maybe it's a factor of age. I'm so imbued with the rhythms of the great British poets I'm apparently stuck with that. Now William Carlos Williams, I'm with him right away. And I have always enjoyed Whitman and Emily Dickinson—I praise her very highly.

I prize a little-known work of Oscar Wilde's I read once and have never since been able to locate. It was a long moral essay, tongue-in-cheek, about a minor poet of the early 1800s who had been hanged for murder. Wilde excused the murder in a few compassionate paragraphs, pointing out that this was the sort of unfortunate accident into which any young man of excitable temperament might fall, and he sought the reader's forgiveness for the misguided criminal.

But then, with all the critical apparatus he might have used on the collected works of Shakespeare or Dante, he analyzed the man's poetry, its form, its rhyme systems, its moral enlightenment and its epic sweep, all of which he found markedly deficient if not downright deplorable. In a splendid conclusion, phrased much better than I am going to do, Wilde gave it as his opinion that the London authorities had been justified in hanging this fellow, but unfortunately had strung him up for the wrong crime.

Funny stuff. Wilde was a curious anomaly. On the frontier he was a hero—they loved him because he was such a nut.

What other writers make you laugh?

Humorists I like are Robert Benchley and some of Max Shulman. And I have great affection for my neighbor and good friend, S.J. Perleman. He used language better than any of us writing today.

Do you like Woody Allen?

I've read a lot of Woody Allen. And I try to see his movies. I find him very self-centered and exhibitionistic, far more than I would be. There's a little more self-revelation, self-pity and self-denigration than I like. But he had a short story about the recreation of a great Hungarian writer from a tab of laundry lists which had been found in his effects, a take-off on pretentious literary criticism. I liked that very much.

Are you familiar with Howard Stern, whose two books have both topped the bestsellers list?

Yes. He's irrelevant.

What about Bill Gates, whose book knocked off Stern's? A great visionary or just a great businessman?

He's a very compelling fellow. I listen to him very carefully. He's taken on all the competitors, kept his cool, and winds up the richest young man in the world. Though the castle he's building is a monstrosity.

What about women writers, any favorites?

Some time ago I thought I ought to find out what the women writers were up to and spent all my spare time reading them with enormously good results. I was very much struck with Anne

Rice's book *Interview With a Vampire*. I liked Joyce Carol Oates's *them*, Joan Didion's *Play It As It Lays*, Sylvia Plath's *The Bell Jar*, Mary McCarthy's *The Group*, Judith Rossner's *Looking for Mr. Goodbar*.

Where do American writers stand in an assessment of world literature today?

Fifteen or twenty American writers stand with anything being done in the world today. Joyce Carol Oates, John McPhee, John Updike, Philip Roth, Tom Wolfe.

Did Wolfe's book on the astronauts help you when you were writing Space?

When I was researching *Space* several people wanted me to read Wolfe's *The Right Stuff*, as well as Mailer's *Of A Fire On The Moon*. But I avoided them at the time. Later when I looked at Wolfe's book on the first page I read he repeated a simple statement in about nine different ways in order to hammer it home. It's marvelously effective—a device that in normal hands would be really quite offensive.

What did you think of the movies they made of his books?

He's way better than the movies they've made from his books. *The Right Stuff* was quite an ordinary movie and *Bonfire of the Vanities* was a disaster as a movie. Maybe he has such a scintillating style that cinema can't catch it. Whereas a book like John Irving's *The World According to Garp* makes a splendid movie because it's more within a manageable form.

Are there books by American writers which you wished you had written?

Carson McCullers's *Member of the Wedding* is an absolutely marvelous piece of story telling, wonderful dialogue, a bizarre setting—that's a precious work. *McTeague* by Frank Norris is one that I most wish that I had written. I hold James M. Cain in high regard because he had that mordant touch, he knew how to create that feeling of a dark alley down which a lot of people spend most of their lives. Irwin Shaw's *The Young Lions* was the kind of book I would have tried to write had I felt competent at that time. I've always read his short stories with real delight; they are Fitzgerald updated.

James Reston and Robertson Davies both died in December, 1995. What did you think of them?

I knew Reston's work well. He made a place for himself, which was quite surprising since he was a Scotsman, not an American. But like Kissinger, he filled a gap. I never read Davies but I met him and liked him.

Davies once said that "You should never write with a view to improving or educating people, you just bore the socks off of them."

I don't agree with that. We're just in two different ballparks.

What writers showed promise but never fulfilled their potential?

James Baldwin and Ralph Ellison are writers who had a larger responsibility than what they have fulfilled.

What about Joseph Heller?

The measure of Joseph Heller's importance is that he put a new phrase into the English language.

John Grisham's novels jump right onto the bestsellers' list. Where does he stand, in your opinion?

He's able, has done a lot to commend him. He runs the risk of becoming a Johnny One-Note, telling the same old story.

You haven't mentioned D.H. Lawrence or Gabriel García Márquez in your assessment of modern writers.

One of the reasons I'm so fond of D.H. Lawrence is that he does things that the rest of us can't do. And Gabriel García Márquez falls into that category very beautifully. I love explosive, poetic writing. *One Hundred Years of Solitude* is a marvelous invention. He merits the highest praise. He deserved the Nobel Prize.

Who else deserves or deserved it?

From the point of view of the vitality of his writing and its broad scope, I think Norman Mailer deserves that recognition. As does John Updike and Joyce Carol Oates. It was a grave mis-justice that Thornton Wilder didn't get it. He was good in three major fields: the novel, drama, the essay. Edmund Wilson should have got it. So, too, Robert Penn Warren and Bernard Malamud.

What did you think when Toni Morrison got the Nobel Prize?

The black Mafia had me as an enemy for some time on the grounds that James Baldwin was an infinitely better writer than I was and it was outrageous that I got the acceptance that I did and he didn't. Well, the same group, having lost Baldwin, whom they were grooming for the Nobel, issued a broadside which I re-member vividly, signed by fifty or sixty black writers and artists, excoriating the Pulitzer committee for never having given her a Pulitzer Prize. I think they talked about a boycott, though I'm not sure about that. She eventually got a Pulitzer. And they were able to mount a fantastic campaign, and they got her the Nobel Prize. She's a damn good writer. Some black writer was due to get it, and she got it.

Are you familiar with the Japanese laureate Kenzeburo Oë?

No, I'm not. I used to know the Japanese writers very well, was involved with the Nobel committee years ago. On a long air-plane trip from Copenhagen to the Far East I sat with a titled Swede who said he was going to Japan to identify somebody to give the Nobel Prize to, they felt they had shortchanged the Ori-ent. I recommended Mishima very strongly. He was still alive, but they took Kawabata. I have a suspicion that years later they must have regretted that.

Any regrets over Seamus Heaney's selection for the '95 Nobel Prize?

No. It was time for an Irishman to get it.

What about yourself?

I have a form letter which I send to people who write to me about the fact that I have not received a Nobel Prize. It begins: When I think of the great men of my generation who did not get the prize—Proust, Henry James, Conrad, Tolstoy . . . about fif-teen names—and compare them with some of the clowns who did—I'm especially bitter about Knut Hamsun, who turned quisling in Norway during the war and vilified every precept of what a writer ought to be, the man had no conscience, no courage, no character—I say I would much rather stand with the former than with the latter. Then I have a postscript saying: Of course, I realize the impropriety of some of this in that if you look at some of the good people who did get it, anybody would be very proud to be with them.

You haven't been completely neglected. Don't colleges often bestow honorary degrees on you?

I have more prizes than I feel I'm entitled to. I get about six honorary degree invitations in a year, and I limit it to two. I suppose I must have close to forty honorary doctorates now.

Which one are you most proud of?

Few people have probably ever heard of Dropsey College—it's the top Jewish research institution in the world. When they gave me an honorary degree for the solidity of my work in Hebraic studies, I was really quite gratified by that. And when another college gave me an honorary degree for my work in science, it was rewarding.

How personally satisfying is public recognition?

I think that a person in any field who is given public acceptance is measured by the creative way he uses it. If you just use it for getting a good table at Sardi's or jet-set attention, it's quite sad. If you don't capitalize on that for the welfare of society, then you're a total jerk. That's why I have so much respect for Marlon Brando, for Robert Redford, in a curious way for John Wayne when he was alive, although I didn't like his politics. For Camus, for Sartre, for Günther Grass, for Solzhenitsyn, for Joan Baez.

Part of public acceptance is attending dinners in your honor. Do you go to many?

Over the years Art Buchwald, Walter Cronkite and I have shared a correspondence. We get invited to all these affairs where we are to get an award of some kind, usually a plaque that costs $1.16 and the names are often misspelled. Then at the end it says, "We would be very pleased if when you receive it you would acknowledge it with a thirty or forty minute commentary." We formed an alliance some time ago that under pain of death no one of us would buy a ticket to a testimonial for the other two.

Is Buchwald as funny and Cronkite as solemn in private as they are in public?

Buchwald and Cronkite are dear friends. Buchwald, as most people know, is terribly funny, and when I'm with him we laugh at least four-fifths of the time. What is less known is that Walter Cronkite is one of the great comedians of America.

How'd you get to know Cronkite?

I met Cronkite on an exploration trip to Tahiti. We sailed over very turbulent seas to the island of Raiatea. Somebody had wired ahead that we were coming. As we entered this tropical lagoon, about as far away from any place as you could get, there was a very beautiful girl at the end of the pier with a violin playing the Brahms Violin Concerto. One of the most extraordinary experiences I've ever had.

You've met and worked with a lot of extremely intelligent people. Have any of them been touched with genius?

In my lifetime I have met only two geniuses, a word that ought to be used with great care because genius is extremely rare. Genius implies a certain intensity and an intellectual gear that is different from what most of us have.

One was Bobby Fischer, the chess player, and the other was Tennessee Williams, who simply looked at life and drama and the human condition differently from the way I do and than anybody else I know does. Both men found that to be the vessel housing genius was an intolerable condition, and each was destroyed by that burden.

Which of them do you hold in greater esteem?

As a writer, Williams has to take preeminence. He used words and human situations more brilliantly than any of us. I had dinner with him in Rome or Spain. We had a long night together. He was just geared into something in a way I wasn't at all. Very impressive.

But Bobby Fischer is quite compelling. My encounter with him was instructive. Television hosts like David Frost earn huge salaries by enlisting guests whom they pay nothing, the pay-off is the publicity bestowed by the telly. Frost, being a generous soul, decided to show his appreciation by renting a Boeing 747 and flying some sixty or eighty of his guests from New York to Bermuda for lunch.

The roster was sparkling—politicians, media stars, actors, musicians—and when it came time to seat us Frost asked me: "You ever heard of Bobby Fischer?" and I told him: "I followed his great triumph in South America against Petrosian."

So I was seated with Fischer, and within a few minutes it became obvious that he had never heard of me, nor Senator Javits, nor anyone else aboard that plane. But when he found that I had followed his great duel in South America, he adopted me: "What do you do?"

"I'm a writer." With delight he told me that he was, too, and from a bag which he kept with him always he produced four stout books on the playing of chess. I asked him if he thought I could learn, and he studied me with professional care: "If you were bright enough," and the way he said this betrayed his snap judgment that I would not be.

During the flight to Bermuda he spoke only of himself: "By the eighth grade I knew more than any of my teachers, so I quit. I could play Karpov anytime, anywhere, and beat him." He found my conversation so limited that in the midst of it he took out a magnetic chessboard, arranged the pieces, and ran through several games while still speaking of himself.

When he reached Bermuda he disappeared, rented a bicycle, and pedaled like mad while the rest of us had drinks. When he returned to ask if he could sit with me at lunch, since he already knew me, he stopped dead, pointed at a beautiful woman member of our group, and cried: "I saw her on television. Four years ago." It was Kitty Carlisle, recent widow of Moss Hart, and he ran to her, telling her in the most minute detail of her performance that night, what she wore, what she said, how she laughed, everything. It was an amazing performance and when I asked her about it, she said: "I'd forgotten, it was so long ago. But he had everything right."

On the way home I told him who all the other passengers were, but he recognized none of them. He told me: "You have an interesting mind, but not quick. I don't think you'd make it in chess."

Not long thereafter he shocked the chess world by insolently throwing away the first game—or was it two?—and then creaming his Russian opponent, Boris Spassky, for the world's undisputed championship. I am not sure he knew what country he was in. I sent him a note. It came back—he didn't know who I was, never heard of me. Very insulting, like I was just another tourist who imposed on him. And I had sat and talked with him for maybe ten hours. Sometime after that he fell apart on religious matters, surrendering by default his crown.

As the author of a book on sports, do you consider chess a sport?

I don't. It's a contest of brain and will power and attention, not a sport. But you better be in topflight condition to face those grueling sessions when one lapse means defeat.

What about golf?

It's something else. It has its own unique niche in society. The gala country club life. It's a delightful game for elderly executives or even young executives who want to make big deals about selling manufactured products. I can't take it seriously.

Deep-sea fishing?

I don't consider deep sea fishing a sport either, but I've done it in Hawaii, Tahiti, and in Key West. I love the motion of the water and the boat, and I once caught an eighty-pound fish off Tahiti.

Do you consider yourself an athlete?

I have played sports vigorously all my life. Not everybody needs sports, but for those of us who do need it, the need is a very real thing. My hometown newspaper describes me to this day as a high school athlete, never as a high school poet or wizard at mathematics—because in a small town like that, what mattered is whether you played games or not.

Who have been some of your favorite athletes?

I knew Lefty Grove, who pitched for the Philadelphia Athletics, and thought him to be quite fine. In all the years I knew him, he never had a sore arm when it was time to pitch against Boston or New York. He won all those ball games and often times with a poor team.

The matador Domingo Ortega was the same way. I knew him as a young man when I was very impressionable, about the same time that I knew Lefty. Ortega was one of those marvelous bullfighters who dominated the sport because he was so classically perfect and so very good.

I also got to know, but not well, El Cordobès. Although I didn't like his bullfighting, I did like him very much.

Cordobès was a tiger, a lot like the sumo wrestler Taiho whom I knew during his years of greatness. That was a real privilege. He was not a giant of a man, but he put together a record in Sumo wrestling that has never been equaled and probably never will be. I knew him through several championships and then on the night he stopped, where he went through this tremendous tearful ceremony of cutting his hair.

If you could have been any athlete, who would you choose?

I would probably choose among three: Bill Russell, the great Boston Celtics center; the Phillies great pitcher, Robin Roberts; or Hal Greer, who played basketball for the Philadelphia 76ers. I don't think I could ever have been Bill Russell or Robin Roberts, but had I been a good player I might have been like Hal Greer, who stayed in there and played more games than anybody else, was the fireman, was a fine man in the clutch, a high scorer, and had tremendous personal integrity and organization.

And what athlete would you compare yourself to?

Robin Roberts is the athlete I'd be happiest being compared with. In the latter days when he had lost his really powerful fast ball he was losing low-scoring games, one-nothing, two-one, three-two in eleven innings. In other words, he was pitching absolutely superbly and the Phillies weren't giving him many runs but he was still winning nineteen or twenty games. I have great respect for the man who they get to and knock him completely out of the park and he comes back the next day and this time he's in control. I see that as an analog to life and I would like to be that way. I would not be at all unhappy to be known as the Robin Roberts of the literary world. I think Zola and Theodore Dreiser were that.

If you were to write a sports novel, which sport would it be about?

Baseball. Philip Roth's book on baseball *The Great American Novel*, is hilarious. And Roger Angell's *The Summer Game* is bloody good. Even better is Roger Kahn's *The Boys of Summer*. There is a book about blacks and basketball by Jay Neugeboren called *The Big Man* that is as good a sports novel as has ever been written. It's as good as Mark Harris's *Bang the Drum Slowly*. I also like David Wolf's *Foul* on Connie Hawkins—not a novel but perhaps the best book on basketball. *Caught in the Pivot* is a fantastically good book by a coach, Tom Meschery, on coaching the North Carolina basketball team. But for me, it would be baseball.

Why?

Baseball is a miracle in that whoever devised the ninety feet between bases must have been one of the brightest men that America has produced, because it's so within the relationship of the bat and the ball and the long throw to first and the steal to second and so on. There is a decency about it. You don't spike the second baseman unless you really have to; you never throw a bean ball unless the guy at the plate is a real good hitter, things like that. I find it very congenial. Also because the players stay in it longer, they have longer lives, and therefore they build much finer personas than is possible in basketball or football. I feel an affinity for this game. The analogy with what I do is very strong: the leisurely way it unfolds, the way they take time, and it can build up to some tremendous climaxes.

Is there any particular player who might inspire your baseball novel?

It might be somebody like Jimmy Foxx, one of the great tragic figures who came up to the big leagues at the age of sixteen, one of the most finished ballplayers that ever came off the sand lots. In later years I was able to follow his career into the dregs. Very few great athletes have ever fallen as low as he did, living in a shack in Florida with $18 a month and nobody to look after him. I contributed to a fund that was raised to at least bring him back to decency. I went down and spent quite some time with him, meeting his family. It's a splendid American story and I would recommend that somebody take a crack at it. And why it would be interesting as a subject for a book is that it was no outside force that brought him down. Every outside force was supporting him. He played for great ball clubs. He wasn't down in the sticks or he wasn't playing for the St. Louis Browns or anything like that. He was at the top. He led the league in hitting, in home runs, he was a hell of a good fielder. Yet, down he goes. Great story.

Another tragic figure was Ty Cobb, recently portrayed in a movie as a cantankerous old man by Tommie Lee Jones.

I had Ty Cobb's son in high school. You got the feeling that Ty Cobb, whom we idolized, was a pretty sad item. He wouldn't come to the school to meet the students. I have read that when

Ty Cobb learned that his son had failed at Princeton he went there and beat him up. His son was very uncommunicative, but he betrayed a lot. I saw that his father never liked him.

Didn't you once get to know DiMaggio?

I had the privilege one summer of knocking around with Joe DiMaggio a bit and seeing what it meant to be a real star, and probably *the* preeminent star after Babe Ruth. Wherever he went, he was the most revered man, extolled, loved.

The Joe and Marilyn thing I understood easily: they were two darlings of the press and the nation; it was logical that they be thrown together. On the other hand, the Monroe-Arthur Miller thing was absolutely beyond me.

When did you first see Marilyn Monroe?

I first saw Monroe when she was dating Truman Capote and they were dancing at the El Morocco. She was barefoot so that she wouldn't tower over him. And she was just radiant. But her makeup was so heavy that I never really saw her, just what she was presenting. She had an enormous can and was not my ideal of beauty at all. She certainly was no Audrey Hepburn. But when she turned that face on, my God, it was something. Just like a sunbeam. DiMaggio loved her very deeply and had great respect for her which he demonstrated when she died.

What other ballplayers impressed you?

Ted Williams is a really classy guy. He told the world to go screw and he made it stick.

DiMaggio and Williams played for the two teams that divided baseball for me. The Yankees, when they were winning, were the establishment; they are the Republican right wing. They represent everything that is conservative and objectionable in life. I don't see how anybody who is seriously interested in the arts from a humanistic point of view could be a Yankee fan. A really good year for me was when the Yankees were ahead by eleven games in mid-July and then Boston comes on strong and beats them out. That is the way God intended that it should be.

So Boston is your favorite team?

I associated with three teams: the Athletics, the Boston Red Sox, and the Giants. I grew up with the great Connie Mack teams of 1928, '29, '30, and '31, one of the great ball clubs of all time. And the bête noire was the Yankees. Then when I taught at Harvard the only recreation I could afford was going out to Fenway Park. Some of the saddest afternoons of my life were in September when the Red Sox would be three games ahead and the Yankees would come in with two double headers and a single game and win all five.

Some of the saddest times of my life were in October, when the leaves would turn color and you would have a hint of snow in the air and the grandeur of summer is over, and here comes the World Series and it was almost always the Yankees and the Dodgers, and the Yankees always won.

In 1994, for the first time in over ninety years, we didn't have a World Series because of the baseball strike. Do you have any thoughts about that?

It staggers me. I wrote an article about baseball where I said I was shocked by the 1923 Supreme Court decision. I was 16 then. That was a horrible mistake. And I've testified before Congress several times trying to get it revoked. It's the core of the whole problem. Justice Oliver Wendall Holmes wrote an opinion saying that baseball was not commerce, and therefore did not fall under the Sherman Anti-Trust Act; therefore the owners could do whatever they damn well pleased. And in the Curt Flood case, the great base stealer, Justice Harry Blackmun wrote the majority opinion, a sickening thing. It idolized baseball, said it deserved special attention because it was part of the American ethic and should be exempt from normal law. Baseball has refused to face the problem of wealthy and not-so-wealthy teams, because they don't have to.

Senator Metzenbaum was very strong in wanting to revoke the exemption. Connie Mack, the senator, and I testified on behalf of Florida before the Senate and House committees urgently advising the Senate to change this. Much as I love baseball, I think that law should be changed. The owners are miserable money-grabbing men who deserve everything they get.

So, did you think George Steinbrenner deserved what he got in the '96 World Series? A championship team?

I was for Atlanta. But I must say the Yankees made wonderful results from their victory, and it was by and large good for the country.

Another problem baseball faced was the decline in interest by the TV networks. Baseball doesn't seem to work as well on TV as it does when you're in the ballpark.

Compared to football, baseball on television looks tedious. Football and television is an absolutely marvelous wedding. It makes basketball look trivial. Basketball is a great game but it doesn't televise well. And college games are more exciting than the pros. Why this should be I don't know. As for ice hockey—nobody can follow ice hockey.

Do you like boxing?

Boxing is beneath contempt.

What about soccer?

Soccer, when it's in competition with American-style football, has no chance because it's so dull. In the early days I predicted that it was so compelling worldwide that it would catch on. I missed the fact that because it was a game of finesse and exquisite art Americans would say the hell with that, let's get out there and knock some heads. It's the same factor that operates in the arts.

And that factor is one of violence and brutality?

Our attitude toward sports is pretty much like our attitude toward artists. Unless it's brutal and macho and manly we don't want to bother with it. We are so addicted to sports in a certain form that any changing of it would be almost impossible.

But I am cautious about that, because in the latter years of the last century there were a lot of deaths on the football field because of the flying wedge that just annihilated the other team, especially the defensive players. Sometimes the player would fall down and his own teammates would trample him to death. A

Yale coach could say to his team that the biggest moment in their lives is tomorrow when you play Harvard; there will never be anything as big as this ever again.

Teddy Roosevelt moved into that as president. He held a big conference and told the athletic directors that unless they cleaned up their acts, within a year he was going to outlaw college football. They did, and the deaths on the field stopped.

There are still too many deaths each year from high school and college football. Maybe that's a small price to pay for the fun the spectator gets out of it. I don't see any likelihood of change. Though I think one of the most amazing things in American sports was the decision years ago by the better Catholic colleges around the country. They could no longer afford two-platoon football, just dropped football and took up basketball. And they got all the values they ever did out of football. Instead of sixty uniforms that are very expensive they could get away with sixteen men with a T-shirt and a jock strap and a pair of sneakers.

It's even cheaper to field a tennis team.

Coaches and sportswriters used to make fun of tennis. Now, a young tennis player comes along, plays into his late forties, and makes a fortune. More money than any of the football players make. It must be quite galling to them—and quite amusing to the rest of us.

It wasn't amusing when Monica Seles got stabbed or when Steffi Graff's father was thrown in jail for not reporting all of her earnings. Any opinion of them?

They have made themselves targets because of the splendid performances they put on. And they're inherently nice people.

What do you think made tennis catch on?

The tie-breaker is what saved tennis. It's very exciting. I'm not sure it's tennis, but I think it's an example of what imaginative men can do to help a sport that would otherwise be doomed. But I am not much taken by the fast serves which result in an ace. This puts a premium on what is a physical freak shot. I wouldn't mind seeing the net raised an inch and a half.

What changes in other sports would you like to see?

If I were to make changes in other sports, I would raise the basket and make the lanes a little wider in basketball. And I would also do something about the last two minutes to avoid it taking fifteen to eighteen minutes to play. I would also get away from the slam dunking, which is juvenile. It is just like the fighting in hockey, exacerbates the worst emotions of the fans.

In baseball, one of the greatest crimes against American culture is the designated hitter. I would also be tempted to reduce the number of fouls a batter can hit after he has two strikes. Because you can get these artists in there who can tick them off without any chance of a play being made and that's not productive. I'd limit it to two fouls and out on the third one.

Boxing I'm quite opposed to. The way we use boxers is pretty much the way the impresario uses a bull, just for the fun of it. I can't take it seriously, though I did find great delight in Mohammed Ali. He was a tonic. I withstood his charm until one night I heard a radio broadcast. They were asking him why he was taking his next fight to Costa Rica and he said: 'Because when you are as great as I am, no mere city can contain you, it requires an entire country.' I figured that any son of a bitch who can get on the air and say that without breaking up, he's in the atmosphere, he's out there. To have somebody say that, quite seriously, and letting you in on the secret, that was high comedy.

Can a cultural history of the downtrodden be linked to boxing?

A study at Harvard made a great impression on me. The researcher looked at the boxing programs in Boston over a hundred and fifty years. In the early days they were all Englishmen. Then after society got established and the young men from good families didn't have to go into boxing, they were all Irishmen. After a while they were still young Irishmen, but actually they were Jewish—from Poland and Lithuania and so on—they just didn't fight under their own names, they would fight under Irish names. After a little while there were no Irish Jews, now they were all Frenchmen, still fighting under Irish names. And then after that the boxers were all black. So it has been a way for the young male to get ahead in boxing in New England. And I think that applies universally.

You've made some controversial remarks about the Harlem Globetrotters being sort of the Amos & Andy *of sports. Do you still feel that way?*

During the heyday of the Harlem Globetrotters I felt that they did more damage racially than good. I don't fault Abe Saperstein for putting the team together, and I didn't fault Meadowlark Lemon, one of the fine comedians of our time, for being the star of it. The Globetrotters did give employment to some very wonderful young men who might not have gotten it otherwise, but it was a really disgraceful commentary among our society that that was the only outlet they had.

Sports can sometimes turn into freak shows, as you observed about Spanish midget bullfighters. Is that appalling to you?

In Spain, in the little towns, they have a horrible thing called *los toreros enanos*, the midget bullfighters. They get the most misshapen dwarfs they can find in the peninsula or import them from other countries, and they dress them up like full-fledged bullfighters, and they get little calves and turn them loose. The whole damned population comes out and cheers and whistles and laughs.

How did you come to write Sports in America?

When I saw the one hundred and twenty page special football edition of the *Dallas Herald*, I thought, My God, sports are even more important than I thought they were. Anything that loomed that large in American life warranted some serious attention. It's been used as a college text and has been the subject of discussions on campuses all over the country. I'm invited everywhere to elaborate upon the problems with sports in America.

Are college sports programs often corrupt?

The corruption of the universities in this matter is appalling. It's quite sad that five great institutions in the West Coast would be suspended because their players were taking courses they have never seen and which in some cases didn't exist.

Do athletes tend to be more conservative than liberal?

In all my research I've come to the conclusion that athletes tend to be Republican. Those who go to college tend to be picked up by businessmen who sponsor them, make the way easy for them, give them jobs, oftentimes allow them to marry their daughters. And these men are almost always conservative and Republican. Almost all coaches are Republican, because they see in the conservative party a more orderly way of life, a little closer to dictatorship, which they seem to prefer. Also, an athlete tends to live in a world of frenzied high finance and crazy deals and automobiles under the table. He feels at ease with that. He feels the business world is where this is continued. I don't know any Democrats in sports.

How would you change college sports?

Any time a young man got an athletic scholarship I would make it good for ten years, so that if he did go into the pros he could then return and still have three years of eligibility left to get a real degree and get on with his life.

And I would also think that a young man who was drafted in either football or basketball, where there are no inferior leagues which the professional teams pay for, making the colleges and universities really adjuncts to the pros, a portion of any hiring bonus ought to go back to the school he came from. Or even a percentage of his income for the first five years. It's disgraceful the way the professional teams have been allowed to use and dominate and direct university sports, which they use as training grounds.

Are you opposed to integration between the sexes when it comes to sports?

I don't think sports should be sexually integrated between the ages twelve and twenty-two. Girls should not play with boys.

Is it fair to expect sports heroes to serve as role models?

Sports heroes as role models are a very dangerous commodity. They really do intrude their emptiness or their criminality. It's better to just keep them as football players.

How do you feel about athletes who abuse women often being treated leniently?

I've never been comfortable with the way we often look the other way when our athletes are involved in misbehavior.

In Philadelphia a member of the Philadelphia Eagles football team lived, like many people, across the river in Camden. He was a big brute, an inside tackle, married. One day the police get a call by his wife who says, 'There's been an accident, you'd better come over.'

When they get there, they find that she has cut his throat and he is very dead. Now there was a hell of a brouhaha over it. This fine young man, good tackle, helped them win ball games, and this dame has cut his throat. At this point she goes to trial, still the demon, still the one who was castigated with this horrible act. When she takes the stand she not only claims, but she has proof, it's in the records, that she called the police five times. 'This brute is beating me up.' Five times the police came over, three or four guys. And when they entered the kitchen they would see that it's their boy and they would say, 'Wait a minute m'am, this is just a family squabble now isn't it?'

And the judge asked, 'You mean you called the police five times, and they never arrested him?'

She said, 'Arrest him? They would take one look at him and ask about the game on Sunday, then they would sit there drinking beer, and then they would go.'

So you just know that's what happened. On the sixth time she said, 'The hell with you.'

Nicole Brown Simpson might have benefited from knowing about that case.

The O. J. trial was the trial of the century. And may have the same kind of repercussions as the Dreyfuss case, the trial of the last century. It was the equivalent of Jack the Ripper, a phenomenon that will be written about for the next hundred years.

It seems the country experienced a nationwide letdown after the verdict.

Yeah. I followed it intimately. I was a junky. It was instructive as to our legal system, but it taught a very bad lesson. Those scenes when the verdict was announced were very disturbing. The students at black schools cheering, the ones at white schools silent. Any sensible man or woman had to conclude that he was probably guilty. That he beat the rap. But you don't make a national holiday of it.

Would you watch the video he hawked?

I'm not sure. I find the whole thing so damaging to the American psyche that I wouldn't want to contribute to it any more.

What did you think of Simpson's defense team?

Johnny Cochran was a sharp item. Scheck was a strong voice. Robert Shapiro is brilliant—I want him when I'm in trouble. They were able to transform a murder trial into an attack on the Los Angeles police, solely because they had the money to do it, and they did it brilliantly.

Did you ever have any doubts yourself about his guilt?

Yes, I had serious doubts. I knew it was going to be hard for the state to prove. In Scotland they have a wonderful verdict—guilty, not guilty, and unproven with the supposition you were guilty. I thought from the beginning that the outcome had to be a hung jury, so the verdict surprised me.

Though you're against it, were you surprised that the prosecution didn't even ask for the death penalty with O.J.?

That's where it began to fall apart. District Attorney Garcetti's performance on that was hard to believe. I had no hope for the trial from that moment on.

Did the jury's three-hour deliberation also surprise you?

Yes. That was shameful. I thought it was going to be a trial. It was a manipulation.

Do you think that he really believes he didn't do it?

He could talk himself into it, yes. In my life I've seen certain things like that. Things that I've kidded myself into believing they happened.

What was your prediction of his civil trial? Did you think the mostly white jury would convict him?

I thought he would be acquitted again. The civil trial showed that the guy was as guilty as sin, yet I was surprised he was found guilty. I think his posturing and signing of autographs and lecturing people at airports is repulsive.

Should it have been televised, since the criminal trial was?

Yes.

If you were to run into O.J. in a restaurant and he extended his hand, would you shake it?

As a novelist, I would. I knew O.J. in his heyday. I saw him at his best.

Then I was the guru of that remarkable decathlon where they had stellar athletes from all over the world competing in south Flordia, where they could not compete in their specialty. I was the major domo, the guy to keep the thing going straight. We got off the airplane at Tampa, and there was a pretty rickety bus there waiting for us. And O.J., obviously disgusted, had to get in the bus. He was seated behind me. Two men trembling with fear dashed up in a stretch limo and one of them jumped out and asked, 'Is O.J. Simpson here?' He got up and they said, 'You're not supposed to be on this bus.' They took him out and put him in the limo. He never said a word. He played the grand seignor. It was totally distasteful. Almost anybody would have said, 'Hell, with all this space, let's take a couple.' Not O.J. The bigwigs at Hertz had told the Tampa office they had better take care of O.J.

Then we got to the playing field. And some of the competitors could not take it seriously and I rode herd on them. But the man who took it seriously, and fought every point and every call that I made, was O.J. And he won almost everything he got into. But I was most impressed with him at the weight lifting. Then there was a sad moment when a British competitor complained that O.J. had been given an advantage. They pressed the issue with me and to my shame I found in favor of O.J. In retrospect I think

I stiffed the Englishman. O.J. made no gesture to offer to do it over again, to say, 'I don't want to win it this way.' He wanted to win it. So I saw O.J. in a very ugly position twice.

And taking all that into consideration I have been most impressed by the 911 call Nicole made, which seems self-evident on the face of it. I was married to a woman of another race for forty-odd years, and we never had one quarrel. There was no possibility of my striking her. That 911 call showed how different we were. After hearing that, I intuitively felt that he was guilty.

Moving on to another tragedy involving a sports star. What do you think of the loss of Magic Johnson as a basketball player after he tested positive for AIDS?

His performance when he announced it was impeccable. But I think the public overplayed it hideously. To make Magic a national hero when he can say in public that he slept with all these women—I just can't think of him as a hero in that respect. Martina Navratilova pointed out that she was the adored darling of everybody in the tennis world until she came out and said she was a lesbian, and she wondered how the public would have reacted if she said she had the AIDS virus. She certainly didn't think she'd receive the same love and acceptance the public accorded Magic.

Are there any sports films you've liked?

The movie *Rollerball* I thought was stunning, also *Slap Shot*. I liked *The Man Who Skied Down Everest*. And *Requiem for a Heavyweight*. And *Bang the Drum Slowly*. The combination of Robert De Niro and Michael Moriarty was very good, very rich. The scene in which Vince Gardenia is giving a great pep talk to his players and it is being translated into Spanish, I cite as almost the acme of invention.

Are most athletes naturals or can they benefit from instruction?

A very knowledgeable sports specialist told me that despite a kind of automatic skill in handling myself, that even somebody like me had practically no chance of just on his own stumbling upon the right strokes in either golf or tennis. That these are solutions that have been worked out over many years and the chance that you'll stumble on them is remote.

Can the same be said of writing?

I cannot imagine anybody writing a novel without having read half a dozen of the really fine novels, to see what they are and how other people have handled it, and what you're driving for. With young people, if they do not wear glasses by the age of twenty-two, they'll never be a writer. They just haven't read enough.

If I had a daughter or son who wanted to be an artist in almost any form, there are only two courses that I would want her or him to take for sure. One would be ceramics with a potter's wheel, so that you could feel form emerging out of moving clay. I never studied ceramics until late in life and it sort of brought together what I knew. The other would be your rhythmic or athletic or ballet dancing, to get a feeling of what movement is, so one would discover the freeing up of one's own body and get that kinesthetic sense, which is at the base of a great deal of art. Instead of rhythmic dancing it could be tennis or high-grade swimming, or maybe track and field.

With all the breakthroughs in genetics, do you still side with those who believe that you can succeed mostly through learning?

I think that our genetic structure places severe limitations on us. And maybe what I prized so highly in Titian and Michelangelo and Hokusai was a genetic freak, for which they deserve no credit whatever.

Several interests have occupied me throughout my life, but the one that has stayed with me has been the speculation on whether a human being's life is determined more by society or by genetic inheritance. I spent a whole half century believing it was society and the differential experience. But recent developments in genetics have made me feel that probably I was on the wrong track. Maybe genetic inheritance is far more important than I ever believed. This is a sobering possibility. I came to the conclusion that genetic inheritance is a limitation of great finality, but that what a person determines to do about it is still of major importance.

Have you written about it?

When I was writing *Centennial* I worked with the foremost experts in embryo transplants with animals. They wanted to bring

French cattle into the United States because they knew they would prosper on a particular kind of grass and plains. They couldn't do that because of hoof and mouth disease. So they brought them into Canada. They would artificially inseminate the top cows with the top bull semen and then they would strip the ovaries and implant them in rabbits. Then they would fly the rabbits into the United States for dog food, but inside them would be these germinating cells. The secret was to take them from the rabbits and implant them in the biggest toughest cows they could find, a breed of no significance whatever. And from the embryos that were germinated in Canada, brought down in rabbits, and transferred right away into these big cows, became the perfect Limousin and Charolais cows.

Hell, we're talking about us! We're next in line. You could do that with a human. Germinate them in Canada, put them in a rabbit, fly them down here and get some big heavy peasant woman, black maybe, who worked in the cottons fields, and get a super human being out of them.

We're pretty soon going to have an atlas of the chromosomal and genetic patterns, and then they can damn near do anything they want. They've already identified one of the genes that predicts colon cancer in men. When it isn't there you don't get colon cancer. That just blows my mind.

So can a lobotomy.

Exactly, and the early lobotomy experiences ought to be a warning to all of these fields. It had such immediate results that they overlooked the long-range results.

Pig organs are being used for human transplants, and baboon bone marrow was injected into an AIDS patient. This practice could unleash the spread of new viruses which could potentially wipe out whole communities.

We're on the margin of the great developments in these fields. I think you take all the precautionary steps to avoid trouble, but if I were that young man with AIDS I would take the chance.

With all the changes we've seen in the last few decades, from the home computer to genetic implants, is it frightening for a writer like yourself to have to learn and comprehend things that never existed in your prime?

Back in 1955 I said that if anybody was frightened by events of recent years, he ought to turn in his chips right now because this was going to be the mood of the world for the rest of this century. Thirty-nine years later I say it again: if what happens terrifies you then you're too tender for this world, because many of the things that are mere speculation today are going to come to pass.

**THE WEIGHT
OF THE WORLD**

10

Back in 1981 you wrote me a letter saying you had been to Poland, advising me to stay in California and not to emigrate because it was a troubled country that would take three years to clean up. You have a clear idea of what's going on in the world, and your books are often timely. How do you do this?

In an introduction that a classical scholar gave before a speech I was about to make, he said there are many trouble spots in the world today—in South Africa, in the Middle East, the Near East, the rising of Japan's power, the revolution in Poland, the uncertainty of the future of Communism and the surrounding states, the absorption in the United States of two outlying territories like Hawaii and Alaska—and that I had written long books about each of these areas years before they came into prominence. "How he stumbled upon that is a mystery," he said. And it remains a mystery, except that I am a cultural geographer. I look at these things and brood about them, calculate and estimate them. It is not the powers of a seer or a prophet that I possess, but I have a deep-seated sensitive antennae about what is going to happen. I'm aware of things. I don't think I have any unusual insights, but I sure have fantastic information-gathering capacities. If you look at the mullahs in Afghanistan, you don't have to be too bright to figure out that these guys are on a collision course with the rest of humanity. I knew that forty years ago. The collision course didn't hit until you get the Ayatollah, but hell, I've known his cousins all my life.

Are we worse off today than when you were a boy?

I don't believe the world's any grimmer today than it's always been. Nations come up and go down, but I doubt that the world as a whole modifies very much over time. That great Dark Age that we speak of was the Age of Illumination in India and Arabia.

So in spite of what's going on in Somalia, Bosnia, the Middle East, the AIDS epidemic, you're not pessimistic about the future?

I am essentially an optimist. I have to be. If you look at what's happened to me, how could I be otherwise? With that said, however, the events of the last ten years have slowed my optimism. The triumph of capitalism over Communism, or freedom over tyranny, is overshadowed by the way they are screwing up the aftermath. That's the basic human condition.

One would have thought that with the breakup of the Soviet Union Eastern Europe would have celebrated new freedoms instead of turning on each other.

Man is so goddamn perverse. After you live under Communism for seventy years and you know that it's false, then when you get free the first thing you want to do is bash your neighbor in the head. What's happening in Moldavia and Romania and what was Yugoslavia—it's so regressive, so meaningless.

You experienced that kind of turmoil firsthand when you wrote The Bridge at Andau *in 1956.*

A very vivid period of my life in Hungary. During the Russian invasion, we helped Hungarians get visas, got Jews to shave their beards and not use any Jewish words; it's probably the thing I'm most proud of. Almost everywhere I go in the world, if word circulates that I'm there, some Hungarian will come to see me and will tell me that he was one of them that I brought out.

You once predicted the breakup of the Soviet Union would occur but not until midway into the next century. How surprised were you when it happened in this decade?

The speed at which Communism culminated took me by complete shock. For the last twenty-five years I have been on one or another commission that fought Communism. We were very effective behind the Iron Curtain, especially from Munich. But I take no pleasure in seeing it end this way, with this confusion. The trouble in Georgia, the fighting between the Armenians and their opponents. I was sick about Gorbechev's fall. Then I remembered the end of the last war when Winston Churchill, who almost personally kept the honor and integrity and drive of the British together long before we got in the war, when they were really on the ropes, and yet come '45 the Brits no longer wanted him. Christ, they took Clement Atlee because they knew intuitively that the day of Churchill was gone and they needed something else.

Do you think the Chinese suspected Nixon's downfall when he visited China in 1972? You accompanied Nixon on that trip—how well do you remember it?

Perhaps the Chinese had given this some thought when Nixon first went to China. Bill Buckley and I were the last two men on the plane that accompanied the president. And we saw the Chinese leadership treating Mr. Nixon very poorly. There was nobody out to meet him, no acceptance. A few weeks before, the emperor of Ethiopia had been there, and the leadership turned out the whole city for him. Then they put some powerhouse people on Buckley to find out what he was thinking and two on me, the equivalent of the head of the Associated Press. Buckley had especially warned them and I did more privately and maybe more forcefully that if this continued we were going to play the Russian card. That was the phrase we used. Meaning that you could rebuff us if you wanted to but that threw us into the arms of Russia.

But Nixon recovered from that bad start and had a triumph in China.

Didn't you also go with Nixon to Russia?

Yes. Again, I was his last man on the plane. We went to Russia, to Iran, to Poland. He wasn't quite as conspicuous in his success there. But he did a lot of good waking them up to the fact that he was pretty much where Kennedy had been in the Cuban crisis.

Weren't you involved in some altercation with the Soviet ministry of culture that led to your being thrown out of a bi-cultural meeting?

I had a big fight with Ekaterina Furtseva, one of the dictators of Russian culture, when I was there with Nixon. It was one of the crucial events of my life. I could not take the nonsense that this woman was promulgating about Russian-American cultural relations and about the Jews. I challenged this woman and either left or got thrown out of the meeting, I have never known which. I think they were about to throw me out and I may have beat the gun by a few seconds. It was quite a fiery moment.

What is it about the Jews that creates so much hatred?

I just cannot get into focus why so much of the world has persecuted or debased the Jewish people. Look at what happened in the Desert War. The Palestinians sided with Saddam Hussein and they prayed for our defeat, they cheered when they bombed Tel Aviv, and yet at the end we made Israel the enemy and the Palestinians the heroes. I think that ninety-five percent of Americans are that way, against Israel and for the Arabs. That's the biggest irrationality.

Even on American campuses there are ads being run in the college newspapers saying that the Holocaust never happened.

When I was in college there were quotas against Jews in medical schools. I got to know more American Jews in Scotland when I studied there than I did in the United States because sixty percent of the students in the four Scottish medical schools were American Jews. It was one of the great national disgraces, far more serious than the chance incarceration of the California Japanese during World War II, though I still can't get *that* one out of my mind.

Discrimination, of course, is something you've covered in many of your books, including the problem of apartheid in South Africa. Did its official disappearance meet your own timetable?

When I left South Africa the first time I visited, I said that the white people could get away with their domination through the rest of this century. The Boers, that is the Afrikaners, were too powerful and had all the guns. If things go poorly as they have been, it will end in disaster before the end of this century. Of course, one says that in relation to Libya, Angola, Zaire, Mozambique and Zimbabwae.

The population in South Africa is one of the best in the world. The blacks are an utterly superior group of people, and the whites are a mixture of highly educated and skilled English and Dutch, and one certainly has got a right to assume that they can unravel their problems. The trouble comes when the rednecks in the back country try to prevent it from being done.

The ultimate manifestation of apartheid was Soweto. For a white policeman to stop a black woman and ask for her pass when she'd moved through a part of South Africa in which her ancestors had lived for a thousand years was so preposterous it was painful—creating an illusion that the blacks were inferior second-class citizens.

So I did not expect to see South Africa turn into a one-man, one-vote free democracy in my lifetime. I was one of the most surprised observers of the South African scene, to see the marvelous way in which de Klerk and Mandela have been able to bury old animosities and begin new lives for their nation. The country's transition was a highlight of this last decade.

Still, after Nelson Mandela defeated Frederik W. de Klerk for president, they disagreed on the scope of legal exemptions for apartheid-era crimes, with Mandela calling de Klerk a joke.

That's to be expected.

Do you think we've seen an end to blacks being considered inferior second-class citizens there?

No. South Africa will develop much the way that Brazil has. Brazil claims to be a non-racial state, but when I was there on various visits I saw that at the higher levels blacks and whites did not intermingle very much. I found no blacks in any commanding positions in universities or business. But, I must admit, there was no social prejudice. It was just that the two races kept apart, and I think that will probably be the case in South Africa.

What do you think is the biggest problem Mandela faces?

The big problem will be Mandela's ability to satisfy the aspirations of his black people. After all, they have been so badly underrepresented in South African managerial life that it will be some time before that can be corrected; and patience of the blacks might begin to run out. But he is a clever man and the Boers are brilliant in many ways, and together they may be able to solve the problem.

Another African hot spot is Rwanda—the genocide committed by the Hutus against the Tutsis. What are your thoughts about that human tragedy?

I traveled the borders of Rwanda, got over the line a couple of times and wrote it off as a sad result of Belgian rule during a short period of its history. I am taken completely by surprise and do not fully understand the terrible animosity between the two branches of the black race that are competing in Rwanda and Burundi.

Another trouble spot is Northern Ireland. How do you come to grips with that one?

I must get twenty letters a year begging me to go there and write about that. That we could have a religious war after all these years. It's such a horrible scar on human society. A week before the pope was shot in Rome he sent his personal emissary, a priest I know, a very bright Irishman, to Northern Ireland to try to persuade the terrorists in that stricken country, Catholic and Protestant alike, to lay down their arms. The man got nowhere. John Paul's own people continued to shoot up the countryside. I have worried that if either side dominated overwhelmingly, it would create reverberations in cities with very heavy Catholic/ Protestant divisions like Glasgow in Scotland, Birmingham and Liverpool in England. It's so terrible that I decided not to go and write about it.

A ceasefire in Belfast was the result of Clinton's visit, but it didn't last. Think there's any chance of that working?

I sympathize with the people in North Ireland, but when I look at their leaders, like Ian Paisley, there's no one to even touch him, let alone support them. It's too much. I don't think the ceasefire in the Near East, in Ireland, or in Bosnia will hold. Human beings are lethal in their hatreds. When we occupied Japan at the end of WWII, there was not a single murder of an American, except in brawls over girls—no revenge. I remember talking with a colonel who had led the fight against the U.S. and asked how could this be. He said, 'We just decided it was game, set, and match. And we just changed.' That was one of the miracles in my lifetime. I don't see that in Ireland or in Bosnia.

Well, at least the Irish voters finally overturned the ban on divorce.

High time. That's been a terrible imposition there. Divorce shouldn't be easy, but it ought to be available. I can sympathize, but that's carrying the dictates of religion a little too far.

So you don't think there's much hope for the peace treaty to hold in Bosnia?

It's a marvelous try and I applaud it. It could be a step in reaching some kind of balance.

We've got 20,000 troops there, of the 60,000 sent in.

That's a jungle, God, the different groups.

Those different groups came to the world's attention with the splitting of Czechoslovakia and of Yugoslavia after the breakup of the Soviet Union. Do we take sides in these new nations' attempts at redefining boundaries?

I've always been suspicious of Czechoslovakia. It was never a very solid country. I'm not surprised it fractured. Go back to about 1500, when that area was in great turmoil and ruled by a succession of pretty damned incompetent kings. The Turks infiltrated the area to get rid of the Greek-Orthodox Catholics and the Norman Catholics to the north. The Turks were monsters, but they got a foothold in present Bosnia, and those people, instead of fighting Turkey, converted to Islam. The hatred between the Serbs and the Muslims started from that period and has not died down. And in Yugoslavia, I feel the American sympathy for Croatia is misguided. We're doing it because Croatia is Roman Catholic and Serbia is Greek Catholic. Serbia is also strongly socialistic, Croatia is not. So it's understandable that there would be this drift toward Croatia, but to justify that you have to close your eyes to the fact that in World War II Croatia was one of the infamous countries of the world, created by Hitler as an independent state between 1941–45 as one of his stooges. They murdered Serbs, Jews, gypsies; they voluntarily sided with Hitler against all the freedom movements. The Roman Catholic cardinal at the time was especially terrible in leading his people on their pro-Hitlerian rampage. But being friends with Serbia today is equally ridiculous. She has behaved poorly—the bombing of Dubrovnik is just unacceptable, and her ethnic cleansing in Bosnia is unalloyed Nazism. However, you don't embrace the Croatians because of Serbia's misbehaviors.

It would be in the interest of the world if Serbia controlled the whole area, but that's not popular to say in light of Serbia's very bad behavior. It's a real witches' brew.

Each time a nation divides or changes governments it alters its own history. How does this affect a writer of historical fiction, especially a writer who lives in the changing country?

I think that nations sort of begin anew every twenty-five years. In the late sixties the French government had a program for people like me who might be able to do France some good—to teach us French. I learned French six weeks after I started this intense drill. The point I want to make is, in order to do it, I tried learning the way a French child would. I got from the French library fifth, sixth, and seventh-grade history lessons in French. Now, you talk about chauvinistic. There was only one country: France. In one lesson, the family goes to an American-style cafeteria, and the father refuses to eat there. He says, "No Frenchman would eat at a place like this. We eat in restaurants, we sit down where a table is covered, food is important to us." And the kids all streak out of the cafeteria and go to an honest French restaurant. And it was all that way. You were aware that there was an England, but they never accomplished anything. No English writer or artist or musician or anyone. I imagine if I had studied German, it would be the same thing.

When one of the V.J. days was celebrated, the French government brought out a beautiful poster celebrating the recapture of Paris in 1945. Into Paris marches General DeGaulle supported by a French general, a French engineer with blueprints, three or four ranks of French soldiers, and way in the back a rather scruffy-looking American, and off to the side an even scruffier-looking Englishman. They are the people who freed France. It was infuriating! DeGaulle convinced France that at the height of the crisis, they drove the Germans out. And the point I'm making is, if you say this nationally, then that's what happened. This is what the French have agreed upon as the history of that period. That their brave resistance troops recaptured Paris, drove out the Germans, and there were some Americans around and a few Englishmen. Societies do that. Nations need to renew themselves.

The U.S. has also played its part in rewriting the history of war-defeated nations.

That's true. The United States helped West Germany and Japan with their tremendous economic growth by assuming responsibility for their military. It gave their economic base a chance to proliferate and has placed a very heavy responsibility on us. We have had to tax ourselves heavily to pay for them.

Earlier I brought up your letter to me after you had been to Poland. How did you know that was going to be a hot spot when you decided to write your book about that country?

I knew that Poland was going to be in the news, I didn't know in what way. The fact that Lech Walesa came along and Pope John Paul II came along were purely accidental.

In '81, I was in every corner of Poland. I knew that the Russians were going to move in within a week. But they surprised us by not moving in, instead allowed General Wojciech Jaruzelski to play their battle for them, holding them off to keep them from really occupying the country. But the true believer wasn't willing to grant that. And the Pope, being a true believer, knocked Jaruzelski down terribly. I rubbed the Pope the wrong way by prematurely praising Jaruzelski.

You knew the Pope when he was a cardinal. What's your opinion of him?

The Pope is a sharpie, though I find him a very confusing man. He's a very conservative theologian and very liberal socially. That's a curious mix. The Polish Church was the most conservative on earth. If you were a Pole and were going to lay your life on the line by remaining a Catholic, you didn't want a watered-down version, you wanted the old fire-and-brimstone. Karol Wojtyla was the epitome of this. But he's a real operator, a real strong man—a pragmatist in politics and an idealist in doctrine.

Like many great men he's been through fire, he's been hardened, tempered. He has a great sense of humor and a wonderful wit. He's great at one-line jokes, many of which were political in nature. And after every session it was, 'How did I do?' I've seen him a number of times in the Vatican and we've always talked about television and the media. He knows how to use the media better than any preceding occupant of the chair, except perhaps Pope John XXIII, who did it in a different way.

Does he also know what you think about the Church today?

The Church is in very great trouble. I believe we're in a Copernican age when a great, great many things are up for redefinition and reallocation. And at any such time any conserving agency—and the Church is one—plays a very valuable role in telling everyone to go slow. And it plays a negative role in sometimes trying to stop what is happening. Any outsider who sits in the papal chair also sits with an Italian Curia around him that is extremely powerful, extremely conservative, extremely patient. I don't think any Pole is going to whip that Curia into line easily. This is a planned policy of great brilliance. And this pope has a very clear vision of what his position and his potential is within the Vatican.

He also must be a hell of a salesman. Knopf paid $6 million just for the U.S. rights to his book, Crossing the Threshold of Hope.

I read a few excerpts. It's a nothing book. But my God, what press.

Did you see that the pope said you can't rule out evolution?

I did. It was the proper thing to say. He's no dummy. It's a break with Church doctrine, but then John XXIII broke with Church doctrine.

Did you think Lech Walesa would lose his presidency to an ex-Communist, Aleksander Kwasniewski, in Poland?

Yes. I know one of his closest advisors and had a long conversation with him recently. They have been unhappy about his behavior as a spoiled brat. It hasn't been dignified.

The vote in Poland was said to be more of a rejection of him than a desire to return to the Communist past.

I can see these countries wanting to return to the Communist past, just as the people in the South wanted to return to antebellum days. That is a very alluring invitation. The tensions of freedom hit every room in the house, the kitchen, the workshop.

You've been a close observer of leadership around the world. Are there many heads-of-state who turned out better than you suspected they would?

Olof Palme of Sweden, Indira Ghandi of India, and DeGaulle of France—they may have been exactly the people that their countries needed at that time, irritating though they may have been. I found Israel's Menacham Begin an anachronism, and I think Israel suffered a tremendous psychological setback when they chose Moshe Dayan and Begin as their heroes to present on the international stage. But I felt the opposite about Anwar Sadat of Egypt. He had a degree of courage greater than any I've ever exhibited. He had to go up against the kind of volatile opinion that eventually destroyed him.

It seems that, whenever there's a move toward peace in the Middle East, it gets sabotaged. Even after Arafat shook hands with Rabin in front of the White House, Arab and Jewish extremists continued their reign of terror.

The continuing events in the Middle East between Arab and Jew have dampened my optimism that they may one day get along. It is strange that these two Semitic races should be such mortal enemies. However, subterraneously, there is a very lively interchange between these peoples. If you're a political leader in one of the Arab states and your wife gets glaucoma, you call a secret number and that night she's spirited into a Hadassah hospital, where she's treated. Then, the next day, those same Arab leaders are firing statements again about what they're going to do to Israel. But that's mostly for local consumption.

How surprised were you to see the Palestinians get control of Jericho and the Gaza Strip?

Considerably. I did not think that there was enough social pressure in Israel to make this possible. I am delighted with the way the warring groups are tentatively getting together. But future relationships between the Palestinians, the Jordanians, the Israelis, the Iraqis and the Saudis are muddy. Any time you have a sovereign state in two separate portions you're asking for very serious trouble. Pakistan tried it; it didn't work. That's the problem between the Azerbaijanis and the Armenians, two separated enclaves. There is little likelihood that the Palestinians will line up with the Jordanians as they ought to, so I expect them to be an agitating thorn in the entire area.

The terrorist group Hamas has certainly made any peace overtures difficult for the Palestinians and Israel. Yasir Arafat, who shared the Nobel Peace Prize, was stoned by the new terrorists, who don't want to give in at all.

Yeah, he's in tough trouble. It's that Churchill/Atlee switch again. And you can't project yourself into their shoes.

It's almost miraculous that Arafat hasn't been assassinated.

Well, King Hussein has been a target for forty years, and he's survived. But anything can happen in that area.

Including a Jewish zealot murdering Rabin.

Self-righteous religious right-wingers are the enemy of society. They do terrible things, wrapped in the cloak of righteousness.

Syria has lauded Israeli Prime Minister Shimon Perez's vow for peace. Do you think Syria and Israel will ever live peacefully?

Syria is much tougher than I would have expected. Hafez al-Assad's a brute.

That's probably what the Arab world thinks of Israel's Prime Minister Benjamin Netanyahu. What's your take on him?

I think he's a tonic. I'm glad to see him. He's what Israel needed to bring some sense into that situation. People forget he was educated in America.

He's taking a lot of strong stands; some say they're on the verge of war again.

They're on the verge of war twenty-four hours a day. You sweat it out.

So you don't think Israel should give up any land?

I personally don't, but I don't think I would say so publicly.

What's going on there does make one feel there will never be peace in the Middle East.

We're going to face a world confrontation with Islam, because they demand it. A petty minority is all that is needed. Ten percent can really wreck the place. And an obsessive patriot can upset a hell of a lot of apple carts.

Are we seeing that kind of minority wrecking Mexico? In 1994, along with the election of a new president and the devaluation of the peso, there was the Indian uprising in Chiapas, the assassination of Luis Colosio, and then the PRI Secretary General Jose Francisco Ruiz Massieu, and the resurgence of drug violence and kidnappings for ransom. What's going on there?

Mexico is a mystery. I used to live there. They've had this national revolution party in office for the last fifty years, and it's ridiculous, because they're right-wing conservatives. Every year they meet to reaffirm their belief in the Mexican Revolution and they think of themselves as a revolutionary country. Mexico has all the advantages that the U.S. and Canada have, but they have been unable to find a way to spread the riches of the country to the country. They really have been incredibly stupid to fail to solve that simple problem, which other nations like Australia, New Zealand, Canada, the U.S. solved so relatively easily. And it grows worse. All the money goes to wealthy people, none to the workers. Just ridiculous.

Is it also ridiculous that Norway doesn't want to join Europe? For the second time in twenty-two years they voted against membership in the European Union. Does that surprise you?

I'm amazed at that. There may be a right-wing no- nothingism free in the world that hits everything.

Well, France rejoined NATO and finally stopped their nuclear testing in the South Pacific.

They're a hard country to fathom.

Can you understand what's going on in Nigeria, where the government ordered the executions of nine activists?

That's shameful.

Isn't there anything the world can do to stop such immoral and infuriating behavior?

You can never outlaw the outlaw behavior of an outlaw group. They can do it anytime they want to.

What about the immoral behavior of England's Prince Charles, where he admitted to having an affair while still married to Diana?

Compared to the analogy with Edward VII, he behaved pretty well. Edward VII faced the same problem, the Queen Mother refused to accept it, and he was left drifting. Same results. Charles is a paradigm of virtue compared with Edward.

There's not much virtue among the Taliban rebels in Afghanistan, which has taken over a great deal of the country.

That's one of the biggest mistakes of my life. I allowed myself to be chairman of the committee helping the Afghanis who were exiled in Pakistan. And I did not foresee that if they won they were going to be exactly like Khomeini's people in Iran. I was very stupid about that.

How great a mistake would it have been had Quebec voted to break away from Canada?

I'm very pessimistic about that. The superpatriots will build a majority, maybe in the next election. But the rest of Canada is not going to take that muscular behavior of Ontario. It leaves the Atlantic Coast provinces unattached to the main body of Canada. It's very similar to Pakistan, and those bizarre arrangements don't last. If Quebec does go ahead with this, which they might even in this century, I would expect an ultimate drift of the eastern provinces to the U.S. And there's always the problem of the western provinces getting fed up and having their affiliation southward to the U.S. We don't want it, they don't want it, but that's going to be the drift.

If you have a son in Manitoba, he cannot get a job in the post office, or any government agency, unless he speaks French. That's absolutely insane. If he has political aspirations, he would be wise to learn French. But not if he's just going to be an ordinary citizen. No, that's a time bomb.

When historians look back on the twentieth century will it be dubbed the American century?

Our behavior from 1941 on converted this century into the American century. The first part of the century, I think, belonged to Karl Marx. But from '41 on our behavior was pretty impeccable. It's certainly drifted off now. We have paid less attention to the values of our society than we should have. When I was young, I had hardly a negative experience. Nobody wanted to give me drugs. Nobody wanted to con me. Nobody assaulted me sexually. Nobody wanted me to become an alcoholic or a gambler. I had moral support and I knew it. But the young person doesn't have that today.

So what does your crystal ball tell you about America?

I am quite confident that we are good until about the year 2050. I think we can absorb the errors and we can absorb the civil disturbances and we can absorb defeats as we did with Vietnam. After that, I'm not so sure.

The societies which have been exceptional have been extremely indigenous and homogeneous, they have had a very strong central, cultural, ethical, and moral set. Greece would be a marvelous prototype. Not Rome, I've never had a high opinion of Rome. Medieval France, yes. Bismarck's Germany, yes. Maybe the most distinguished after Greece would be England of 1750 to 1940. I don't see the United States in that pattern. I see a new rule operating of a heterogeneous society which has developed some kind of glue to keep it together where others have not, and it may be that that's our genius and that we will continue to invent new kinds of glue to keep the hodgepodge together. Otherwise, we might be in very serious trouble. Fifty years from now Japan could still be a well-codified, well-organized state with a central drive and a central intelligence, and Germany could be the same. The United States, because of our peculiar structure, might be fragmented.

So it's a homogeneous country like Japan that will dominate the next century?

Many years ago I concluded that Japan and the United States differed in this respect: Japan was a homogeneous country—very resilient, very powerful, with high vertical integration. And the United States was composed of fragments which might fly apart at any moment. I thought this when Japan was at the bottom, during one of the great adventures of my life, when I went to Japan alone, traveled all over, got a feeling of the country which led to *Sayonara*. So I am not a Johnny-come-lately on this, I have written about it and thought about it a great deal. Japan is reborn every quarter of a century, and they can do anything. Who the hell knows, they might even align with China.

China certainly does loom large on the horizon.

The Chinese are one of the most formidable and marvelous people that have ever developed. They're strong, they're resilient, they have brains. And, curiously enough, they are willing to go about things slowly. They absorb everybody who comes their way. We in this country often think of the Ming emperors, but they were outlaws, they were not Chinese. All they did was remain in total control for about three or four hundred years, and they passed. They didn't have any sticking qualities. True, they were in control about a hundred years longer than the United States has existed, but in Chinese terms, that's a very brief time. I have infinite respect for the Chinese. And neither Japan nor China faces the kind of internal problems that we do.

Let's talk about some of our problems. The race issue may be just as troubling now as it was during slavery.

Recent reports are very disturbing: that black youths die earlier, often at their own hands; that they don't have the sense of self-respect that whites are allowed to have; that their family pattern is under terrible stress.

Racism is a deep and profound malaise and will always be with us. And it will take wildly different forms. Look at David Duke in Louisiana. When he ran for governor he got some forty percent of the vote in an area where there was a powerful black minority who automatically voted against him. What's he, or someone like him, going to do in some place like Montana, where there isn't that dominant black minority? I'm very scared of that one. Preaching hate is very popular.

Do you remember the killings of all those black children in Atlanta in 1981? They convicted a young black man but I always believed there was a group of people unrelated, each jumping on the bandwagon for the hell of it, motivated by common racial sickness. The media played up the killings and that extreme publicity attracted kooks on their own. What baffled and staggered me about that one was that the kids who were done in were exactly the kind of kid that I was at that age: broken home, no father, drifting around, very self-oriented. One kid worked at the supermarket for $20 a day. Well, that was the kind of boy I was. I had experiences with a thousand people, to think that any one of them could have been so sick as to do me in gives me great pause.

What positive signs do you see among the races?

In certain conspicuous areas there has been improvement: appointing blacks to offices and electing them in free elections; providing scholarships and giving them a real education; and in the military the role of the black is much better. Though not so much in the space program where, right from the start, if you panned the cameras at the great group that's supervising in Houston, they all look exactly like me. Not a black face, not a Chicano, not a woman. To get in that room, all you have to do is have an A– in engineering, do well at M.I.T. or Cal Tech or Stanford or Louisiana State or Purdue, have five years of intensive research in aviation. And the blacks? Any good black doesn't want to be an airline pilot, he wants to be a manager of Sears Roebuck or someplace like that.

Or thinking about becoming the next Barry Bonds or Toni Morrison.

In sports and the arts, all a black has to be is as handsome and as gifted as Harry Belafonte or Lena Horne or as fine an athlete as Barry Bonds or Michael Jordan and he has no problems. It's a really disgraceful commentary that we should have structured it so these were the only outlets they had. So overall I'm very pessimistic about it. God help the poor slob in a nine-to-five job at a filling station—he's the guy that's in trouble. Of course, that represents 99.7% of the black population. Ronald Reagan was elected more than a dozen years ago in strong part by a white backlash against the gains that blacks had made. There's still a strong Ku Klux Klan element in our society, usually hidden but certainly surfacing now more than ever before. I think the behavior of the blacks right now is extremely perilous, because the rap groups and many of the philosophers are really calling for an all-out racial war. And when that happens they've got to be the losers.

Race has figured into many of your books, though it's not something critics often highlight.

In all of my books I've testified to the fact that people of different skin color and nationalities and religions can be delightful people. But any society which negates or diminishes the contribution of a large segment of its people is in serious trouble. That's basically my attitude on race, though I'm not completely faultless. When I first married Mari I was in the habit of using the word "Jap," which is a perfectly splendid invention. It's short, it's accurate, it takes up little space in a headline, it's completely definitive. It seems an ideal word to me. She told me, "You know, we don't like that word because of the way William Randolph Hearst used it to crucify us." I kept using it and she said again, "We don't like that word because it was used so pejoratively throughout California to throw us in jail." I used it a third time and she said, "If you ever use that word again, I'm going to take a ketsup bottle and knock out the rest of your teeth." Then I understood.

Besides racism, what else troubles you?

What I have been thinking about lately is the diminishing of American productive capacity and skill, which is quite frightening, and the decline of education, which is very sad. The lower-middle group, they aren't going to get jobs if this keeps up.

We are going to have to face the fact that we're going to have a permanent unemployed group. And we must figure out some way to distribute goods to them and keep them in the purchasing circle. We just cannot put them off to one side as non-participating citizens. We don't have enough jobs, apparently, nor will we have in the foreseeable future, to employ them all, because our machines are so tremendously effective that we can produce all we need with maybe 75% or even less of our workforce.

We are becoming a consumer nation rather than a producing nation. We think we can run this great country on hot dog stands and electronics from Japan and shoes from Italy. What are we making ourselves?

Are there other countries we can look to for inspiration?

Back in 1949 it was obvious to me that Japan was going to buckle down and reorganize, though I was surprised that the Toyota company developed into the great company of today. At that time they had little cars with a small stove that burned charcoal where the gas tank would be. And the fumes from the charcoal ran the car! But very little else surprised me about Japan.

So is the answer then to study Japan?

If I were a young man interested in the things that I've been interested in all my life, I would study England now more than Africa, or Islam or South America, simply to find out what will happen, and what might happen here. I'd start the most intensive study of Great Britain to see where they are, what they're doing, what trends are afoot, where they've gone wrong, where they've succeeded. Because we are fated to follow them at a lapse of about eight or nine years. If you look at the way Britain handled the great Leyland motor company and the horrible mistakes they made with them, you'd find that we did exactly the same with Chrysler and Ford. The only differences between the companies are that labor has a stronger hold in Britain than here and that we do not have a highly structured caste system in our country compared to India or England.

Are the roots of our problems the schools and the lack of quality education in public schools?

In state after state there are terrible stories coming out about education. Cutting education. Some towns even refusing to pay teachers' salaries even to keep the schools open. There is a weakness in resolve. And then there are these goddamn lotteries which are supposed to bring more money into the schools— appalling that governments would tolerate the despots and sponsor them. The money does go to education. But then the legislature cuts back that same amount from what the citizens should be paying through taxation. So the education comes out poorer— actually, they cut more than they get, or they get less than they cut. It's smoke and mirrors of the worst damn type. It just infuriates me!

I've taught all my life—every grade from kindergarten through the post-doctorate at Harvard and elsewhere. Education is terribly important to me. And schools are in worse shape than when I went to them. The top students that I meet are as good as I ever was. But the great middle group, the workers of the nation, they are in decline, if not fallen. They are way below what they were in my day. *Way* below. Our nation is in great danger.

What happened to our school system? You certainly are a product of a strong and healthy education. So am I. Can we ever get back to the way it was?

When I was a young man, the teachers wanted the students to do well; the students wanted to excel; the administration supported the teachers; the parents also supported the system; and so did the courts. There was no way of going into court and taking court action against a teacher because he disciplined a child. The community wanted you to be good. Today, the courts have played a terribly negative role in this, taking all power away from the schools and giving it to anybody who wants to bring the most trivial complaints, like getting a court order to protest a low grade. The courts have intruded into the conduct of educational institutions to the point where you're not allowed to flunk a student or hold him back or deny him a diploma anymore, although in adult life you get flunked every day. I wouldn't put up with that for one day, which is probably why I'd be fired at the end of the first week.

I don't think I could teach in a high school today where I'd have to be afraid that the student was going to slug me. Because if I'm not free to strike a student, certainly the student is not free to strike me. What this says is that there is an irreducible number of students who ought not to be in school. No matter what the law says, or what kind-hearted people say, they ought to throw them out.

Where will those troubled kids go?

I'm strongly in favor of alternative education, but I would not allow them to be in school and disrupt the learning of the serious kids.

I have felt in recent years that maybe the permissible leaving age ought to be fourteen. There are a lot of kids in school who should be allowed to drop out of the academic system, enter schools that teach technical competence—learn the restaurant business or how to be a repairman or a mechanic.

Are our colleges any better than our high schools?

The first two years of college and university are now little more than advanced high school. A lot of the smaller colleges are going under—probably a hundred of them have already closed and about three hundred more should close.

If you were in charge of education in this country, what changes would you make?

I would have free admission to every college. Then I would have a protracted freshman year. By the entrance to the sophomore year the student should be totally capable of competing with you and your cousin Victor and the bright girl from Sioux City. It might take one year, it might take three. There should be financial help, as well as every kind of academic help, so that the freshman year would be an accordion-type thing. But at the end of that he would fit right into the mainstream and we would have a splendid system.

As someone who has spent a lot of time on campuses is there anything you've seen that has encouraged you?

At the University of Texas recently there were a lot of kids on campus and a scruffier lot I never saw! But they had energy, they had enthusiasm, and the good ones were taking three books home from the library. I had great hopes for that group, but the rest I'm worried about. When I go into a classroom these days I say I will not read any of your papers unless they are typed as if you were submitting them to a New York publisher or magazine.

I automatically assume that anyone taking a writing class had done moderately well in their English studies, including sentence structure and vocabulary. I would not be at all impressed if a would-be writer said she got an A in English at Smith or at the University of Chicago. Anybody ought to be able to do that. But I could get very excited if the girl said: 'I've studied architecture and I have a feeling for form and I see how they build these buildings, how you put certain things forward and other things back and this balances that and you don't want it totally symmetrical.' I would say now that kid is really thinking about what art is. And you can get it in any subject—science, tennis, psychology. I would think that I suffered from not having good courses in psychiatry, learning the analysis of weakness, for instance.

But someone who wanted to be a writer should also have interests in other fields, history, theology, or the age of exploration.

With layoffs happening in every profession and job insecurity probably at an all-time high, how important is work for work's sake?

The work of the world is done by a very small percentage of the population. We'd better protect that group or our society is really in jeopardy. I don't see how you can have a major city unless you have people in there who know about sewage disposal, food supply, medicine, government, taxation.

That second tier of capable, tested, proved workmen, male or female—they are where we're falling way behind.

Are you a strong advocate of rigorous testing to certify academic excellence?

What disturbs me in the intellectual field is the program of Ralph Nader's to do away with all external testing and evaluations of human behavior. Nader must have had his head in a pickle barrel to come up with it because he knows that the life he leads and the life he wants other people to lead is drawn on the basis of very severe external testing and evaluation. The IQ tests have a predictive value in identifying those people who can do well in math, chemistry, English, and the handling of abstract ideas. I do not want to see this stopped.

Where do you stand on bilingual education?

One of the worst things that could have happened to our education system is enforced bilingual education. It is wrong. If allowed to continue it would insure that we create rather than inherit a situation probably much worse than Canada's with its linguistic minorities or Belgium or Cyprus or India.

I've looked into this in the Hispanic systems. The temptation of the teachers is two-fold. One, to make the class a constant attack on the American system: that we are unfair to Hispanics, that we don't give them a fair chance. The other is they have a vested interest in keeping the kids from learning anything, in keeping the kids in a linguistic ghetto. Their jobs depend upon it.

If you are, by bad luck, historically a bilingual nation, well, you're stuck with that. God did that. But geez, to introduce it yourself with a law is just an invitation to separatism.

Did you know that Bob Dole, before he left the Senate to run for president, called for the ending of most bilingual classes?

Did he? I'm glad to hear that. I'll be damned. The tragedy of Dole was that he was easy to respect but hard to love.

Back to bilingualism. Is this something that only the Supreme Court can stop?

What has happened is the terrible decline in the quality of the Supreme Court. There's nobody of any reputation, there's no leader there, there's nobody speaking to the great tenets of law. Maybe there will be some revulsion as there was in the 1930's against the nine old men. Now we have the "nine stupid men."

So the Court is a source of disappointment to you?

I think the Supreme Court is almost failing to serve its primal function. The only thing that gives me hope is when I look back at someone like Justice Black, who was once an avowed Ku Klux Klanner. But when a larger horizon was opened up to him, he was equal to it and he became one of the great adornments of the bench.

So there's still hope for Clarence Thomas?

To think of that man on the Court for the next fifty years . . . Jesus Christ! Justice Clarence Thomas's free speech decision was so dead right-wing, so anti-labor and anti-freedom, it's terrifying.

I assume you were glued to Thomas's confirmation hearings.

What happened during Thomas's confirmation hearings, which came shortly after the rape trial of William Kennedy

Smith, was a disturbing glimpse into power and privilege. One set of values emotionally were all with the woman, Anita Hill; and the same people who were strongly in favor of her, in the Kennedy trial were strongly in favor of him. Though in my opinion young William Kennedy Smith was a worm—you see something that you think of behind the floorboards. He was repulsive to me. But it shows how volatile public opinion can be. Miss Hill was probably telling the truth and she was an abused woman, and the other woman was not telling the truth and was rather a pretty shady character.

Are you aware of the book Strange Justice: The Selling of Clarence Thomas? *And that the* N.Y. Times *condemned him as the "youngest, cruelest justice."*

Yes. The thing that I cannot tolerate is the fact that that son-of-a-bitch is denigrating his own sister who stayed out of college and worked as a waitress so he could go to college, and he ridiculed his own nephews, saying that all they did was hang around the post office. That is just intolerable. That disqualifies him as a decent man.

What do you think of Clinton's two choices for the Supreme Court: Ruth Bader Ginsburg and Stephen G. Breyer?

They were a hell of a lot better than Scalia and Thomas. But for a Democratic president to select them, after years of drought in Democratic appointments to the court, it depressed me. We should have had two men like Holmes, or Cardozo, or the great judges that Roosevelt sent up.

So you'd agree then with the L.A. Times that Judge Breyer and Judge Ginsburg appear to put President Clinton on the same path as his Republican predecessors, who sought to build a court more likely to adhere to the status quo than to boldly reshape the law or expand individual rights?

We have been marking time in the Clinton administration on this great point of balance between the three branches of the government. Bill had done nothing to establish a more honest balance. I hope he has two more appointments in his tenure and that he will take steps to correct those imbalances.

Are Ginsburg and Breyer inclined to make consensus rulings? And has the trend of the high court been to avoid dramatic decisions? Georgetown law professor Mark Tushnet spoke of "the downsizing of the Supreme Court" and the court's "avoiding the high-profile issues." Is he right?

Yes. The two new judges give every indication that they will avoid dramatic decisions and intellectually limit the court almost tragically.

One of the highest-profile issues is abortion. I know you're against it for personal reasons, but you don't think it should be the law of the land, do you?

I believe that women have to have the right to these things.

We've talked about America's problems regarding race, education, unemployment, abortion; what about another major problem for which there may not be a solution: violence?

I think it's ingrained, cherished, and beyond any possibility of being disciplined. Americans love violence in all its manifestations. With world soccer available, we prefer American-style slam-bang football. With the rich potential of television, we prefer gangster shows and auto chases. With traffic controllable, we seem to enjoy killing 50,000 people a year with our cars.

Then there are the abberrations, which seem to be becoming part of the American landscape—like the Jon-Benet Ramsey murder, or that young woman, Susan Smith, who made a plea on national television for the return of her two "kidnapped" toddlers, when in fact she had strapped them in her car and drove it into a lake.

I followed very carefully that case of the six-year-old beauty queen, Jon-Benet Ramsey. I think there was something extremely sexual there that hasn't come out. My guess is that the father might have been having some kind of relationship with the little girl, his wife discovered it and in a fury killed the girl. Whereupon he steps forward to take the responsibility. It is something like that. I wouldn't gamble on that particular orchestration, but it's something like that.

As for the Susan Smith case, I saw her on television several times, pleading with the "kidnappers" to let her have her two boys back. And she was terribly impressive. Your heart just went out to her. This poor woman, bereft in one shot of two sons. When she went on TV a fourth time, at 10 A.M. of the day in which late in the afternoon she was going to confess, that is behavior so damn bizarre I can't categorize it. It escalates onto a new level. I have a feeling it is something that you allow the forces of society to handle. I'm against the death penalty but I guess you have to have a loophole for the totally irrational case.

Do the forces of society allow for the prison murder of Jeffrey Dahmer, whose cannibalistic behavior no one condoned?

I am against the death penalty, because it is applied so unevenly and it's so prejudicial for black guys.

But, in recent years, there have been crimes so horrendous that are beyond rationalization. Dahmer falls into that category, as does the miserable son-of-a-bitch who raped a 14-year-old girl and cut off both her arms. When things like that happen, you sort of look the other way.

We also look the other way when it comes to passing sensible gun laws; we seem to prefer the spirit of the wild West.

I am against the proliferation of guns and the perpetuation of the American myth: that every man shall have a right to gun down any other man.

I've written with great affection about the great guns of early America, the Kentucky rifle and the Hawkens. But they were six feet long, not repeaters. I can see no reason in the world why repeating revolvers should be sold over-the-counter or carried freely by the populace.

When I lived in the west, states like Colorado, Wyoming and Idaho, they said they'd secede from the union before they gave up their guns. Autos carried bumper stickers, 'The West wasn't won with a registered gun.' I helped manage Senator Joe Clark's bid for reelection in 1968 and he made the fatal mistake of admitting that he thought it was improper for citizens to go around shooting each other. The gun lobby assassinated him.

Where were you when President Kennedy was assassinated?

I was in Israel. Friends had invited us to the evening services at their synagogue. I noticed that our friends were uptight, very subdued; they were looking at Mari and me very intently. When the service was over, they took me aside and said, "We have very disturbing news. Your president was murdered two hours ago."

You knew both Jack and Bobby Kennedy, didn't you?

I knew Kennedy well. I was his manager in Pennsylvania and campaigned heavily for him with Stan Musial and Arthur Schlesinger. And I took Bobby Kennedy around Pennsylvania when he came, he and I were buddy-buddy. Jack's personal life turned out to be pretty much of a scandal and I felt let down. When I heard the news of his assassination, I went back to our hotel and I typed a memo, as I often do, speculating on what had actually happened.

And did you think it was a conspiracy?

I said that there was a connivance of the agencies of government to get rid of this guy. I stipulated three or four groups that it might be. Later I saw that I had been hysterical and that my kind of guessing was not needed and I backed away from it completely.

Do you feel safer when you're traveling outside the U.S. or within its borders?

I have felt much safer overseas, where they don't have the tradition of gunning a guy down for the fun of it, than in my own country. I suppose one is much safer in South Africa or Spain or Israel than here. When I lived in Bucks County on one occasion the hunters shot right through our house. If I had been sitting at my desk the bullet would have gone right through my head. It's shocking—the figures on death by handguns should make anybody with any sense gasp. But what the hell are you going to do about it? America likes lawlessness, condones it within reason, and does not want to see it stopped.

Our history and our legends have deified the gun. It means something quite different to us from what it does to an Englishman or a Japanese. That's why our gun-murder rate is so fantastically higher than theirs. Guns to Americans are aphrodisiacs.

Men are macho when they have them. Women go bananas over the gunslinger. I used to argue that if England and Japan could control murder-by-gun so could we. Now I see things differently. Americans want their heroes to gun down the opposition, and I'd hate to be the United States marshal who invaded Texas or Kentucky to confiscate their guns. We've created this myth of the gun and I guess we'll have to live with it. Of course, if we gun down six or seven more presidents we just might change our attitudes, but I doubt even that.

What about organized crime?

Organized crime is terribly pervasive. We had a scandal in Washington where most of the pizza parlors are controlled by the Mafia through some very clever and imaginative control of the provolone and mozarella cheeses. And the Mafia seems to have taken over a lot of other things that we're not necessarily aware of.

After the bombings of the World Trade Center and the Federal Building in Oklahoma City, has terrorism finally come to America or were these isolated cases?

The threat from urban guerrillas makes a complex society like ours terribly vulnerable. A handful of people can disrupt it, and the brighter they are the more ingenious will be the destruction. In the late '60s, when I was writing *The Drifters*, urban guerrillas had not started, but I knew what was coming very clearly and had a pretty good fix on that. It's one of the most overlooked things I've written. I have a scene where the urban guerrilla comes to enlist a black student for a bombing party. I was already sixty years-old when I wrote that and it wasn't long after when urban guerrillas began changing countries like Italy.

Did you read the Unabomber's manifesto which the New York Times *published?*

His statement made sense. It tended to ramble. I understand the serial killer much more than I do the serial bomber. The serial bomber has to make the bomb, find a way of delivering it, cover his tracks.

Is nuclear energy another problem or part of some bigger solution?

There are certain categorical imperatives in life; one is that you have food and energy. I know something about atomic power and nuclear power and I am terrified by it, but I simply do not see it ending civilization. It may damn well end Detroit or Seattle, but not the entire world. Any source of power, including nuclear, should be very carefully explored.

Most of America's problems seem to be urban. Are big cities as we know them unlivable because they are too fractured?

New York today is definitely diminished, due to the heavy taxation, the insecurities, and the fact that decisions are being made elsewhere. The swing of society is throwing the leadership of the country into the hands of California, Texas, Florida and that arc. If you knew Harlem in the 1920's, it was so exciting to go up there and hear the new music and associate with people you would never meet in college: blacks, Catholics, Jews. Then to see Harlem deteriorate to the point where you can't even go there. . . .

It's how I feel about New Haven. The burden that Yale suffers from being there is really quite sad. When I was visiting there the head of one of the colleges said, "Michener, I saw you walking home. Please don't do that alone. Our secretary was walking from one building to another on campus and was caught and raped the other day." Now for a nice little 19-year-old girl to work at the heart of one of the great colleges of the world and not be safe to walk from one building to another is pretty shocking. Why we can't do anything about it just baffles me.

Does what happened to Orange County in California, where they filed for bankruptcy protection, also baffle you? It's the largest such bankruptcy in American history.

It's also terribly symbolic. Orange County may be one of the richest and most conservative counties in America, yet it allowed itself to be bamboozled by these phony investments.

It was smoke and dreams. And it's curious only because it involves such a broad piece of landscape. I don't know how they allowed it to happen. It must have been a unique combination of circumstances. Tremendous good luck at the beginning, and then everybody went in to get aboard. It's going to be billions! $8 billion was invested and they borrowed on that $12 billion—that's $20 billion!

Have you been following the passage of Proposition 187 dealing with illegal immigrants in California?

I look at 187 through the perspective of Miami, a hellhole of racial hatreds and malperformances. If I looked only at Miami, I would say that 187 was overdue. But as an active national policy, in which California presupposes, it has very powerful drawbacks.

Can there be a fair immigration policy in this country?

I've been a close friend of Alan Simpson and it seems that nothing can be done.

I had trouble with 187 because it denied health care and education to children of illegal immigrants.

I thought the Supreme Court handed down a ruling twenty years ago when this happened in Texas, saying that a child had these rights. But the bottom line is, if I lived in California I would have voted for it. Not living in California, I would not want to see it spread.

Another initiative that passed in California and Arizona in '96 was the medicinal use of marijuana. Were you surprised?

I was indeed. I think that's a hell of a way to conduct the medical stance of a nation—by popular vote! I don't think it will hold up constitutionally. At least I hope not.

Are there places in the U.S. which give you hope?

There are a few bright spots, none brighter than Annapolis, where the governing powers sold off the decrepit areas to young people who would undertake to resuscitate them. They have made this one of the most charming state capitals in the U.S. Wherever they have touched, the values have just skyrocketed. If I were a mayor of a city I would have an Urban Homestead Act tomorrow. I would sell off this real estate at a buck a house with stipulations as to what should be done. I would endeavor to do what Annapolis has done, and what San Antonio and Denver are in the process of doing.

Maybe the most encouraging thing I've seen, apart from Annapolis, is Minneapolis, where they said, 'Let's look at this crazy city of ours. In the winter it is unlivable and anybody who stays here ought to be certified as nuts. So let's take the downtown area and connect all the buildings on the second floor with ramps and runways.' The owner of the Miami Dolphins, Joe Robbie, who has been an employer there, says that from his office at noon he can go to forty good restaurants without putting on his coat.

**THE POLITICS & POLEMICS
OF THE LAST DIE-HARD LIBERAL**

12

You once ran for Congress, which you took pretty seriously, didn't you?

I have a very high sense of social responsibility. A writer doesn't write constantly; there are broad periods of time when he's doing other things. And I decided to run for Congress in 1962.

What would have happened had you won?

I suppose I would have served my five or six terms, and then in the big election of 1980 I would have been kicked out as being too liberal and I'd be about where I am now.

But would you have written Caravans, The Source, Iberia, Kent State, The Drifters, Centennial, Sports in America, Chesapeake, *or* The Covenant, *all from that period?*

Probably not. I must say I never took refuge in the fact that I might have been better off having not won. I was bitterly disappointed about losing. I wish I had won.

Even if that meant not having written the books which have made you who you are?

I would be willing to sacrifice my writing career to a political career. I place that very, very high on a scale of values, maybe the highest.

What did running for office teach you?

It showed me my own limitations. It also showed me that one had to learn how to balance one's own beliefs with other agendas and concerns.

On the Sunday before election day my opponent and I were campaigning in Allentown, Pennsylvania, to drum up votes. The Republican incumbent had never lost an election and he was determined not to lose this one. And the majority of those people didn't even know there was an election in two days, and those who did had no idea who their Congressman was. And they certainly didn't know anything about me.

It was a sobering day, that Sunday. I thought I had a chance of winning and when I lost I was pretty upset about it. It still bothers me.

I still find it hard to believe that you'd equate serving in Congress with creating the body of work you've created. What you've done seems to be so much more solid and permanent.

I look at my former neighbor, Richard Schweiker, and think he's playing just as important a role in American life as I ever did. I would have been happy to have been someone like him or like Indiana Congressman John Brademas, who left Congress to become president of N.Y.U. If I could have served the way Brademas did or the way Al Gore's father did, I think I would have left a glowing record. I knew Senator Gore moderately well. I served as the secretary to a commission that he chaired on what bases to hold onto in the South Pacific, and Gore was very impressive, first rate.

Who was the ablest leader you ever knew?

Chester Nimitz of the U.S. Navy during World War II. In public life, the ablest man I've worked with was Frank Stanton of CBS. Among the political leaders I had an enormous respect for Senator Fulbright of Arkansas.

You were sorry not to have been elected to Congress, but in retrospect, and in all honesty, can you really see it as a regret?

Although I tried hard enough to get it, I am sort of glad that I wasn't in an elected office, because I think the temptations would be so great and so omnipresent every day that sooner or later I would be trapped in some conflict of interest. I'm afraid that I would be caught in some stupid thing like somebody giving me fifteen CD's on grand opera worth about $35 each. That's five hundred and twenty-five bucks. I could see myself caught in that.

What about your wife, would she have been drawn to the perks of office as well?

I think Mari would have been especially vulnerable. She would have said, "Yes, my husband has one of the major jobs and I am his wife and it's entirely proper that I get a small fur coat."

Did your throwing your hat in the political ring politicize you in a way that changed your future?

As a result of my running for Congress I wound up serving as the Democratic leader in the Constitutional Convention which rewrote the laws of Pennsylvania. I lost every issue I fought for: cutting the size of the legislature, electing judges on a merit system, changing the way the justices of the peace were paid according to how many people they found guilty, taxing both the American Legion and the Church for property they didn't use for specific purposes. But they still appointed me the chairman of the very powerful committee that put the new laws into effect. I served on six government commissions for the State Department, the Postal Department, Voice of America, NASA. So it's good and proper to be at the center of things.

I was on a commission to reorganize a corner in the State Department. And another dealing with the supervision of the U.S.I.S. and all the cultural and intellectual operations abroad. For the Postal Department I was on the committee that commissioned Arthur Singer to create fifty separate drawings of the birds of each state on one sheet of stamps. That series was one of my prime sponsorships. I also voted against an Elvis stamp, but that came into being after I was gone.

And became the most successful stamp the post office ever issued. Did that give you pause?

No. It's a phenomenon that I will never understand. And it grows rather than diminishes.

Didn't you also testify before the Senate against the cutting of funds for the space program?

I did. I gave a very strong paper on our scientific future and what a democracy ought to be doing. My testimony helped save some of the endowments, and as a result they put me on the board that supervised NASA. I served on a committee that counsels with the House and Senate on aviation and space policy.

What kind of things did you deal with?

Space stations, exploration of other planets, the mining of asteroids, the advanced scientific concepts of the large space telescopes, and the utilization of the sun and moon, especially the idea of throwing up a gossamer-type net to collect power. In space, where you have no wind and no gravity and no disturbance, a filament of the finest nylon you can spin is just as rigid as a steel beam because nothing is affecting it, it's just there. So you can take a space ship up and throw out a fin that might go five miles and be a quarter of a mile high, like a giant fish net, and it can collect power from the sun and give you all the energy you need. As a matter of fact, that's something we're already doing on a small scale. We spent a great deal of time dealing on marking off the boundaries of space. We started out feeling that a space station was right around the corner but reluctantly we came to the conclusion that this was not practical in the next two decades. I've done a lot of studying on logistics to set up space colonies, but it would use up so much of our Earth's resources that maybe the trade-off would not be positive.

These are big questions. Think we'll ever have answers?

The pope promulgated the Treaty of Tordesillas in 1494 in which he divided the world, which was just as mysterious to him as space was to us, giving half of it to Portugal and the other half to Spain.

Not long ago NASA called me back to do the same job. I testified again for two days before Congress and we reversed one negative. We had an array of eight of the nation's top scientists battling us, and there were three of us—a woman astronaut, a hell of a bright medical doctor, and me. They shot us to pieces. They said there was no merit to what NASA wanted to do. I was the clean-up man and led the fight and by God, they adopted our interpretation. We prevailed that time. We said space is part of the human experience and must be pursued within the limits that the budget allows.

You must have been excited about the Galileo mission and the data coming back. Voyager explored Neptune in '79, Saturn in '81, Uranus in '86, and got within 800 feet of Jupiter's volcanic moon. Is NASA's future a series of small spacecraft that could be launched to various planets as often as once a month?

The future is in unmanned flights and robotics. Jupiter is a great target, and a significant one, so I think the explorations there will continue.

Think we'll ever see manned flights to the moon again?

I don't see it in the U.S., China or India might want to do it when they get the capacity.

With all the changes that take place so rapidly now, is it possible to accurately speculate where we'll be even twenty years from now?

I attended a two-week meeting of about thirty of the brightest men in the world who were trying to speculate where we are going to be around the year 2010. I was the only layman there. After we had talked a while a professor from Cornell pointed out that in 1938 President Roosevelt convened a group like this to give him advice on what might happen in the next decade and these men of great sagacity and terrific reputations failed to predict penicillin, radar, television, the atomic bomb, and rockets. All of which came into existence within the next five years! So the possibility that even with the broadest imaginations we could sit there and predict what might happen in even the remaining years of this century was remote. Though we're getting some indications: if you compound what we know about the manipulation of DNA and what the wizards are able to do with computers and what the most primitive types are able to do in urban guerilla warfare.

Regarding war, one can see how struggles begin, but not necessarily why they proliferate. When we entered Vietnam, were you for or against our involvement there?

I wasn't against the Vietnam War at first, but I changed my mind when I was working in Washington, in the government military archives in Alexandria. I was there on the afternoon that President Johnson announced that he was sending a really substantial body of troops into Vietnam. There was a German archivist working there and he blanched when the news came in. He said, "This is the first footstep down the slippery slide."

Is there anything one learns from war that can help prevent the next one?

First in Korea and again in Vietnam we tried to force a war that the entire nation did not support. We thought we could get away with a nickel-and-dime war, and we couldn't do it. We should have learned in Korea. I was distraught about Vietnam because I could see it was a terrible mistake, recapitulating.

In *The Bridges of Toko-Ri* I have a passage about the essential immorality of trying to prosecute a war without declaring a state of national emergency in which the penalties and the hardships of war are divided equally among the population. We got away with it in Korea, but in Vietnam that blew up in our faces.

Our ambassador to the U.N. spoke about the possibility of going to war against North Korea if they don't comply with nuclear inspections. How dangerous a situation is this?

Certainly the ambivalent statements in 1948 and '49 about our unwillingness to defend Korea and similar statements prior to the Gulf War about our giving Saddam Hussein a free hand to do whatever he damned well pleased weakened our national stature considerably. So maybe this outspoken blast against North Korea was a corrective to that namby-pamby approach.

You've written about World War II, the Korean War, the Hungarian Revolution, the war between Mexico and the U.S., but not about Vietnam. Why not?

I was then quite an older man, and I thought it was the responsibility of younger writers. But I half-blame the reactionary Walt Disney, who had a very limited vision, and some of the other cartoonists, for giving our nation silly fairytales to believe in. Woody Woodpecker gets annihilated every three minutes, and nothing ever happens to him, he always triumphs in the end. We went into Korea, Vietnam, Iran with a Mickey Mouse attitude, that everything was going to turn out all right in the long run because we're the good guys.

What did you think of President Reagan's petty war in Granada?

I served on a very powerful committee with Reagan's secretary of defense Caspar Weinberger when we went into Granada and kept the press out. We warned Weinberger that the easiest way to defeat an army is to have the home folk march away from him. And if you do that often enough, then you get a military that runs on its own, becomes a dictator, and the people rise up and rebel. We begged him not to do it. But they didn't listen, and then they did it again, worse than ever before, in the Gulf.

Was Bush right to have fought against Iraq?

I think Bush was dead-right in stepping in and keeping Saddam Hussein from taking over Saudi Arabia, which he would have done in another week. I backed Bush all the way, because I was sure that Hussein would be in Riyadh if we didn't stop him. But not to finish it, not to pursue Hussein, and to interpret it as a great military victory when you had no opposition, it's a mystery. To have parades around the nation for an affair like that—I questioned the sanity of our population. I mean, we didn't get rid of Manuel Noriega in Panama. And then we didn't get rid of Saddam Hussein. Hard to understand.

Is it also hard for you to understand the elimination of the draft?

It's hard to comprehend our going to war with a volunteer army. In Korea we got away with fighting an overseas war without conscription. I warned against that then. I'm not happy with any democracy that tries to fight a foreign war without declaring a national emergency to do it. Otherwise you leave the guys like me home to make a bundle, and you send guys like poor Lou and poorer Ned to fight. We allowed the petty victories we had in Granada and Panama and the desert to make us think that we can do that with impunity, at no cost to the nation. We're just crazy, because no nation's been able to do that. The decision to go to an all-volunteer army was one of the colossal errors of recent history. It has produced a very shabby military. That was true of ancient Rome, true of Greece, and certainly true of the Turkish empire. We better not go down that road.

Besides opposing a volunteer army, you also oppose the way we elect our president. Why do you see that as perilous?

I was concerned enough about the way we elect our president that I wrote a book about it, *Presidential Lottery*. I was disappointed that people did not take it more seriously, because sooner or later that's going to blow up in their faces. It may be one of the most important things I ever wrote and it has been lost in obscurity. However, the Senate interrogated me on it, and they understood what I was saying and were rather startled. I have never advocated abolishing the Electoral College; it's just the operation of the college that I object to, the system of awarding the votes. Every state regardless of population gets two senators, and you have quite a difference between the big and the little states. I am not against a general one-man one-vote popular election. But I failed in my attempt to get a Constitutional amendment on this. It's an intricate problem.

Another intricate problem, which has touched you on a personal level, has to do with how Congress views the value of the written word, specifically the worth of a writer's manuscripts. How has that affected you?

Congress passed a law saying that the manuscripts of a writer is worth to the Library of Congress only the cost of the paper and the typewriter ribbon used to type it. So if you found tomorrow the original of *Hamlet* with Shakespeare's annotations on it, it would be worth maybe two pounds six. About seven dollars!

To think that Arthur Miller's *Death of a Salesman* is worth seven dollars, that's goddamn crazy! The minute that happened all of us stopped giving our papers to the Library of Congress. Because the papers of Congressmen were valued at the old rate. So that the papers of some horse's ass from Utah, who was against everything good this nation ever represented, because he wanted to further the Mormon tenet or something—not a good Mormon but a horse's ass Mormon—is worth $300,000 and *Death of a Salesman* is worth seven bucks. Up to then they had all my papers. Now they are all scattered—in Colorado, Alaska, Miami, a little town library on the Eastern shore . . . wherever I work.

I could never be president of this country. I don't have the patience; I don't deal with willfully stupid people well. If Congress brought in an act like that, I would have vetoed it by one o'clock in the afternoon!

You bring up an interesting point. There are a lot of men who are qualified to be president, but they never run. Do we basically keep the best and brightest from the Oval Office?

Prior to the Civil War, we had about as drab a body of leadership as we've ever had. Except for James K. Polk from Tennessee, who was really quite wonderful in his way—sort of the Harry Truman of his day.

But Zachary Taylor, John Tyler, James Buchanan, and Franklin Pierce, these men were pretty poor. And we survived that leadership. We also survived the pitiful leadership after the war of Ulysses S. Grant and James A. Garfield, Chester Arthur, Rutherford B. Hayes, and Benjamin Harrison.

So I can only conclude that American democracy inherently does not want good leadership. We always passed over the very great men we had like Daniel Webster, John Calhoun, Henry Clay, John Fremont, and the people after the Civil War like Carl Shurz.

We pass them up because we don't want first-class men in that position, we want somebody who is a stupid bum like us. We're afraid of good leadership until a time of crisis, when we call upon a Woodrow Wilson or a Teddy Roosevelt or a Franklin D. Roosevelt.

How do you think military men have fared as president?

We idolize our military generals, but if you look at American history, how have we fared with our military presidents? We had Washington, Andrew Jackson, Zachary Taylor, Grant, McKinley, Teddy Roosevelt, Eisenhower. It's been fifty-fifty. We've gotten some very good ones, and we've gotten some real dodos—William Harrison, for example. If we can survive some of the incredible civilians we've had, I guess we can survive some of the incredible military men.

Would General MacArthur have made a good president?

General Douglas MacArthur's personal vanity and his arrogance cost him the presidency. He was a marvelous military practitioner and very attractive, but Truman had to do what he did and he was entirely right to do it. General Bradley was correct when he testified that MacArthur in Korea was advocating the wrong war at the wrong time and the wrong places against the wrong enemy, which was a pretty damning rebuttal from one military leader to another.

Had the former chairman of the joint chiefs of staff, Colin Powell, decided to run against Clinton in '96, would he have had a good shot at becoming the first black president?

Colin Powell is assessed by hopefuls in the Republican party at a much higher level than the facts would warrant. He is a splendid addition to our country from Jamaica, where his forebears lived, and he conducted himself superbly when I followed him at the Pearl Harbor celebrations; he really made not a single mistake. He would probably be a good vice president, but as president I cannot see him.

Why do you think Powell didn't go for it?

The extreme right scared the hell out of Powell in that big meeting they had where they warned him that if he made a move toward the presidency they would have to oppose him.

What do you think about Hillary Clinton and her chances of one day running for president?

During the primary campaign that Clinton won for the Democratic nomination, I foresaw that one of the strengths and weaknesses of his incumbency would be Hillary. She is a marvelous woman, way ahead of her time; she is in the tradition of Eleanor Roosevelt, has my complete support. I applaud all that she has done, and yet I know from bitter experience how the Republican party simply hates her, not because of her attitudes, but primarily because she is a woman and they are not ready for this. She bears the burden of years of macho supremacy, and it is painful for me to see this woman, so brilliant, well trained, and well prepared, treated savagely by both the opposition and some members of her own party. The president has been badly hurt by the good-ol'-boys syndrome in American life that denigrates and ridicules any woman who tries to play a major role. They have really ganged up on his wife miserably. But I say hurray for Hillary. I shall be in her corner the entire way, and I would be delighted to have the chance to vote for her for president or vice president.

What did you think of William Safire calling her a "congenital liar" in his N. Y. Times *column?*

Way out of line.

Who would you rank as the best presidents?

On my list of the top five presidents, Lincoln would be at the top. Number two would be F. D. R. Three, Jefferson. Four, Washington. And five would be Teddy Roosevelt.

Isn't it often true that when one branch of government is strong the others are less so?

By and large the ordinariness of the president has been offset by strong Supreme Court justices or by strong leadership in Congress. When Congress and the justices have been pretty bad, we've had strong presidents. So, mysteriously, the system works.

We have the oldest continuing form of government in the world. Go back to 1787–89 when we put our Constitution together—every major country has changed its form of government since then but us. Even England diminished the power of its monarchy and almost wiped out the power of the House of Lords. Sweden took one of Napoleon's marshals to be their new king and used the device that he was the son of the present king, who had no children—just dictated it, and everybody accepted it. Switzerland has been through five or six major changes. China, Russia, Japan, all of them. *We're* the successful country.

Among presidents, how would you compare those who served prior to the Civil War with those who served since World War II?

Clinton, Jimmy Carter, Nixon, Kennedy, and Eisenhower are at least as good as the crowd that ran the country then.

Look at Richard Nixon, certainly one of the most complex men of our times. And the Nixon that I knew was a very good man. I liked him. He was very good to me, even though he knew that I never voted for him and had written the official campaign biography for Hubert Humphrey. His fall was one of titanic dimension, the equivalent to anything in Aeschylus or Sophocles. He was as big a man as any that they were writing about. And there was that same problem of euphoria and power going to the head. It was Greek all the way through. The House's attempt to impeach Andrew Johnson didn't parallel Nixon's case at all. That was just niggardly politics—a bunch of real bastards got after a reasonable man. They failed at impeaching him, and he served out his term rather well, as a matter of fact. But Nixon's resigning the presidency under the cloud of impeachment was of another dimension.

Was Ford right to have pardoned Nixon?

One hundred percent right. Any further penalty he suffered for Watergate would have been very unjust.

Could the brouhaha surrounding Watergate have been avoided?

It didn't have to happen at all if Nixon had just come forward. Hobart Lewis was his personal friend, and he and I went to the White House with a plan: a bipartisan statement backing him and saying that an ungodly mistake has been made and will be corrected. It called for him to make a confession, which he might not have been able to make. But if he did, it was perfectly clear he could have been saved. Eisenhower or Kennedy would have resolved it. I think there was something very incriminating in the missing 18½ minutes of tape which was clearly erased by Nixon and his secretary, Rosemary Woods. I say that because I'm pretty sure that's what I would have done, and probably just as ineptly.

What happened when you went to the White House?

Rosemary Woods wouldn't allow us to see him. She said the only people Nixon had talked to in the last six weeks were Bebe Reboso and another of his cronies. John Connolly had been trying to see him and had not been able to for three weeks, she said. Nobody gets in to see him. But he had done it to himself. The men around him were third rate. And his farewell statement was so extraordinary that we have to assume that there had been a total deterioration.

After Nixon's death there was a great deal of positive oratory about him. Are we seeing history being revised?

There is a saying dating way back before the invention of English that one should never speak poorly of the dead. I think it begins *De mortuis nil nisi bonum.* There certainly was a vigorous drive on to rewrite history and put him in a somewhat more favorable light than he deserved.

What do you think of H.R. Haldeman's diaries?

He certainly punctured some balloons. Haldeman was the brighter of the two men, Haldeman and Erlichman, but they served Nixon poorly.

Did you do anything to help Carter get elected?

I came out for him strongly in Pennsylvania at the invitation of Senator Joe Clark. We did a great deal to help him win the primary, the one that put him over.

How high were your expectations for the Carter presidency?

One hoped that he would come to Washington and be able to fit in. But he was a complete naif. It was heartbreaking. The lesson was simply that you cannot run a great multiplex democracy with fifteen guys from Georgia who have never been to Europe and who have never been to Oregon or Stanford or the University of Texas.

Just as Nixon's inner group of maybe sixty men—most of them from California, had never been elected to office, hadn't even run for sheriff—who fell into disrepute, Carter's men were not tried and tested by the electorate. Neither were those who advised Reagan.

When it came time for Carter to run again, did you support him?

In the summer of 1979 I was convinced that Ted Kennedy ought to run for the presidency because I knew that Mr. Carter couldn't get reelected, but I also knew something far more important: that he was going to take down a lot of good men with him, just as Barry Goldwater had in '64.

There are many times when a political party is in a position where it cannot win the big election but it ought to put forward a candidate who will not damage people in the lesser elections. The Democrats didn't do that, and they suffered a very heavy penalty.

But Ted Kennedy?

Ted Kennedy, of course, had too much baggage, from the tragedy at Chappaquidick to his divorce. That's a very curious thing in American politics, that a Republican candidate can be divorced from a very fine woman and remarry and it doesn't hurt him at all. A Democrat is divorced, and it proves that he's a bum and an outcast and a pariah. The fact is that we allow Republicans to steal money from banks because they wear blue suits. If a black Democrat steals ten cents from a 7–11 convenience store, he's sent up for five years!

Ted Kennedy narrowly won reelection in '94.

I never doubted that. He has that rock-solid Irish support. And he's a damn good senator.

You obviously were no fan of Ronald Reagan.

When Ronald Reagan became president, he said, let us turn the government of this country over to the fine and noble and all-wise industrialists. Not a bad idea, because our nation was built in part upon that. Then I thought, with a shudder, wait a minute. These are the same industrialists who have been running Ford and Chrysler and General Motors for the last twenty years. Are they going to be infinitely wiser in managing the nation than they were in the management of their own companies? We were in a similar position when Joe McCarthy was running wild. It was a blessing then that a Republican president came in to draw his fangs and Eisenhower, in his very tardy way, did. If we had elected Stevenson in '52, the entire Republican party would have had to rally behind McCarthy, and some very terrible things might have happened.

Reagan's background was very flawed. When I was covering the Republican convention, I was visited by two Irish women from his hometown who vowed to me that Reagan was a grandfather, which he had decided to forget. I brought that to the attention of the people I was working for, and they said we don't want to know that, so they edited it out. I think rightly so. Just as it was agreed that you weren't going to show Roosevelt as a cripple.

So scandals of a sexual nature are best left uncovered?

I remember in the Korean War when there was possibly a major scandal which we were all in on about a general who had a Korean mistress. An older man said, "If he has the power and responsibility of sending 100,000 men into battle, don't you think it's better for him to be at ease at night when he goes to bed, than farting around somewhere with a bottle of booze?" You're not going to judge him—or the French marshal who stopped the Germans and saved Europe during World War II— by the fact they were in somebody else's bedroom at four in the morning.

What do you make of the sexual harrassment case brought against President Clinton by Paula Jones, who claimed he exposed himself to her when he was governor?

The Paula Jones case has made me wish that I could go back to Bill Clinton's grade school and find some young woman who has developed into an attractive adult about Bill's age who would come forth and charge him without specification of having made very improper sexual advances toward her in her day. And then when the press was gathered, we would find that it consisted of having kissed her in the hallway in Public School 41 when he was nine and she was seven. The Jones case stands at about that level of nonsense. The pattern was set by Mrs. Bill Cosby when her husband was accused of adultery. Her performance was magnificent, in which she said, in effect, 'Why should I worry about a one-night stand that happened thirty-three years ago? That's beneath my dignity.' That was refreshing. I would suppose that the Paula Jones deal was just as fake. To think that the statute of limitation does not put a terminal date on such preposterous attacks on the highest office in the land is not disturbing, it is outrageous, and I wish the whole nation would come to its senses. What would the present press corps have said about Harding and his mistress or Eisenhower and his dilly-dallying with that lovely British driver, or Jack Kennedy and his proclivities? Throwing such an attack on a sitting president is a tragic case of historic error.

Jumping back to Ronald Reagan—do you think his Alzheimer's affected him when he was in office?

No. I met him three times. All he wanted to talk about was sports. He was very hep.

When he was president, where did he go wrong?

Reagan, unfortunately, screwed up, modeling his presidency on the advice of these seventy and eighty-year-old California millionaires and the extreme right. And what did we get? No anti-gun legislation, no additional freedoms for the black, none for women, no concessions to outside powers. And we went deeper and deeper into debt. The nation retreated into a kind of fortress. We became anti-scientific, anti-arts, anti-speculation.

How threatening were the extreme right and the religious fanatics who came to prominence during the Reagan years?

In the eighties we developed a very able cadre of American ayatollahs who tried to do to this country what the Ayatollah Khomeini did to Iran. Jerry Falwell and Pat Robertson were the prototypes. I would give a passing tip of the hat to the great Reverend Jim Jones who served a very useful purpose in reminding us what can happen when the ayatollahs go crazy. The Moonies were a very destructive force. Scientology is frightening beyond imagination. Scientology had devised a tactic of using the American courts to persecute anybody who even spoke about them. They were very able and adroit until they broke into Federal records and really committed a major crime to which they pleaded guilty. It's a rough doctrine those people have preached. Old Ron Hubbard was a brilliant operator and he set up all sorts of protections and enticements.

We were in the same position that the Romans were about fifteen years after the crucifixion of Jesus, when their sons and daughters began leaving home, going into the catacombs, following a charismatic leader. The analogy of Jim Jones and the leaders of Synanon and Scientology is an exact one.

My concern at the time was not primarily what Sun Myung Moon was going to do to the individual children he picked up, but what Falwell and his men announced they were going to do to me and to the society of which I have been a proud and willing part. These people do not serve society well. A great many of them interpreted Reagan's election as a license to go gunning for liberals. They wanted to knock off all the baddies—the pornographers, *Playboy*, movies like *Taxi Driver*; then the near-baddies like Jane Fonda and that great singer, Joan Baez; then in that third line, guys like me, Kurt Vonnegut, Judith Rossner. The

Moral Majority had a fairly large hunting list. They got rid of the liberal politicians in '82 and wanted to exterminate from public life everybody they called a scientific humanist. They would have liked to have gotten rid of the Jews and anybody else who didn't believe in their God and the New Testament.

So how strongly did you oppose this movement?

For a while they had me concerned. History showed what happened in Germany, Spain, China, Japan. Why should we think that we are somehow marvelously exempt from what's happened in fifteen South American countries? We're not at all! We could be next.

Which is why I suppose that I will spend the remaining years of my life bearing constant testimony to the dangers of totalitarian action in the field of moral domination. I don't think it will diminish in my lifetime. Though when Jimmy and Tammy Bakker fell, and Jimmy Swaggart self-destructed, and to a certain extent Oral Roberts in Tulsa and Jerry Falwell, it was a victory for all good people, thank heavens. We do not thrive under a theocracy. And I am Jeffersonian to the limit on that basic principle. I despise these sons-of-bitches. I see them as evil, corrupt men and women.

What about some of the mystic religions of the east that set up followings in America? Any cause for concern there?

Some years ago I visited the University of Colorado and saw in the student union advertisements for eight different gurus who were coming to that university to explain the secrets of life. And one wondered if, really, you needed eight. When you look at the societies that have been produced by Hinduism and the guru sects, I think you can say without the yahoo that there are questions as to whether it is majestically superior to what Christianity or Judaism have produced.

Putting prayer back in school has become a hot issue again. William Buckley wrote in a column: "The best lesson to teach the idiosyncratic minority is that the majority has certain rights. The majority should have the right to say something pleasant to God when school assembles in the morning."

There has not been much discussion of the fact that these

people are preaching that this is a Christian nation. It is not a Christian nation. It is a polyglot, many-varied religious nation. I think people ought to stress that. It's the world we live in.

After Reagan, the country still wasn't ready for a turn. How depressed were you when Bush took over?

With the election of Bush and Quayle in '88 liberalism was made the enemy of the nation. I really found it bizarre that Dan Quayle could sit in judgment about me—in his attack on liberals he was attacking people like me. They wanted to muzzle us, to deny us a voice on the courts.

Then Bush went to Japan with some of our industrial leaders— that was really something! Every aspect of it was stupid. I wouldn't want Lee Iacocca to conduct my foreign policy. If he wasn't able to withstand Japanese competition any better than he did, how could he have advised us on how to deal with them?

Has the greed of the Reagan-Bush years been exaggerated?

No. I understated the greed of the Reagan-Bush eighties. The amassing of wealth by a few at the expense of the many was just wrong. In state after state they cut back on education, on health services. I never expected any American politicians to do that.

What did you think of Ross Perot?

If there was one good thing about the entry of Ross Perot into presidential politics, it was that he brought the problems of our national debt into some sort of focus. But I was very afraid of Perot. He was, and is, a dangerous man. He promises that he can make the trains run on time and if that doesn't scare you, then you haven't been reading modern European history. He's done other things that bespeak of a man of good sense and character. But the other aspects of his character are open to question.

Such as?

I think he's a fascist, a racist, a man who would use his power to destroy you if you fucked him in any way. Certainly evidence of his going after people who competed with him in business proves that. The fact that he's pragmatic doesn't have anything to do with his being just or right.

Just look at the way he investigated his former classmate at Annapolis who also started a computer firm. Perot decided to drive him out of the market and did everything he could: he put the FBI on him, he leaked things which might cause him to be hauled before a Senate committee. He circulated rumors in the industry that the guy couldn't be trusted. Just terrible things. Classic Joseph Stalin tactics. And if he wanted to do that against you or me, he could do it.

Was Perot ever a serious threat?

Perot was strong. You had to go back to the great Republican Convention of 1952 for comparisons. That's when Robert Taft was the darling of the Republican party and had won all those primaries. He had chits out all over the country, people who owed him. He was Mr. Republican. His weakness was he could not be elected president. I was fairly close to some very important Republicans at that time, and they knew he couldn't be elected. They led the movement to bring in Eisenhower. They knew nothing about him, not even what party he belonged to. But they knew they couldn't win with Taft.

So the Democrats went with Clinton, who I interviewed when he was governor, and who made a strongly favorable impression.

Clinton doesn't seem to have a grasp on foreign policy. Would a stronger president be able to do anything about the events in Bosnia, Rwanda, North Korea?

I think that comparing Bush's policy in the Gulf up to the time of his precipitant ending of that war with President Clinton's fumbling policy on the countries you've mentioned, and especially Haiti, puts Bush in a strong light and Clinton in a weak light. I regret this. I do think, however, we should remember that Clinton has inherited some of these problems from his predecessors and he is doing maybe as well as he could with his particular background.

Clinton seems to have had more than his share of problems not only with foreign policy but also with his advisors, which he keeps changing.

Is Clinton suffering from the same kind of inability to delegate power that Jimmy Carter had?

When Clinton won the election in that dramatic vote the first thought I had was, "Can he avoid being the new Jimmy Carter?" And the more I studied the situation and the more I saw the Arkansas cronies flocking to Washington the way the Georgia cronies flocked to Washington in Jimmy's day, the more fearful I became. All my fears have been substantiated and they continue. I think that Clinton's main problem is not Rwanda or Bosnia, but to avoid a repetition of the Carter debacle. I have great warm regard for Jimmy Carter. I think his behavior since leaving the presidency has been impeccable and a remonstrance to some of the former presidents.

Clinton also has to deal with an opposition party that seems more concerned with doing him in than with important interests of the country, especially health care.

We may have moved into a position in which any constructive idea that a president may bring forth will be opposed by the opposition party to the point of stalemate.

The president must also deal with the fact that his party has lost its majority rule in both houses of Congress for the first time in forty years. Was the '94 election a revolution?

It really was. But it didn't surprise me. And I'm a stronger liberal now than I was two years ago. I can't believe that my time-worn, time-tested beliefs going back to Jefferson and Jackson and Lincoln, Teddy Roosevelt and FDR will be in obscurity permanently. I think the '92 election proved that. But the '94 election was a body blow. Though we had this before, when Reagan stormed into the White House. He took twelve senators with him. Six years later eleven of those dodos lost, because they had paraded themselves as total incompetents. And that might well happen again.

Were you surprised that Ann Richards lost the governorship of Texas?

I was indeed. Should not have happened. But the swing was so great that people voted automatically.

Almost happened to Feinstein in California, against Michael Huffington.

He seems to be a real horse's ass. Hard guy to love.

With the way the country has turned, were you surprised that Oliver North lost?

I was surprised he lost. We haven't heard the last of him. But thank God he didn't get six years in the Senate.

How galling was it for a liberal like yourself to see ultra-conservatives Newt Gingrich and Jesse Helms winding up as the Speaker of the House and chairman of the Senate Foreign Relations Committee?

Gingrich's revolution and its implications were enormous. He was *Time's* Man of the Year 1995, but that vanished with inspection. He's a loose cannon careening about the deck of the good ship Columbia. He's a smart guy, but his motives are extremely cloudy. It was my hope that people like him and Phil Gramm would self-destruct and that seems to be the case. In the '96 election he was money in the bank for the Democrats. It's outrageous that a man like him, who evaded military duty, should now put himself in a position of dismissing me from American life as not a patriot, when I volunteered for service when I was exempt from it and saw two long tours of duty in the South Pacific and even more dangerous work in Korea. His censure in the House and $300,000 fine was putting him where he ought to be. It was very good to see Newt digging his own grave and diminishing his position.

How about Jesse Helms?

I think we'll have a lot of trouble with Jesse. I had a fantastic run-in with Jesse, when I was up for confirmation before the Senate. I was tremendously impressed by the man. He was courtly, gracious, he gave you every opportunity and applauded you when your ideas coincided with his. But he was a real thrust-at-the-heart with a sharpened dagger.

What do you think of what he said about President Clinton needing bodyguards if he visited North Carolina?

That's so shocking—it's precisely the language that was current in Texas prior to Kennedy's arrival when he would be shot.

Helms has been making controversial remarks for years. In 1990 he said about NEA funding to certain artists: "What is really at stake is whether or not America will allow the cultural high ground in this nation to sink slowly into an abyss of slime to placate people who clearly seek or are willing to destroy the Judaic-Christian foundation of this republic."

Here we go way back. The U.S. is not a congenial society for the creative artist. We're held in contempt as being unpatriotic or unmanly or un-anything. Every literary figure who has run for political office in my lifetime has lost, because he was seen as not a real American. Mailer lost, I lost, Gore Vidal lost, Buckley lost, Bill Mauldin lost. We do not fare well, because people intuitively suspect us. Every athletic figure who has run for office has been elected, because you know he's reliable. Because we idolize the sports figure.

Helms threatened to make Sen. Carol Moseley-Braun cry after they had debated on the Senate floor over use of the Confederate flag. "I'm going to sing 'Dixie' to her until she cries."

That's the talk most of us reserve for the back room of the bar. You don't make it public.

Do you know the majority whip, Trent Lott?

Very well indeed. I spent three days with him. Absolutely delightful man. Sophisticated, knowledgeable, a tough in-fighter for his party. Impressive. It surprised me to hear he was an ally of Gingrich.

The GOP had a ten-point plan that's at least worth considering. Think we can see a balanced budget by the turn of the century?

It's not totally irrational, though it's terribly hard to effect.

Crime control—they want to toughen the death penalty provisions, add new mandatory minimum sentences, put more money into prison construction.

We're at such odds there it's not worth discussing. They want to make a frontier society—be my guest, I can't do anything about it.

What about welfare reform—they have a Personal Responsibility Act that would ban welfare benefits to unwed mothers under eighteen and cut off assistance after two years to families covered under other federal-state welfare programs.

It seems quite cruel to me. I've been through that experience myself in several dramatic instances, and it's just awful to penalize children for what adults have done. I'm all in favor of penalizing adults for what children have done.

Regarding education and children, they would establish school voucher programs, set up a nationwide tracking system to find parents who fail to make child support payments, strengthen child pornography laws, and provide tax credit for people who care for elderly relatives.

Those are good aims. Though the school vouchers worry me, because our educational system has been very advantageous to this country. The GI Bill of Rights was a godsend. I'm a case history of a good educational system available to lift me out of the ghetto and allow me to do what I've done, so I would never revoke that. I don't want to see the system weakened. It ought to be strengthened.

The Republican version of a middle-class tax cut would give a $500-per-child tax credit for families earning under $200,000 per year and allow people to open IRA accounts bearing tax-free interest upon withdrawal.

Those are good moves.

National security. Their proposal called for increased defense spending and legislation to prohibit U.S. troops from serving under United Nations or other foreign command.

Boy, that's a tricky one. We're almost saying that the U.N. is defunct. I'm not willing to make that judgment yet, although I have fought the United Nations because of their blatant anti-American policies. I was a delegate to one of the great Paris conventions where we got rid of UNESCO—high time. But I'm not proud of it, was quite sorry to see it happen, although I was one of the major engineers to see that it did happen.

The U.S. pulled out of UNESCO in 1984. Why?

It fell into the hands of a Senegalese pirate named Amadou M'dou, who hated the U.S., despised a free press, and was a petty little empire builder. He treated Arthur Miller and me with contempt so grievous that we declared war on him and ultimately got him fired, along with pressure from a lot of other sources. He was terrible. We took care of him.

Senior citizens. Several tax cuts were proposed, along with raising the Social Security earnings limit.

Those are good measures. But I hate to see them funded by cutting back funds for children.

Capital gains tax cut. The GOP proposed to halve the capital gains tax and adjust the purchase price of an asset for inflation.

That's a provision for people like me, and it's based on the principle of trickle-down. I have seen damn little evidence of trickle-down in the last twenty years. The rich get richer, the poor get poorer. Because you and I are such miserable sons-of-bitches that we get the financial advantage and hold on to it, and there's very little trickle.

Legal reform. Tort reform to set limits on punitive damages in product liability and medical malpractice suits.

Very strongly in favor of that. Because they're using that without tort reform as a punitive measure, the deep-pocket theory, and I've seen examples of deep-pocket that are just repulsive.

What about the "loser pays" provision to allow judges to order losers in lawsuits to pay the other side's legal costs.

I've been involved in that a great deal. You get sued and there's no basis for it; it's really transparent folly. But to prove it in court takes so much money that I settle out of court. You could get $6,000 from me almost any time you wanted to. You could cite your visit here, say you gave me the ideas for my books or that I stole your ideas, and when we look into the charges they're so thin, almost evanescent. The lawyers work out the best deal they can, which usually comes to $6,000, of which the lawyer gets maybe sixty percent. It's happened three times with me, and I was very happy to get out of it.

Have you ever sued anyone?

No. God, I wouldn't dream of it. There is no way that I could sue you for something you said or wrote, because to prove damages would be so costly that it wouldn't be worth it. And it gives greater circulation to the idea anyway. I would draw the line, obviously, if I were accused of treasonous attitudes or behavior. And maybe an infamous attack on my wife. The attack on me I can absorb.

The last of the GOP points was congressional term limits.

I'm not in favor of that. You need bright people, and by bright I also include knowing. I'm not sure I would oppose it strongly, but I am opposed to it.

Where do you stand on the issue of physician-assisted suicide? Cardinal Bernardin, before he died, wrote to the Supreme Court asking them not to judge in favor of it.

Looking at the experience of Holland, I'm in favor of voluntary termination when life is unbearable. I have said that it would be impossible for me, but I'm not so sure now.

A lot of Republicans would like to see the voluntary termination of President Clinton. And yet, in spite of the backlash and setbacks, he's getting a lot done.

Yes. I would advise him to adhere to his principles, keep hammering away at them. The problems of the inner city are so pressing that it takes an idiot to deny that they exist. And if Justice Scalia and Thomas want to mount a campaign in the

Supreme Court to deny or reverse those rights, I think we have a battle.

Also high on Clinton's list is the size of the national debt. Can anyone make a dent in that?

Of my current fears, the debt would be second after education. That debt in the end is going to stagger us. I'm pretty sure that one of these days we'll devalue the dollar. Just knock off two zeroes, pay off the debt and start over. That doesn't hurt the very wealthy because they retain their relative position; it doesn't hurt the very poor because they're not involved anyway. But it certainly knocks hell out of the middle class. Make the dollar worth a penny. We're heading that way right now without doing it. Don't worry about the dollar, worry about the three trillion dollars, that's what you've got to diminish. Maybe the only way to do it is just to knock off the two zeroes. Germany did it, Japan did it. And they got back on the main track and became the wealthiest nations in the world in the process of a very few years. They were smart enough to manage it. We certainly would be.

That's a pretty drastic proposal.

Nobody's talking about such a drastic move yet, but the debt will never be reduced the way they're going about it. Nor can I see any other moves that would reduce it.

Are we burdened with too much taxes?

We're allowing the infrastructure of the whole country to go to ruin. We are not heavily taxed compared with other countries. We have these crazy ideas that you can save the money and we'll have it to spend sometime later. The first priority of the Clinton Administration should be to rebuild the nation in all ways. Housing, railway, bridges, highways, schools, libraries, hospitals, just do what needs to be done and pay for it as we generate activity. That's what great nations do.

As we approach the millennium, where do you see the nation heading?

I think the nation will drift, constantly more to the right, and leadership of the world will pass to Europe, because we are dealing with entirely new forces now in the EEC and the revitalized Europe. And certainly a very powerful Asia. Not just Japan, but Korea and Singapore and the new China. We're not home safe by any means.

Are you glad you were born in this century?

I have always been happy that I was born in America in 1907. I am especially grateful that I lived in the age of aviation, because it has played a vital part in my life, and also, curiously, that I lived in the age of television, quite a remarkable invention.

You live in the decade that you're in. And each one of them is meritorious on its own account. Obviously there were decades in which I would have been happier. But you're stuck with the six or seven or eight decades into which you were born. And goddamn it! I'm going to live with them.

In spite of your success, would you caution people with artistic tendencies to think twice before pursuing that path?

Because America doesn't particularly prize its artistic talent, it's a tough, tough game for anyone so inclined. Any of us with any artistic talent are all cousins, and who has it easy varies from decade to decade. The painters had it fairly easy in the sixties, but couldn't make a nickel in the thirties and forties. The poets have had it very tough for a long time. Dramatists come in about even. I happened to come along at a period when the novelist was on the table. If I had not been able to make a living, even though I might feel in my heart that I was just as good as Bernard Malamud or John Cheever, I would have been out on the road three nights a week, on every show I could get on.

In retrospect, is there anything you've done that you would change, knowing what you know now?

I think that I would be the same guy with the same complex motives and the same strengths and limitations. I don't for a minute think that I would avoid the great errors.

I've lived a very intellectual life and am the way I am because of my early life experiences that account for my liberalism, my economic attitudes, and the fact that I probably work too hard. I have never allowed very many people to get too close to me. I've had my own battles to fight. I had a very hard life, but I was pretty *duro*, as the Spaniards say. I developed slowly, like an oak tree, not like a pine. I had a profoundly good education, and over the subsequent years I continued to educate myself.

I'm talking about the propulsive force that keeps a man like me going if he is going to write books of the lengths that I have done. I'm not sure that I could clarify what mine were, but an intense self-respect would be one for sure. I am a driven person who hates to do things poorly.

George Orwell called writing a "horrible, exhausting struggle." Has it been that for you?

Having written more than forty books, I can attest to that but also to the joy of seeing the damned thing finally on the shelves and in a score of different languages.

Do you feel what you've written will last?

I don't believe that what I have written will be quickly dated. In the field of Japanese art it definitely won't be dated, because it will be a standard. *Caravans, The Source, Iberia*—these books will last. Some of the novels might date, but there is no evidence of that yet. *Hawaii*—and it can be the prototype for all the other books as well—was a compilation of about five or six novels. It could have been published as a set. With a little bit more work on each one I could have mined these veins for thirty years. There ought to be a great novel about the Japanese and Hawaii; about the Chinese; about the coming of the Polynesians; about the Big Five; the coming of pineapple. It's all there to be done. But it's now thirty-eight years later and nobody has even attempted it.

Why do you suppose no one has?

Because all you need to be eligible to write a new *Hawaii* is to have lived in Japan, reached forward to China, lived in the South Pacific, made the travels, lived in New England, in Walpole, have spent about twenty years thinking about it. And people aren't willing to do that. The same with *The Source*. Every one of those chapters is a novel. But it hasn't been done. It isn't done because to do it you have to be two things: you have to be an artist, and you have to be willing to do your homework. And that is a tough combination. Over the years I have become more aware that I have been a freak. I've known a dozen others who soared like a lark at dawn, then faded with the first rays of a merciless noonday sun. I was lucky that my acceptance came late and in careful monitored doses.

So you admit to being among a small elite?

No, I am not an elitist. I did not come from an elitist background and I have never felt that I was a member of the elite. My affinities have always been with the working group, with the people who are doing the hard work. And with the cannibals on the frontier. I get along with them perfectly well.

Do you consider yourself a religious man?

Many people find their greatest solace and their greatest meaning in life in religion. I don't. I have never been at ease with or known what I thought about religion. Though I don't know whether God exists, I take it very seriously. Mari and I contributed as liberally as we could to churches because we believed in them without question. I don't think I would want to live in a community that didn't have any churches. But doctrine doesn't excite me very much. I find mine in art, and in the interaction of society in which religion is a component and I deal with it the same way I deal with economics and good sewage systems and taxation and military service and good elementary schools. It comes in exactly at that level with me.

So it's really up to man, and not divine intervention, to set things straight?

I had a humiliating experience in Pennsylvania when I lived beside a little stream of beautifully pure water. Just the most glorious place. Then people started dumping refuse, especially chemical refuse, in it, and they destroyed it. A friend of mine came to see me, and he said: "You are concerned about everything and you haven't even looked at what is happening on your doorstep." When I went down and looked, I really was quite heartsick because they had done this stream in. There was not a bullfrog, a fish, there were none of the succulent weeds they live off of. By taking vigorous action, we were able to flush the stream clean in three years, and it is now as good as it ever was.

How important is it for the average person to know about the arts?

I have tried all the arts, because I think one should respond to the art of his time and should be aware of what good people are doing. When I am through with writing a book I turn to music or painting. I also look at postcards of great works of art, which I have collected since I was a boy. I leaf through them at least once a week. And several museums have had shows of my paintings, most of which are now at the University of Texas.

I tend to have considerable respect for people who do what I can't, whatever it is. Somebody could crochet real well, and that's something to me. The so-called Pennsylvania Impressionists are a group of damn good artists who flourished in Bucks County and painted mostly landscapes. We are gathering the works of these men and women for display in the museum of my name, formerly an old jail in Doylestown, opposite the Henry Mercer Museum.

Mari left them some money to take the next steps: adding another wing or a museum in tribute to the individual artist. We have a tradition of maybe fifteen great writers who have lived there: Oscar Hammerstein, Sid Perelman, George S. Kaufman, Moss Hart, Dorothy Parker, Pearl Buck. I come on at the end of the list. It's a pretty dazzling array.

Do you have any favorite work of art?

One of the happiest pieces of art I've come upon in my lifetime is a signed drawing of diplodocus, the dinosaur I wrote about in *Centennial*, which a museum in Houston commissioned for a show they did on dinosaurs. I am extremely proud of diplodocus. I felt that I had done something in bringing to the attention of a lot of people the fact that this extremely ancient creature was a living thing.

What about helping to promote other writers' books?

I have very grave doubts about the advantage of a blurb from another writer. I would think that a blurb from me is damn near valueless. If a young black writer could get a blurb from Walter Mosley or Toni Morrison, that would mean something. A poet who got a hearty recommendation from Robert Penn Warren or Robert Lowell when they were alive would mean something.

Would you say you are content with the life you've led?

I'm not *content* because I've seen too much of the world, and I know too much of what is brewing. I've seen fantastic poverty, death, starvation. But how one reacts to his total universe is another matter. Within that I am happy.

As the years have passed, your productivity has increased. Don't you get tired?

My wife sometimes asked why I didn't just relax and enjoy the fruits of what I have done. That was never even a remote possibility. I'm ninety now, going on ninety-one. It's very hard to keep a life of eight decades moving forward. There ought to be a touch of levity and joy. To have fun in life is an obligation. In recent years I've met so many men who retired twenty-five years before. That really frightens me, to think that they dropped out of the competition so very early. We all share mounting headaches, working within parameters that we can't fully define, and against forces in which we're pretty powerless. I'm pretty much a fatalist, but that doesn't make me passive or indifferent. We all have to do what is germane to our life's melody. You write the way you're able to write; you behave the way your genes enable you to. If you can get up Monday morning and brush your teeth and get out of the house, you're doing as well as I'm doing. I don't judge other people; I just like to see them make something of their time and to be contributing at least into their early seventies. You ought to stay in the ballgame as long as your health allows and as long as you've managed to avoid senility.

AFTERWORD BY
JAMES A. MICHENER

When Larry Grobel already had many pages of notes, answers to his questions about my life and work, I let him know that, because of obligations, I could not spend more time in conversation with him. So, conniving wit that he is, he came up with a proposal: "Jim, why don't you ask yourself the really crucial questions that I might have overlooked. Ask yourself only the goodies and answer them as fully and as bluntly as you wish."

At first glimpse the proposal was dubious. My credo has been: "Media people are at least as honest as I am. We'll talk. They'll take notes. And I've got to trust them to report fairly what I've said." This has proved an effective gambit, so I saw no need to embrace Larry's suggestion.

But then I remembered an article in which my Florida neighbor Issac Bashevis Singer had been invited by the editors to interview himself, and I remembered it as so effective that when I next met Singer, for we were teaching together, I asked him: "How did that interview work out?" And he said: "Fabulously. I covered all the untouched spots. And I could be sure that my answers were reported correctly, because I was doing the reporting." He added, "When they sent me the galleys, I improved sentences here and there."

I concluded, "If the device was good enough for a Nobel premiado, it's justifiable for me," and I proceeded to ask myself a few crucial questions.

How do you see yourself in the American literary scene?

Professional writers do not sit about daydreaming on such subjects, but the answer is quite simple. It's found in the word *transpire*. Years ago, Albert Erskine, the erudite fiction editor at Random House, approached me apologetically, "Jim, I've never before put the arm on you for a back-cover quote for one of my writers. But now I have to. I have a young fellow who, I'm convinced, is going to be the next William Faulkner. Unbelievably good. Name's Cormac McCarthy. Southern boy with a pen of pure gold, but his books do not sell. We can't give them away. He's completed this new manuscript, a real leap forward. Will you read it and give the young man a boost?"

I read it, couldn't make head nor tail of some parts, but agreed with Erskine that the kid could write. So as an act in the collegiality of writers, editors, and publishers, I penned an accolade.

"This novel reports the various actions that transpire in a small Southern town."

As soon as Erskine received my copy, he telephoned. "Jim, thanks for the quote. But since we've been trying to sell McCarthy as a polished stylist, I'm afraid we can't use your quote as given because you seem not to know the definition of the word *transpire*."

"*Happens*," I said.

"Wrong," Erskine replied. "Do you mind if we change it, to avoid a glaring solecism in support of a style master?"

"Be my guest." And when I looked up the definition, I learned to my surprise that indeed I did not know the meaning of the word. *Transpire* was cousin to *perspire*. The latter meant "to excrete perspiration through the pores of the skin." My word meant "to pass perspiration through the skin itself," but because of the process of leaking out, it had almost immediately enjoyed a secondary meaning as in "Although yesterday's meeting had been secret, it soon transpired that a major change had taken place." My usage of "it happened" appeared in the dictionary, but with the condemnatory caution that it was avoided by serious users of the language and by writers who attended to their style.

So what happened?

I was insulted and agitated, because I have great affection for my language, and when I started exploring—I spent about a week on this project—I found that from the misuse of the second meaning, "to leak out," a third had evolved, "to happen," which had been used by many of our best writers both in England and America. And when the next edition of the big Webster came out—you can look it up—it not only gave "to happen" as acceptable but cites me as the authority for this usage. And wait a minute! When the big *Random House Dictionary* appeared, it gave as the preferred first meaning of the word: "to occur, happen, take place."

How could your adventure with such a word acquire the importance you implied?

Because it alerted me to the literary career of Cormac McCarthy. Erskine had been right. The young man was a genius. Critics loved his work, but in those days his books did not earn back their advances. The MacArthur Foundation gave him one of its genius awards, two hundred and fifty thousand dollars, someone told me. But it was pointed out to me many times that Random House could afford to continue publishing fine books like McCarthy's and others in that vein only because Random also had on its lists less applauded books like mine, which earned the house millions. In the decades when I was a huge bestseller, Random paid me only a portion of what I demonstrably earned, but I never complained. I told them, "If you spend my earnings to publish fine novels, important nonfiction, and especially our poets, I'm satisfied. It's a decent bargain . . . good for our society . . . good for the country."

So in a few words, how do you see yourself?

As a writer who has been able to entertain and instruct millions of readers in all languages, and in doing so help to keep a publisher solvent so that he could afford to print the books of fine writers who did not find large audiences.

Were you aware that you were creating a new literary form, the extended historical-romantic novel?

I don't think I did invent anything. The great picaresque novels of the past paved the way with their broad roaming in landscape. Certainly Thomas Mann's *Buddenbrooks* demonstrated how to keep attention focused on one family, and in English Galsworthy excelled. In using verifiable historical material Tolstoy's *War and Peace* established the norms, and Herman Wouk's *Winds of War* adapted them to current material. I learned from all of them.

Afterword

Did any one such book exert special influence?

Like all literate people, I'd always heard about Eugene Sue's phenomenally successful *The Wandering Jew* (1845) but had never read it. I thought I ought to know what had been done before me, so I checked it out. What a frolic! It dealt with Ahasuerus, the Jew who taunted Jesus on the way to the Crucifixion. Legend says that Jesus replied, "I go, and you will wait till I return." This was interpreted to mean that Ahasuerus would wander the earth endlessly, a concept which tantalized medieval moralists, whose retelling of the story gave it such universal currency that the Wandering Jew was seen by watchful observers in all centuries and in all continents. Sue told his chaotic story in ten monumental volumes (the novel appeared as a vast serial in newspapers and achieved wild acclaim). I can see no reason for anyone's reading the novel now except for amusing literary archaeology, but I came upon it just when I needed it, for it taught me several valuable lessons. (1) Sue spends such an intolerable length of time describing each of his characters that the reader soon tires; I decided to avoid that, believing that a phrase can be as effective as a page. (2) Sue uses coincidence in plotting to a degree that is laughable. One ship sets out for France from a distant part of the world, another from the antipodes, each has as a passenger a major character and they must meet to keep the story moving. In a violent storm one ship wrecks the other and the characters meet. I vowed to avoid that nonsense. Later, however, I was forcibly struck by the blatant and effective manner in which Boris Pasternak uses coincidence in *Dr. Zhivago*, from which I conclude that it can be done in a serious book, if done well. (3) Sue uses historical incidents arbitrarily, and so do most writers of historical fiction. A historical incident should be dragged in only when inescapable for the development of the story. (4) Finally, Sue cannot resist the scene that tears the landscape apart. He's good at depicting the big event, but he overdoes it till the effect is humorous, not startling.

You don't seem much impressed with your illustrious predecessor.

Wrong. I meant I would not recommend him for the general reader, but for the aspiring writer whose taste goes to many characters and intricate plot development I recommend *The Wandering Jew* enthusiastically for its descriptions and its daring. The opening chapter is about as stirring a chapter one as there is in literature, almost the equal of Thomas Hardy's opening for *The Mayor of Casterbridge*, in which a wandering shepherd auctions his wife to whoever wants her as she stands on a table in an inn where the men have been drinking.

But in your books you start very slowly.

Yes, and with conscious intent. I am embarked upon a massive project, and I judge that my readers will not stay with me unless the territory in which the protracted action occurs is so solidly based—no nonsense, no tricks—that when the meat of the narrative arrives a hundred pages later, the reader will be engrossed in the setting, almost mesmerized into remaining with it.

I've been told that a lot of people start reading your big books and quickly put them aside as being too onerous.

Correct. A fourteen-year-old boy told me in a letter: "When I reported in class that I was writing my paper on *Centennial*, Miss Shoemaker said: 'I tried to read it, but it was too long,' so I told her, 'If you keep reading it does get better.'" On the other end, throughout the year I receive letters from other readers who complain that my book ended too soon. Customarily they say something like, "When I saw that the end was approaching, I rationed myself because I did not want to leave that land and those people who had become so much a part of me."

So why do you make the openings so difficult, pages before human characters appear?

Falling back upon the explanation of the Mississippi riverboat gambler, who was asked, "Why did you jump the ante to fifty dollars when it had been ten?" Said he, "To weed out the ribbon clerks, so that us real gamblers could go at it." I'm aware that many readers ought not bother with my books. Too difficult. They wouldn't enjoy them if they did finish, so I invite them out.

What percentage of the total available readership can a writer like you aspire to?

I thought about this when I worked in Israel, which has excellent writers. If they insist on writing in Hebrew, the language of the nation, they have a population of only four million worldwide from among whom they must find their readers. So although Israel is a literate nation that cherishes books, there are probably only about one-and-a-half million who might conceivably buy a novel in Hebrew. When an American writer publishes a novel, he has nearly four hundred and fifty million potential readers worldwide. Those of us who write in English are fortunate indeed.

Are you content when others categorize you as "a historical novelist?"

No. It's not accurate. My books may start out with a strong historical base, but they end very much in the present. It's the present that interests me: how we got here, how the past influences all we do. What category to place me in? I really don't know. Perhaps *storyteller* would be most accurate. Simply *novelist*, without an adjective.

Are your books also translated into foreign languages?

Customarily they go into at least a dozen, often many more. I have sometimes answered that question honestly but spuriously: 'My books have gone into fifty-two foreign languages.' It's true because *The Bridge at Andau* did appear in that number of tongues, but it's spurious because after the Soviet Union crushed the Hungarian Revolution of 1956, my book was rushed into print and circulated throughout the world. Many were little more than hastily printed pamphlets, which summarized my reports of the worst examples of communist barbarianism.

You wrote a good deal about Communism, didn't you?

Two books, *The Bridge at Andau* and *Poland,* and articles when I worked on the various national commissions. But even as I inveighed against communism itself as a destructive world force, I always spoke well of the Russian people, for I was convinced that we must one day join forces. I supposed it would not come until after my lifetime, maybe around 2010. I've been astounded to see the monolith crumble so soon. I knew from my travels that it was frail around the edges—Lithuania, Ukraine, Uzbekistan—but I did not realize it was also rotting at the core.

Have you never written short stories?

My long novels contain numerous fairly able short stories, which appear in the guise of individual chapters. I hold four of them in high regard: the story of Bloody Mary and her daughter Liat in *Tales of the South Pacific*; the story about the hoopoe bird and King David in *The Source*; the adventures of the dinosaur diplodocus in *Centennial*; and the marvelous true account of Admiral Lord Nelson struggling to find a rich wife in *Caribbean*. I had the touch of a short story writer but lacked both the instruction and the challenge when I was young.

Did you ever write poetry?

Any young fellow who does not attempt to put his inchoate feelings into poetry will probably never make it as a writer. As a boy I rewrote the ending of *The Iliad*. In college I tried to capture the tragedy of Thomas Chatterton in blank verse. Quite a few short snatches of my poetry appear in my novels. I can recite long passages of Wordsworth, Keats, sonnets by the masters, and much of Milton.

Why are you so interested in American poetry?

Because I see the fate of poetry as the paradigm of what's going to happen to American fiction. Consider. A century and a half ago poets dominated American letters. Henry Wadsworth Longfellow. James Russell Lowell. Ralph Waldo Emerson. John Greenleaf Whittier. On their incomes they lived well, ate well, and graciously accepted the accolades of the public. The poor novelists couldn't begin to live on what they earned on their books. In less than a century poets threw away their position of leadership. In my early days only Edward Arlington Robinson, Edna St. Vincent Millay and Stephen Vincent Benét could earn a living with their poems. Robert Frost and Carl Sandburg survived, and some others, marginally, but quietly in the night poetry strangled itself, so far as the public was concerned. By the 1950s and especially later, poetry became an erudite conversation among elites, at which point the public and the publishers dismissed it. There were exceptions, but they tended to be few in number and most often admired by the poetic fraternity rather than by the public at large.

Has it been the same in other nations?

No! And that's the mystery. Poetry has never enjoyed a more vital role in national life than it does now in countries like Russia (whatever its new name will ultimately be), Poland, Spain and parts of South America. This too I cannot explain. Can it be that we Americans are intuitively barbarians?

Do you worry that by 2050 novelists, too, will lack readers?

Indeed I do. I see fiction, which is now king of the walk, beginning to take the same fatal steps.

Like what?

Like losing its readers. Like allowing well-intentioned critics and college professors of literature to make reading such a cabalistic experience that only someone who has been trained in a highly specialized vocabulary of technical terms can understand what's being argued.

You can't be that worried. Your books are still doing well.

I'm not worried. I'm scared. And for two reasons. First, television is such a remarkably effective invention that it could in time replace both books and newspapers. Indeed, it's starting to do so right now. I never knock it. I believe a child can acquire a fairly good cognitive education via the tube. Our business, military and political leaders could come from the ranks of children educated by television. But not the thinkers, the brainy ones who will invent the next clever machine or the next wonder drug, or help establish and preserve the moral norms of the nation. Those kids will always be educated by the book, in whatever form it may take in the future. Second, almost anything in writing and publishing will be possible with the new word processors and printers. It's quite possible that in two decades the printed book could become a treasured relic. This year I earned substantial royalties from talking books . . . on tape . . . listen to them in your car. So what's going to happen to the printed book I cannot even guess. But I do see one encouraging development for writers like me. I work in three different locations—Florida, Texas, Maine—and I find it impossible to lug with me the massive books I ought to consult almost every day: the thirty-one volumes of the *Encyclopedia Britannica*; the huge *Times Atlas of the World*; my big standard dictionary; a *World Almanac*; a compendium of world history; a Rodale thesaurus; a very fine biographical dictionary; a large gazetteer; *Bartlett's Quotations*; a small book giving just the spelling of forty thousand words; and a King James Bible, with concordance. Obviously that's too much to carry, but before long a writer will be able to keep beside him floppy disks which contain all the above data and more, like abbreviated foreign language dictionaries. Most of the items I've listed are already available on individual disks; it's the assembling of them into one system that I await, for surely it will come, and research in writing will become a lot easier.

But at the same time that the word processor makes creation easier, it threatens the book most powerfully. Even the word *manuscript* should be dropped, for no hand will write the future book. It will be composed on a word processor, which means there will exist no record of development of the book's ideas by stages. It will appear to have been born full-bodied. No great loss, perhaps.

But a far more radical possibility looms: the creation of a manuscript not only with a word processor, but in it, a fluid operation of constant change, limitless variation, and timeless moments of creation and sharing with others. The future book will be composed, circulated and read within the domain of the word processor. *Hypertext* this burgeoning new development is called, and it's well-named, because the text is free to roam and soar and dive and change color and character as the mind and imagination of the writer conceives. Also, a group of eight or nine can share in the action. The result is a floppy disk which can be shared with others (published in the broad, true sense of that word) with never a print-out into traditional word forms.

This seems a far cry from what you've been doing all your creative life.

Wait a minute! These concepts have captivated me for years. I submitted a major part of one of my books not in manuscript form but on a floppy, and can foresee a time not far distant when novelists will be required to submit not only a print-out of their manuscript but also a floppy, or just the floppy. I believe that complex articles for the advanced scientific journals are already submitted in floppy.

And don't forget that in my book *The Novel* my secondary hero, the gifted young writer Timothy Tull is writing his work in radically new forms. Had he not died prematurely, I feel sure he would shortly have been off to some place like Brown University to experiment with hypertext, a development which seems to have been made for mercurial talents like him.

As a working writer I've already lived through a revolution during my relatively few years in the profession. Pocket books arrived on the scene just as I did, and they changed everything. In the beginning, when paperbacks sold for a quarter, the returns to the writer who did not hit the jackpot could be so minimal that we paid little attention to them. Now the paperback sometimes drives the action in publishing. In the old days novels were not published in big-type size for older readers. Nor were there talking books that the very busy person could "read" while driving an automobile. When I started there were many magazines that used fiction, and of the ten fiction books that appeared on the *Times* best-seller list each week, some six or seven could be expected to be bought by Hollywood, including some of the nonfiction successes. No more. Nor had publishing houses begun to merge, or fall into the hands of mega-corporations, or be sold to foreign houses. I've lived through tumultuous times in the business of books.

You teach in two different schools, a small college in Florida and a huge university in Texas. What characteristics do you look for in a potential writer?

I have a right to assume, since these are serious, dedicated young people, that they already have a general knowledge of literature, including poetry and drama; that they have a feeling for the English language; that they understand at least the rudiments of the sentence and the paragraph; and that they are generally familiar with at least one other subject than English, say history, psychology, or the general principles of science.

But a correction. I do not do the teaching. I am what they call a T.A., a teacher's assistant. The class is taught by a very bright, talented, already published younger full-time professor, often with tenure, whose responsibility it is to establish the class, give it direction, and determine the grades.

I have two answers to your question. In would-be writers of fiction I assume the basics listed above, but then look for a young person who loves to tell a story and who has courage. I stress the latter because it requires fortitude to sit at a typewriter or word processor, knowing that the job about to begin will require at least two years of tremendous concentration and effort and—here comes the courageous part—with no assurance that anyone will want to read your stuff when you're done, because there is no felt need on anyone's part, individuals or society at large, for the novel with which you are struggling. An architect starting an assignment knows that, when he's finished his demanding labors, someone will want to live in that house; the would-be novelist has no assurance that when she is done, anyone will have a burning desire to read what she has written. When I start a long novel, I am aware that it's going to take three years of unceasing work, and even then I cannot be sure that anyone will want it. Without courage, I could not possibly finish the job. One of the silliest phrases I know is "the long-awaited novel of Chester Jones." The only person really awaiting it is Chester's wife, who's been wondering how they're going to pay the bills next year, or, in an occasional case, some junior editor who is expected to publish four books this year and learns that one of her well-regarded writers with a promising track record is being divorced and has lost forward motion. That editor may have to rely on Chester Jones, good or bad, but the rest of the world does not give a damn whether he finishes his novel or not. What the would-be novelist needs is the elegance of a hummingbird and the irresistible force of a pile driver.

The would-be writer of nonfiction books or articles requires the same basics as the novelist plus a knowledge of not one or two fields not related to English and literature but four or five, and he or she is fortunate if some of them are in the sciences, for there are tremendous openings for writing in those areas. So what this young person needs is not courage but arrogance—or phrased more gently: self-assurance, confidence, unquestioned adequacy—because on any general subject one might want to tackle in the limitless areas of general experience, there would have to be at least a thousand experts who are equally capable, half of whom would be far more qualified to do the book. The difference between you and the other thousand is that you're the one who's going to do it. You're the one who has the determination to get the job done. I've written more than thirty books on a wide variety of subject matter, and in every case I knew there were people, often in my hometown, who were better qualified to write the book than I. But they were not writers and I was, and later, when I heard that they had said: 'I could have written that book better than he did,' I think: 'Yes, you could have, had you been a writer willing to spend three years at it.'

I have little regard for the young person who vaguely wants to excel in demanding artistic careers like acting, singing, sculpting, painting, or working in architecture but lacks the fortitude to commit wholeheartedly to the job. A career in writing demands courage and arrogance, but the latter should be manifested in secret, not in public bravado.

What do you think about the theory of deconstruction, that it is fruitless to look at the life of a writer and deduce anything at all about his writing? That the only thing that matters is what he put on paper?

Recent critical theories like deconstruction have questioned the ability of words to convey reality and have substituted for traditional scholarship a series of brilliant word games which culminate in a doctrine which the originators did not themselves voice but which their adherents have: "The author is dead. Only the words count." This theory has produced one good result. It terminates fatuous college investigations like "Wordsworth and Coleridge in the Lake Country . . . and Dorothy," and gets back to the more important question: "What did the poems say? What did they achieve?" But that is small gain when compared to the damage the movement has done in obscuring literature and misdirecting graduate studies.

You seem rather harsh in your criticism.

Not of the good ideas and the cleansing concepts . . . I see positive good in them. But from the start I have been appalled at the sycophancy bestowed by otherwise sensible American scholars on the charismatic Belgian scholar Paul De Man, who led the movement in the States from his exalted position as professor at Yale. It started with my not wanting to agree that as an author I was dead, and that I'd had little to do with what I'd written except act as an almost unconscious conveyor. But it was when I started looking into De Man the human being that my intuitive fears became a cyclone of rejection, because I learned that when a young man in Belgium during the World War II period, he was an ardent supporter of Adolph Hitler, writing some two hundred newspaper articles extolling the Nazis and excoriating Jews and other inferior breeds. When he came to America he did not have to deny any accusations regarding his past behavior; he never acknowledged it. It was in this period that he promulgated his theory that what an artist writes is dissociated from his personal history.

Why are you so bitter about De Man? T.S. Eliot and Ezra Pound were also harsh on Jews, and they've been forgiven. Relax.

Good point. But I've told you only the favorable aspects of De Man. Not long ago David Lehman wrote an excellent book about De Man, shattering the myths that the Belgian had erected about himself, and showing De Man the philosopher as he really was. On May 24, 1992, Lehman published in the *New York Times* a scathing report on De Man's teaching experience at Bard College, the well-regarded experimental school on the Hudson, in the years 1949–51. It was written by a Professor Artine Artinian of Bard, who had hired De Man. Artinian proceeded to give as devastating a portrait of a college professor as one could imagine. De Man, already married in Europe with three sons, abandoned his family, did not divorce his wife but did bigamously marry a Bard student, who became immediately pregnant. After paying Dr. Artinian two months rent for the house De Man had taken over, he stopped payment. He ran up bills with local merchants whom he refused to pay. He lied, behaved scandalously, and pretty well wrecked the Artinian house, from which he may have taken certain valuable books. He was a disaster, but after he was fired, he successfully covered his tracks both in Belgium and Bard and went on to become a valued professor at Columbia and one of the leading lights at Yale. This is the man who was going to remake the teaching of literature in the United States. His theories, expounded with brilliance and persuasion, swept the American academic community until he died somewhat prematurely in 1984, his glamorous reputation still unsullied.

Why do you harp on about him?

Because my life is dedicated to books, and I want people who traffic in them to be people of rectitude. And if someone climbs to the position of guru to a generation, I expect him to be intellectually, politically, and morally honest. Not above reproach. None of us achieve that. But just basically honest, a man or woman of character.

Let's get back to what you said about the novel as one of the grand manifestations of the book.

Yes, my major concern. Four thousand years before the birth of Christ men and women in caves were composing novels without ever writing them down. When alphabets were invented, Plutarch, those who assembled the novelettes contained in the Old and New Testaments, and women like Lady Murasaki in Japan wrote their work without feeling any necessity for the printed page. The storytellers of the world are an indestructible breed; they will continue to frame their tales and leave it to someone else to circulate them. But that the tales will continue to be told and that writers will continue to be of value to their societies I have no question whatever.

You seem to be contradicting yourself. First you say that the novel could be in danger of following the demise of poetry as a force with broad national readership; then you claim that the writing of novels is a timeless, indestructible human endeavor.

Perceptive. Let's take your points in reverse. Yes, storytelling is an ingrained habit that cannot be eradicated. It will continue forever. But I'm not sure its results will be disseminated in the same physical form as printed books, and I'm quite fearful that if the principles of deconstruction continue to dominate academic thinking and preference, the well-received novel of merit will follow the path of the well-received 1890 poem. It will become increasingly erudite, increasingly committed to a dialogue between elites with the general public growling "To hell with it." If this seems improbable, I simply ask, "Would you as a devotee of poetry in 1850 have been able to imagine its practical disappearance from bookstores in less than a hundred years?"

Do you see yourself as different from other writers?

No. I'm a fairly standard example. I do stay off to myself more than most. I have remained away from the mainstream. But there is one significant difference. I grew up with books. Books to me are inordinately precious, for I could not have survived without them, so I am vitally concerned with what might happen to them in this time of radical change.

We've been throwing around high-sounding generalizations. Let's focus on a spectacular problem that exploded in your backyard: How does a writer react to something like the tragedy at Waco, Texas?

You're right. Waco is not far from where I do my writing. I know it intimately. Fine little city. Excellent university in town, Baylor. Very religious. Very conservative. The kind of area that a self-proclaimed messiah like David Koresh might look for when seeking a congenial place in which to settle with his flock.

Interesting background, but how did it effect you?

Viscerally. You must remember that twice I'd gone out of my way to deal with the charismatic, unstable, unreliable, self-ordained, religious fanatic. In *Space* Dr. Strabismus was a proto-type of Jimmy and Tammy Bakker and Jimmy Swaggart. And in *Caribbean* I spent a lot of time on the damage that can be done by a religious leader who allows the biblical Book of Daniel and Revelation to disorient him with visions and the arrant non-sense that Revelations can induce, with its seven seals, beasts, and the cryptic evil force designated by the number 666. I've made a recurring study of the Revelation phenomenon and had concluded early in the Koresh manifestation that there was a strong probability that he would end his siege in some kind of self-immolation in which he would persuade his followers to join him. But I prayed that at the last minute common sense would prevail and he would be able to save face by some other kind of bold gesture.

When my wife called me to the television that morning and I saw the great claw-like projections from the tanks smashing into the corners of the compound, with no visible reaction for a sur-prisingly long time, and certainly no flame, I said, "He's reacting sanely. Thank God!" But at that moment parallel streaks of flame leaped out from the eaves and I shouted, "Get out!" for, against my better judgment, I supposed that the people trapped inside had free choice in the matter. But those hopes were dashed when that monstrous fireball mushroomed upward from the roofs and the entire structure exploded in one vast fireball.

The television pictures were so revealing and so very much in our viewing room that I became part of the fire. I died with the children, I perished with the deluded men and women from Australia and Great Britain and California. What were they doing in Waco?

Three days later one of my students told me, "Don't worry, Mr. Michener. David Koresh will have escaped the fire and be seen in a Waco supermarket accompanied by Elvis Presley." And thousands more will flock to his banner, for he will be able to prove that God saved him as He had earlier saved Shadrach, Meshak, and Abednigo from their fiery furnace in the Book of Daniel.

Books by James A. Michener

Tales of the South Pacific. New York: Macmillan, 1947.

The Fires of Spring. New York: Random House, 1949.

Return to Paradise. New York: Random House, 1951.

The Voice of Asia. New York: Random House, 1951.

The Bridges of Toko-Ri. New York: Random House, 1953.

Sayonara. New York: Random House, 1954.

The Floating World. New York: Random House, 1954.

Rascals in Paradise (with A. Grove Day). New York: Random House, 1957.

The Bridge at Andau. New York: Random House, 1957.

Selected Writings of James A. Michener. New York: The Modern Library, 1957.

The Hokusai Sketchbooks. Boston: Charles E. Tuttle Co., 1958.

Japanese Prints. Boston: Charles E. Tuttle Co., 1959.

Hawaii. New York: Random House, 1959.

Report of the County Chairman. New York: Random House, 1961.

Caravans. New York: Random House, 1963.

The Source. New York: Random House, 1965.

Iberia. New York: Random House, 1968.

America vs. America: The Revolution in Middle Class Values. New York: Signet, 1969.

Presidential Lottery. New York: Random House, 1969.

The Quality of Life. Philadelphia: Girard Bank, 1970.

Facing East. New York: Random House, 1970.

Kent State: What Happened and Why. New York: Random House, 1971.

The Drifters. New York: Random House, 1971.

A Michener Miscellany: 1950–1970. New York: Random House, 1973.

Centennial. New York: Random House, 1974.

About Centennial: *Some Notes on the Novel*. New York: Random House, 1974.

Sports in America. New York: Random House, 1976.

Chesapeake. New York: Random House, 1978.

The Watermen: Selections from Chesapeake. New York: Random House, 1979.

The Covenant. New York: Random House, 1980.

Space. New York: Random House, 1982.

Poland. New York: Random House, 1984.

Texas. New York: Random House, 1985.

Legacy. New York: Random House, 1987.

Alaska. New York: Random House, 1988.

Journey. New York: Random House, 1989.

Caribbean. New York: Random House, 1989.

Six Days in Havana. Austin: University of Texas Press, 1989.

The Eagle and the Raven. Austin: State House Press, 1990.

Pilgrimage. Emmaus, PA: Rodale Press, 1990.

The Novel. New York: Random House, 1991.

The World Is My Home: A Memoir. New York: Random House, 1992.

James A. Michener's Writer's Handbook: Explorations in Writing and Publishing. New York: Random House, 1992.

Mexico. New York: Random House, 1992.

My Lost Mexico. Austin: State House Press, 1992.

James A. Michener Retells South Pacific. Orlando: Harcourt Brace, 1992.

Creatures of the Kingdom. New York: Random House, 1993.

Literary Reflections. Austin: State House Press, 1994.

Recessional. New York: Random House, 1994.

Miracle in Seville. New York: Random House, 1995.

This Noble Land. New York: Random House, 1996.

A Century of Sonnets. Austin: State House Press, 1997.

A. A. Knopf, loss of manuscript by, 102, 103
Across the River and into the Trees (Ernest Hemingway), 128
Adams, John, 79
Adventures in Paradise (television series), 110
Afghanistan, 77, 82, 168; aid to rebels in, 181; car wreck in, 83; goat-dragging in, 82–83
Africa, 171; appearance of natives in, 79; beauty of, 86
African Americans, 151, 154, 185, 186; the black Mafia, 143; and boxing, 157; and courts, 215; and death penalty, 195; Harlem Globetrotters, 158; Harlem Renaissance, 198; and the O. J. Simpson trial, 160–63; presidential candidacy, 211; writers, 143, 233. *See also* Racism
Agents. *See* Publishing
Aida, 24
Alaska, ix, 50, 94, 168; Glacier Bay, 90; Sitka, 52
Alexander the Great, 80, 82
Ali, Mohammed, 157
Allen, Woody, 140
Altman, Robert, 107
Amelia (Michener's companion), xv, xvi, xviii, xix
American Library Association, 61
American Tragedy, An (Theodore Dreiser), 138
Andrews, Julie, 110
Angell, Robert, 151
Answered Prayers (Truman Capote), xii, 130
Arab-Israeli peace, 81, 173, 178, 180. *See also* Islam; Israel; Jews
Arafat, Yasir, 179
Argentina, 87; appreciation of artists in, 96; Buenos Aries, 83

Armstrong, Louis, 23
Armstrong, Neil, 85
Arnold, Bennett, *The Old Wives' Tale*, 12
Arnold, Matthew, 139
Art, 123, 232, 233; American lack of appreciation for, 96, 97–98, 223, 230; collecting, 115–16; competition in, 129; given to museums, 115; Japanese, 51; in New Guinea, 131; under Reagan presidency, 217. *See also* Writers; Writing
Arthur, Chester A., 210
Aspern Papers (Henry James), 133
Assad, Hafez al-, 179
Athletes: conservatism of, 158–59; in politics, 223; problems of, 160; as role models, 151, 159
Atlanta, Ga., 185
Atlantic Monthly, 36
Atlee, Clement, 169
Auchincloss, Louis, 18
Auden, W. H., 112, 137, 139
Austen, Jane, 43, 53, 132

Baez, Joan, 23, 144, 217
Bakker, Jim and Tammy, 218, 250
Baldwin, James, 95, 114, 142, 143
Balzac, Honoré de, 53, 80, 131, 132; *Quest for the Absolute*, 6
Bang the Drum Slowly (Mark Harris), 151, 163
Barbados, 86
Barth, John: *Letters*, 134; *The Sot-Weed Factor*, 134
Barthelme, Donald, 134
Bartlett's Quotations, 243
Baseball, 151, 152–55; changes in, 157
Basketball, 151, 155, 156, 159; Harlem Globetrotters, 158
Battlestar Galactica, 111

Merimee, Prosper, 24

Meschery, Tom, 151

Mexico: division of wealth in, 180; Mexico City, 89; rights of immigrants from, 25

Michelangelo, 80

Michener, James: on abortion, 7–8, 194; acting, 14, 52, 106–07; on aging, xvi, 3; on AIDS, 66, 67, 163, 165; on Alzheimer's disease, 69; on the American Century, 184; on anti-ERA movement, 64; on architects as artists, 97; as artist, 233; on artists, 40, 98; on Asia, 86; on battleshock, 84; on being adopted, 14–15; on bestseller lists/bestsellers, 128, 238, 245; on biographies, writing of, 34; birth of, 230; book signing on eighty-ninth birthday, ix–x; on Brazil, 172; brushes with death, 31, 83–86; on bull fighting, 19–20, 106, 150, 158; on Canada, 181; on cannibalism, 76; on chess, 149; childhood, 4–6, 7, 8–9, 10, 14, 184, 186, 224; on children, 224; children, adopted, 60; college, 11–14, 20; on communal living, 69; Congress, run for, 202, 203, 223; on consumerism, 187; on crime, organized, 197; on Dan Quayle, 219; death of, xx; death of wife Mari, x, 65–66; on the death penalty, 195; on divorce in Ireland, 173; divorces, 60; drugs, use of, 73–74; on editing, 27, 32, 55–56; education, 10–11, 14, 230; education, higher, 26; on ethnic cleansing, 174; family, importance of, 69; on fishing, 150; fortune-telling, 102–03; future, predictions for, 227–28; gender preferences, 68; on genetics, 164–65, 206; on golf, 149–50; on Granada, 207–08; health, ix, xv, xvi, 2, 3, 117; on himself, 236–51; on his life in New York, 26, 47; on hockey, 155; homes, 88; honorary degrees, 144; on Jamaica, 86; jobs, 7, 8, 11, 12, 14, 18, 21, 25–26, 27, 189; on language, foreign, 46, 75, 86; on lawsuits, 226; and the Library of Congress, 209; on love, 69; on Machu Picchu, 89; on marijuana, medicinal use of, 199; marriages, 60–61; on masculinity, 68; mathematical ability, 11; as Mich the Witch, 102; on the Middle East, peace in, 178–79; millennium, predictions for, 227–28; on misogyny, 63–64; on money, x, xv, 2, 3–4, 113, 117; and the National Council for the Social Studies, 21; on the national debt, 227; and the National Youth Administration, 21; Naval service, 29–31; on nuclear power, 198; old age, xvi, 3, 234; on peace in Ireland, 178; on the Peace Corps, 72; on plagiarism, 100–01; and the police, encounters with, 9; on pornography, 57, 99, 217; and the Postal Department, 204; on presidents, 209–10, 212; reviews by, 124, 128; at St. Andrews University (Scotland), 18; on scientology, 217; sexual harassment, 31, 66; on short stories, 94, 241; on soccer, 155, 194; in the Social Studies Society of America, 21; on the South, 9, 98, 177, 236; on the South Pacific, 30, 35, 63, 77, 88, 203, 222; on the Tailhook scandal, 30; on taxes, 86–87, 114–15, 227; on teaching, 18, 21, 25–26, 189, 245–46; on technology, 166; on terrorism, 197; on trickle-down economics, 225; on urban renewal, 199; values, 41; on violence in America, 194; World War II, 222; writing, early skills at, 11

Works: *Alaska*, xii, 44; *Bridge at Andau, The*, 50, 169, 241; *Bridges at Toko-Ri, The*, 36, 37, 207; *Caravans*, 45, 231;

Violence: Americans' love for, 194; and guns, 196–97; in novels, 121; in sports, 155

Von Sydow, Max, 110

Vonnegut, Kurt, 217

Walesa, Lech, 176, 177

Wallace, DeWitt, 35

Wandering Jew, The (Eugene Sue), 238–39

War and Peace (Leo Tolstoy), 238

Warner, William W., *Beautiful Swimmers*, 134

Warren, Leonard, 24

Warren, Robert Penn, 97, 122, 131, 143, 233

Washington, George, 79, 210, 212

Washington Post, 129

Watergate, 212, 213

Watson, James, *The Double Helix*, 13–14

Wayne, John, 144

Way of All Flesh, The (Samuel Butler), 12

We Are All Murderers, 107

Webster, Daniel, 210

Weinberger, Casper, 207

Weld, Tuesday, 107

Welles, Orson, 106

Welty, Eudora, 98

Wharton, Edith, 18, 128; *Ethan Frome*, 133

White, Dr. Paul Dudley, 2

White House, 26

Whitman, Walt, 79, 131, 139

Whittier, John Greenleaf, 242

Wilde, Oscar, 139–40

Wilder, Gene, 108

Wilder, John, 111, 112

Wilder, Thornton, 97, 143

Williams, Ted, 153

Williams, Tennessee, 53

Wilson, Edmund, 130, 143

Wilson Quarterly, 133

Wilson, Woodrow, 210

Winds of War (Herman Wouk), 134, 238

Wolfe, Tom, 141; *Bonfire of the Vanities*, 114

Wolper, David, 101

Women: attitudes toward, 63; of Burma, 79; compared to lions, 63; compared to men, 63; Equal Rights Amendment, 64; and homosexuality, 67; housework, 57–58; and other women, 64; and religious doctrine, 58, 63; in sports, 159; strength of, 62; traits of, 68; and widowhood, 62–63; witches, 63; writers, 140–41. *See also* ERA; Women's rights

Women's rights: during Reagan era, 217; Michener support for, 65

Woods, Rosemary, 213

Woolf, Virginia, 137

Wordsworth, William, 139, 242

World According to Garp, The (film), 141

World War I, 10; Battle of Gallipoli, 80

World War II, 28–31, 51, 173, 216; Admiral Nimitz during, 203; in the Balkans, 174; battleshock during, 84; in France, 175; Hawaii during, 61–62; Japanese internment during, 61, 171; occupation of Japan after, 96; pro-Hitler writing during, 247

Wouk, Herman, 53, 238; *Caine Mutiny*, 134

Writer's Handbook, The, 118

Writers, 236; characterized, 20; compared to Michener, 122; cutting edge, 131–32; distinguished from authors, 138; ethics of, xiii, 122; image of, 131; Japanese, 143; women, 140–41. *See also* Publishing; Writing

Writing, 20, 231; about writing, 118; character development, 239; character names, 49; coincidence as plot device in, 239; collaborations, 56–57; difficulty of, 54; education, 190–91; effect of films on, 6, 107; effect of Michener's health on, 3; effects on home life, 65; ethics, 122, 123; freelance, 35, 36; goals of, 42; historical incidents in, 239; inspiration, 40, 50, 52, 54, 230–31;